GENRES OF
LISTENING

GENRES OF LISTENING

AN ETHNOGRAPHY OF PSYCHOANALYSIS IN BUENOS AIRES

XOCHITL MARSILLI-VARGAS

DUKE UNIVERSITY PRESS · DURHAM AND LONDON · 2022

Printed and bound by CPI Group (UK) Ltd, Croydon, CR0 4YY
Project editor: Lisa Lawley
Typeset in Huronia Latin and Quadraat Sans Pro
by Westchester Publishing Services

Library of Congress Cataloging-in-Publication Data
Names: Marsilli-Vargas, Xochitl, [date] author.
Title: Genres of listening : an ethnography of psychoanalysis in
Buenos Aires / Xochitl Marsilli-Vargas.
Description: Durham : Duke University Press, 2022. | Includes
bibliographical references and index.
Identifiers: LCCN 2021050315 (print)
LCCN 2021050316 (ebook)
ISBN 9781478015918 (hardcover)
ISBN 9781478018551 (paperback)
ISBN 9781478023159 (ebook)
ISBN 9781478092698 (ebook other)
Subjects: LCSH: Listening—Psychological aspects. | Listening—
Social aspects. | Psychoanalysis—Social aspects—Argentina—
Buenos Aires. | Psychoanalysis—Methodology. | Interpersonal
communication and culture—Argentina—Buenos Aires. |
BISAC: SOCIAL SCIENCE / Anthropology / Cultural & Social |
PSYCHOLOGY / Movements / Psychoanalysis
Classification: LCC BF323.L5 M356 2022 (print) | LCC BF323.L5
(ebook) | DDC 153.7/33—dc23/eng/20211217
LC record available at https://lccn.loc.gov/2021050315
LC ebook record available at https://lccn.loc.gov/2021050316

Cover art: Margaret Watts Hughes (1842–1907), two voice
figures created with the eidophone Hughes invented for
visual capture of the human voice. The Visible Sound
Collection held by Cyfarthfa Castle Museum & Art Gallery,
Merthyr Tydfil, Wales.

This book is freely available in an open access edition thanks to TOME (Toward an Open Monograph
Ecosystem)—a collaboration of the Association of American Universities, the Association of University Presses,
and the Association of Research Libraries—and the
generous support of Emory University and the Andrew W.
Mellon Foundation. Learn more at the TOME website,
available at : openmonographs.org.

To Oskar

CONTENTS

viii   *Author's Note*

ix   *Acknowledgments*

1   Introduction: A City of Listeners

25   1   For a Theory of Genres of Listening

48   2   The Music in the Words

80   3   "What You Really Mean Is . . .": Listening to "That Which Is Not Said"

106   4   The Psychoanalytic Field in Buenos Aires

137   5   The Mass Mediation of Psychoanalytic Listening

174   Conclusion: Final Resonances

185   *Notes*

203   *References*

223   *Index*

AUTHOR'S NOTE

All names are pseudonyms unless they appear with a last name.

ACKNOWLEDGMENTS

Writing an academic book is a hard thing to do—or at least it was for me. It is a process that begins with an idea that mutates, taking many forms, until one day it acquires a more or less definite shape, and then begins to grow. This process happened through many years, and the shaping and molding of what became the structure of the book emerged from the interactions, conversations, mentoring, and dialogues with a range of people, each contributing in different ways, levels of intensity, and intellectual focus. This book is collective in that the ideas explored emerged through all the dialogic exchanges, collaborations, discussions, conversations, and support from many people.

I am particularly grateful to my mentors at the University of California, Berkeley. Charles Briggs welcomed me to Berkeley and provided valuable guidance and advice, as well as encouragement when things did not go as planned. Charles's ethical commitment to the communities he works with taught me that our work as anthropologists can and should have an impact in the world. His continuous support has been key in the overall crafting of this book. Bill Hanks's wisdom knows no bounds. His keen understanding and rendition of difficult texts have shaped my vision of what it means to do rigorous, good, and meaningful scholarship. His work has been and continues to be inspiring. Bill always believed in my work and encouraged me to develop the idea of genres of listening (not everyone did). I will always be grateful for his constant support, friendship, and thorough advice. I want to thank Stefania Pandolfo for her insights, but especially for introducing me to the work of Jacques Lacan. It was through her engagement with Lacan's theories that I began to explore psychoanalysis, both as a practice and as an episteme that shapes how we perceive the world. Patricia Baquedano-Lopez stepped up when I needed help and guidance. Her generous disposition, encouragement, and careful reading of my work made the experience of writing pleasant and a little less stressful. Roger Bartra's mentoring at the Escuela Nacional de Antropología e Historia set the motion to a very fulfilling scholarly trajectory. His beautiful writing and original ideas served as a model for the crafting of this book. The support and guidance of Valentine Daniel during my time at Columbia University (and his love of Peirce) helped me fall in love with semiotics and I have not looked back. The work of Asif Agha, Richard Bauman, Summerson Carr, Alessandro Duranti, Steven Feld, Miyako Inoue, Michael Silverstein, Greg Urban, and Ken Webb has been a profound inspiration for the development of the ideas in this book.

Numerous friends and colleagues have offered incredible critical support and helped sharpen and refine the ideas and general outlook of the book. I am especially indebted to Eric Plemons, whose detailed reading and numerous conversations helped me develop the idea of genres of listening. Saleem Al-Bahloly, Nate Dumas, Terra Edwards, Mara Green, Sharon Kaufman, Elizabeth Kelley, Martin Lappé, Theresa McPhail, Bruno Reinhardt, Chris Roebuck, and Allison Tillack provided critical reading of various chapters of this work in its early stages. More recently, the careful reading and feedback of Omar Acha, Sergio Delgado-Moya, Daniel N. Silva, and Calvin Warren improved the book immensely. Denise Gill's insights and careful editing helped me work through the conceptual framework in chapter one. Their ideas about how to better structure the story line and to make my voice the center of the narrative created a more dynamic text. To the Berkeley Latin Americanists Sarah Selvidge, Sarah Hines, and Celso Castilho, thank you for the conversations and insights. A special thanks goes to my dear friend and colleague Jamie Melton, who read many drafts of the book. His observations and commentaries have helped disentangle difficult parts of it; most importantly, his encouraging words and overall support were the push I needed to finish the book.

Marco Jacquemet and Dawn Cunningham became my family when I moved to Berkeley. I am forever indebted to them for their nourishment— both intellectual and gastronomical. Mia Fuller's emotional support and advice were invaluable. My colleagues at Emory have served as an anchor while navigating the difficult task of writing a book, and they became a strong network of support: Carla Freeman for her wisdom and advice; Jeff Lesser for being an incredible mentor and friend; and Yanna Yanakakis and Javier Villa-Flores for our conversations and their critical thinking. I also thank Emory's Center for Faculty Development and Excellence and the Department of Spanish and Portuguese for their support when writing this book.

I want to thank María Elisa Mitre for opening the doors to the Multi-Family Structure Psychoanalytic Therapeutic (MFSPT) community. Her kindness and willingness to talk to me and discuss the ideas of the late Jorge García Badaracco proved to be key for my understanding of psychoanalytic listening as a genre. All the psychoanalysts and analysands that participated in the MFSPT sessions helped me understand the embodiment of listening. I am grateful for sharing their personal stories and individual journeys. Their words continue to resonate with me.

Sergio Visacovsky and Mariano Ben Plotkin were key for their feedback, guidance, and support at the beginning of my fieldwork in Buenos Aires. They helped me to connect with many analysts and have always been generous with their time and insights. Ezequiel Adamovsky, Carolina Azzi, Mariano Bargero, Claudio Benzecry, Adriana Busson, Alejandro Dagfal, Eduardo Gluj, Paola Peimer, Julia Vallejo Puszkin, Daniel Sazbón, and Nicolás Viotti made my fieldwork in Buenos Aires a meaningful experience and helped me at various stages in different capacities. Héctor Palomino's active role in finding and sending me articles in newspapers and magazines was key to my understanding of the circulation of psychoanalysis in Buenos Aires. To the *humoristas gráficos*—Tute, Esteban Podetti, Rep, Rudy, and Sendra—thanks for your amazing art!

This book would not have been possible without the funding from Mexico's CONACYT program Becas al Extranjero, and the binational collaboration UC MEXUS–CONACYT. The time I spent at the Stanford Humanities Center provided the perfect atmosphere to finish the manuscript. Three amazing editors helped me to transform what started as a convoluted text into a more readable book: Brandon Proia, Christopher Lura, and Teresa Davis. I thank them for their help in shaping my thoughts into legible sentences, as well as David Nichols for his careful work on the bibliography. Two anonymous reviewers at Duke University Press provided incredibly valuable feedback. Thanks to their acute observations and editorial suggestions, the book is now in existence. I hope to one day thank them in person for all their hard work. I also want to thank Gisela Fosado for her patience and guidance through the editorial process.

My sister, Tania, and my nephews, Santiago and Emiliano, are my favorite people in the whole world! And they brighten my life. Thanks to them—and Joel and Valeria—I have a place to call home. Without the constant support of Grandma Rosita, I would not have been able to accomplish anything; I am forever indebted for her love and care. I want to thank my uncle, Adrián Marsilli, who introduced me to anthropology and encouraged me to pursue an academic career. And although they are no longer here, my late grandparents, José Marcelli, José María Vargas, and Grandma Elvia, were pillars in my life. I thank beautiful Precious for her endless companionship at the early stages of writing. And I dedicate this book to my beloved Oskar. He brought so much joy and beauty to this world, and I miss him terribly.

I thank Greta Marchesi, Kathleen Grady, Sapna Thottathil, David Gardner, T. K. and Aggie Ravane, Erin Tarver, Josh Mousie, Dilek Huseyinzadegan, Jeremy Bell, Amy Bach, Paco Barrenechea, Juliana Sphar, and Fred Nolan Clark for being amazing friends during good and bad times.

Last but not least, I owe a particularly large debt of gratitude to Pablo Palomino. He has been my lifeline as I trudged through the process of writing this book—from listening to my constant complaints, to copyediting, to helping me have a brighter outlook on life when things were difficult. His companionship and encouragement are very treasured, and this book would have not been possible without all his support.

Unless otherwise noted, all translations are my own.

Introduction

A City of Listeners

Anyone who listens is fundamentally open. Without this kind of openness for one another there is no genuine human relationship. Belonging together always also means being able to listen to one another.
Hans-Georg Gadamer, *Truth and Method* (1989)

"That doesn't sound right." (No me suena bien.)
Popular saying

Buenos Aires is a city of listeners. *Porteños*, as its inhabitants are called, listen carefully to each other's stories, declarations, silences, and testimonies. In some cases, they listen only to the words and their established meanings; in others, they try to *resonate* with their interlocutors by listening to "that which is not said," offering an interpretation—or translation—of the unspoken words latent in the speaker's speech. This particular way of listening is learned and is based on the idea of the unconscious proposed by psychoanalysis. In the clinic, a psychoanalyst would attempt to achieve a "state of resonance," meaning that the analyst would listen to the words of the analysand (i.e., patient), trying to go beyond the mere denotations of the words to grasp the "real" motives and possible intentions behind the uttered statements. The proposition is that words have hidden meanings that are discernible only to the listener who, much like a radio frequency, *tunes in* with the unconscious of the speaker and is able to listen, not only with the ears but with the body as a whole. Listening to the unconscious is thus an embodied experience where sensations, affective states, "gut feelings," and intuitions roam freely to connect with the hidden meaning of the words expressed by the analysand. Although *resonating* with someone else's speech might seem to belong to the realm of the unexpected, the sensible, or the uncanny, it is highly structured. Psychoanalysts are skilled listeners who have developed a variety of listening methodologies to find the undisclosed in speech (see Akhtar 2013; Freud [1912] 1958; Isakower 1939; Lacan [1966] 2006; Reik 1948, 1964). In other words, psychoanalysts learn how to deploy what I call a psychoanalytic *genre of listening.*

In Buenos Aires, a form of listening based on these ideas—unconscious practices and resonances—circulates outside of the clinic. *Porteños* have developed a sort of "psychoanalytic ear" that they deploy freely in different settings and that emerges through the responses during dialogic encounters in everyday interactions. After a statement has been made, in many cases *porteños* offer different "readings" or interpretations of the hidden meaning of the words, trying to go beyond the denotation to find the unknown in speech. Consequently, it is not uncommon to hear statements such as "I think you mean something else," "I don't hear your voice in what you are saying," "What you said sounds strange," and "Your words are betraying you" during everyday conversations. Accordingly, in Buenos Aires there is a culture of listeners whose personal identities, conceptions of citizenship, and constructions of the political are rooted less in the performativity associated with speaking than in a particular form of listening based on psychoanalysis. I found that in Buenos Aires, this listening is social, produced by a collectivity of individuals and performed in all sorts of interactions surpassing class, age, and gender classifications. The ubiquitous nature of psychoanalytic listening in Buenos Aires prompted me to analyze this phenomenon as a genre. Based on this research and analysis, I argue that, as an interpretive framework, psychoanalysis has permeated a variety of discursive arenas, generating a particular form of listening that organizes the city dwellers' social interactions.

The concept of *genres of listening* emerged from over thirty months of fieldwork in Buenos Aires, Argentina, over the course of six years. When I first arrived in the city, I was interested in conducting an ethnography of what Argentines call *el mundo psi* or psy-world: the web of interrelationships between psychotherapeutic experiences (including psychoanalysis, psychiatry, and psychology), institutions, knowledge, and commonsensical awareness of the self in relation to the psyche that is shared by vast swaths of the Buenos Aires population. My hope was to understand how the quintessentially modern language of psychoanalysis, which lost its prestige in the United States with the rise of other epistemologies of the mind, the self, and individual behavior, has remained so lively in Argentina. But observing psychoanalysis in the clinical setting was a methodological impossibility, due to the private nature of the psychoanalytic session and the contract between analyst and analysand. This prompted me to look for other sites of inquiry where I could have at least an indirect glimpse of the clinical encounter. I began to undergo psychoanalysis myself to understand, firsthand, the psychoanalytic interaction. But the impossibility of recording my own analytic sessions (my analyst was adamant that a recorder would hinder the free flow of unconscious impulses) left me without "data" to analyze.

Unexpectedly, I stumbled onto a fascinating, and to me unknown, psychoanalytic practice: the Multi-Family Structured Psychoanalytical Therapeutic communities (MFSPT), a group that was meeting at the Argentine Psychoanalytic Association (APA) when I began my research in 2010 (see chapter 2). Depending on the session, the group gathered from sixty to eighty analysands and from five to fifteen analysts. During sessions that were open to the public, analysands would share their emotional states and feelings with the other attendees and tell stories about specific personal events. Some of these sessions were extremely moving, to the point of creating a "refracting of affective states" (Collu 2019), a sort of emotional cloud that hovered above the room and "touched" (Derrida 2005) everyone present during the verbal performance. One example occurred when a grandmother declared that she did not want to live anymore after a car crash killed two of her three grandsons and her daughter. As she told her story, the affective atmosphere was so charged that even one of the most experienced analysts said, with evident sorrow, "I don't have words. I don't have anything to say." The rest of us sat there in silence. Tragic stories of loss and desperation abounded in these meetings; on certain occasions, such stories produced particular effects in the group, leaving everyone in reflective silence or "touching" people individually. "There was something in her voice," an analyst told me after the session where the grandmother spoke. "The rhythm of her words told a story beyond the content of her words."

I found this idea that words *sound* in a specific way to listeners, carrying a meaning beyond (or parallel to) their denotation, to be an important feature of psychoanalytic listening as a genre. Words, through the way they sound, interpellate listeners beyond their denotation. And although this may seem a specific trait of therapeutic encounters, the second epigraph of this text indicates that there are everyday interactions in which words "don't sound right," either because the referential meaning does not match the information we have or because the *sounding* produces a gut feeling, a bodily manifestation of distrust or skepticism that we often do not have the language to explain.[1]

In psychoanalytic therapy, this gut feeling, which can sometimes be qualified as uncanny (*unheimlich*), is experienced through the unconscious by the *resonance* that some words create in our psyche. Sigmund Freud and especially Jacques Lacan dedicated extensive attention to this idea. For Lacan, the clinical encounter is oriented precisely toward the moment where interpretation fails and our attention moves away from the semantics of language to *la langue* through a chain of signifiers, prioritizing listening as a way to connect with the unconscious (see Lacan 1988, 237–60). My time observing the MFSPT helped me see how this mode of listening, in which attention to the hidden sense in words generates a resonant state among listener(s), might extend to spheres beyond the private encounter between analyst and analysand. I began to notice parallel interactions between MFSPT sessions and casual interactions outside the center, where people focused on what words invoke in the listener. Suddenly, by overhearing conversations and in my everyday interactions in Buenos Aires, I started to notice a form of listening that replicated the MFSPT setting, where people were constantly trying to resonate with their interlocutor's statement.

The first claim this book makes is that psychoanalytic listening (inside and outside of the clinic) can be understood as a genre of listening. At the most basic level, what I identify as the genre of psychoanalytic listening follows a particular structure and differs from other forms of listening (such as denotational listening, for example). At the same time, the material explored here opens up wider theoretical vistas: if we can begin to elucidate the specificities of psychoanalytic listening as a genre, for instance, could it become possible to imagine other forms of listening that are similarly patterned? To give one example, the idea of *ethical listening* has been explored by anthropologists and philosophers who have tried to understand what it means to "listen through the heart" (Hirschkind 2006), find "attunement with others" (Lipari 2014), and embrace the "ethical responsibility of listening" (Stauffer 2015). In all these works, the presumption is that there is something that can be categorized as ethical listening that differs significantly from other modes of engaging with sound. Can we conceptualize such listening as generic (that is, as belonging to a distinctive genre of listening)? I think we can. To do so, we would need to focus on the particularities of this form of listening. What are its main characteristics (e.g., attention to the interlocutor, neutrality, openness)? What other bodily dispositions does it trigger? When does it emerge? How does it differ from (or complement) empathetic listening? These and other questions could lead us to a possible identification of the broader features of what I call a *genre of listening*.

Other forms of listening that may be categorized as genres could include specialized types of listening generated inside institutional settings. To take an example from a different ethnographic site, I encountered distinctive forms of listening during my work as a translator between unaccompanied minors and United States Citizenship and Immigration Services (USCIS) officers. One officer declared that "in this job, you learn to *listen* to lies." When I asked if she could explain what she meant, she told me that the intonation of voice, the number of hesitations, and other cues were the key clues pointing to dishonesty. Yet she quickly added, "But not always, so I can't really point to a specific thing; *you just know*." Many issues arise from what the officer said. People studying the relationship between language and culture know very well that people do not all respond or react the same way to questions, that questions are not objective artifacts where one can measure credibility (Briggs 1986), and that cultural patterns of communication differ greatly (Gumperz 1982; Jacquemet 1996). This is especially true in the USCIS institutional setting, where there is a cultural distance between interviewers and interviewees—often rural and sometimes Indigenous minors who lack a full understanding of what is going on in an interaction controlled by immigration officers. By "listening to lies," the officer seems to be performing a very concrete and ideological form of listening based on a set of cultural assumptions about communication (Gibb and Good 2014; Kirmayer 2002, 2003).

This form of *suspicious listening* is learned and, as is evident from this case, has concrete material consequences. Listening plays only one part in these interactions, where the officer seeks above all to monitor the accuracy of the asylum seeker's testimony (Park and Bucholtz 2009). But listening is key because, as the officer stated, pitch, intonation, and hesitancies are cues intrinsically related to listening and to how we position ourselves vis-à-vis sound. By listening with a "suspicious ear," the officer contextualizes the interaction and allows the "That doesn't sound right" feeling to emerge, which she was unable to describe accurately ("You just know"). Similar to Freud's motivation to "unmask" the "real" from the "apparent," the USCIS officer is performing an embodied form of listening that I call *generic*. The referential content of language is, of course, key, but in this example the officer is going beyond the denotation, letting herself resonate with the asylee's story.

In this book I focus on listening among the multiple interactional components of communication in order to tease out the listener's role as an active agent of value. I am thus focusing on a genre of practice (Hanks 1996), the embodiment of listening, through the concept of resonance. When we listen, the first thing we hear is sound—not a text but a stream of sound and motion—and these sounds in many cases accumulate and reach a referent at a later time (or not, as the case may be). As anthropologists, for example, we listen to our informants through an *anthropological genre of listening*. Some informants do not know that they are informants, but "we" (anthropologists) know it because we are listening as such. Our listening positions individuals—and ourselves—as occupying a particular social space. Sometimes we listen with a purpose, focusing on what we know is relevant for our research. But at other times, we engage with our informants (and the "data" obtained) by listening through a sort of "free-floating attention" mindset until the "data" finally "speak" to us (an embodied practice). Both anthropological listening and psychoanalytic listening are cumulative. In other words, sounds and words sometimes find a referent—if they find one at all—only after an aural accumulation that can take days, or even years. Thus, anthropological listening is performative in that, by listening "as an anthropologist," we position ourselves as social actors presumably different from others (Marsilli-Vargas 2015).

To understand the embodied nature of psychoanalytic listening, it is useful to look at how musicologist Nicholas Cook, in his influential book *Music, Imagination, and Culture* (1992), distinguishes between two different forms of listening. One he calls *musicological listening*, following Eduard Hanslick's and Heinrich Schenker's formalist view of musical structure. Cook (1992, 166) refers to this form of listening as a metaphorical way of representing music through the analytical, historical, and contextual knowledge of any musical piece, which emphasizes the structure and location of the *Urlinie* (the fundamental line of a musical composition). The other form he conceptualizes simply as *musical listening*, in which the physiological and psychological bodily experience of music happens and where the self-monitoring of music pauses. This second form of listening relates closely to the concept of resonance described earlier. It is experienced rather than analyzed. As happens during shamanic chanting, when the music can get far too quick and elusive for the performer to be able to simultaneously render it and carry out a rich musical analysis, musicians can suspend their attention while playing, experiencing the music with their bodies (Hanks 1990). Cook's work is a good example of why it is productive to distinguish between listening practices. By analytically separating what I would call particular *genres of listening*, Cook is able to understand each form separately, arguing that the perceptual/sensuous field is as important as the analytic component. Hence, discriminating listening from other interactional modalities (although some, such as gaze and bodily disposition, are part of the listening experience) helps in understanding how we listen in different contexts and how listening creates social positioning.[2]

Going back to the psychoanalytic encounter, when copresence between analyst and analysand happens, the analysand may very well bring to the conversation different speech genres and registers. But the analyst's listening is constant, regardless of the speech form being reproduced. The analyst is listening as an expert trying to find the "signifying chain" that organizes the analysand's unconscious. Psychoanalysis, famously referred to as "the talking cure," is also a "listening cure." What ultimately helps analysands is to listen to themselves and to the resonance that certain signifiers (Lacan calls these *nodes*) create in their psyche. The role of the analyst is to suspend attention and reverberate with the analysand's story. Psychoanalysis and phenomenology converge in that understanding is not just a mental activity but rather a pervasive dimension of "being in the world," including what is going on in its *pre-predicative* encounter with the world.[3]

The second claim this book makes is that, in Buenos Aires, psychoanalytic listening as a genre has left the clinical setting to circulate throughout many different arenas, becoming a social way of listening and a mode of organizing social interactions. It is through this form of listening that psychoanalysis travels, reproducing itself in many different settings.

I experienced this firsthand during the summer months in 2012 in Buenos Aires, when I attended a party with some friends. After I casually mentioned that I usually don't dance, a friend said, "You didn't have enough affection [growing up]. Well, that's how *what you said sounded to me*. You missed the embrace, and I identify with that too."[4]

My friend's response took me by surprise, as it conveyed the message that there are specific reasons why someone might dislike performing a particular activity, reasons which may or may not be conscious to the performer. Furthermore, she implied that I somehow transmitted the message of being bereft of physical affection when I *said* that I don't dance. My words *sounded like* (transmitted) a coded message that she was able to *listen to*, even though my denotation did not include any words that could point to a "lack of embrace."

Throughout my fieldwork, I discovered that these interactions, where someone says something and another person "translates" the "real" motives or feelings that words convey, are extremely common in Buenos Aires. Moreover, they are not mere personal interpretations. By focusing on how words *sound* in a particular way, how they *resonate* with the listener, my friend was inadvertently replicating psychoanalytic listening as a genre.

The concept of resonance—a concept that Lacan developed, where sounds reverberate between the signifier and the signified without ever becoming completely reified or fixed—compelled me to understand these interactions as a form of listening. Similarly, in the sessions inside the MFSPT and in such interactions as the one between my friend and me, interpretations coexist with denotation, but the focus is on what the words invoke in the listener.[5] It is, of course, through the dialogic exchange of words that the lay listener is able to bring to light these resonances, but it is overall a listening practice based on how words produce an echo within the psyche of the listener.

The idea that someone can "hear" something other than the denotation in the words uttered by someone else seemed unfathomable to some of my colleagues and associates back in the United States. I remember a conversation with a senior male professor who, after hearing about these recurrent interactions in Buenos Aires, expressed concern: "How could someone know more about my own intentions? No one has the right—or knowledge—to tell someone else what their real motives or intentions are." He continued by classifying these interactions as "intrusions and impositions." This reaction was common among my US colleagues, and it reflects a common conception of the intimate self, rooted in classical liberal theory, which sees the self as authentic, autonomous, and unconnected to others. This concept of the rational, detached individual is implicit, for example, in John Locke's view of language as a vehicle for expressing the thoughts of an independent self (Bauman and Briggs 2003). In Locke's own account, words are said to "excite" ideas in hearers, which suggests an automatic reaction unmediated by any kind of inference (Gauker 1992, 304; Locke [1690] 1975)—that is, language transmits verbatim the unmediated intentions of the speaker. This proposition echoes the views on language articulated by the senior professor. In Buenos Aires, a sociability challenges this conceptualization of the self and understands language not as a transparent vehicle but as containing different voices and communicating beyond the intentions of the speaker.[6] Although on some occasions *porteños* would not accept the interpellation, the majority of people I encountered believe that words have meanings beyond their denotation and are open to a "symbolic exchange," to use Marcel Mauss's (1966) famous conceptualization, where meanings and words are traded, creating reciprocal bonds. Often *porteños* accept that others' interpretations of themselves have value. Thus, in this book, rather than view these interactions as personal intrusions or as technologies of power, as a Foucauldian analysis would suggest, I invite the reader to move away from a framework that conceptualizes social and intersubjective relations as exclusively (or mainly) embedded in a relation of power and instead to focus on the productive exchanges that emerge throughout these encounters.

My fieldwork shows that the lay listener in Buenos Aires who translates the words of others into new interpretations is helping those people *listen to themselves*. Thus, I conceptualize these interpretations as acts of generosity. When the lay listener resonates with the chain of signifiers, or when listeners understand their role as a translator—as an ethical duty or concern—there is no violence or interference but a symbolic exchange.

The recurrence of occasions where listeners imagine it is their right or prerogative to provide a particular interpretation is obvious to Buenos Aires scholars and psychoanalysts: "Lo llamamos psicoanálisis salvaje" (We call it wild psychoanalysis), in the words of a male psychoanalyst wary of conflating the real exchange that happens inside the clinical setting and this "wild" form of analysis. During my time in Buenos Aires, I witnessed people accepting being interpellated and often watched them ask follow-up questions of their interlocutors. On the rare occasion that the person being interpreted felt uncomfortable, the lay listener would not press on a particular meaning, and the conversation moved to a different topic.

Throughout this book, the reader will find many examples of the dissemination of the psychoanalytic listening genre "in the wild." And although I do not claim that these generic forms of listening are indeed a performance of psychoanalysis, they show that in Buenos Aires, on many occasions, people listen to the words as an embodied practice rather than focus only on the denotation. They focus on how words *sound*, on what they invoke in them. (The ethics of listening to the "real" intentions of the speaker is analyzed in chapter 3.)

The idea that psychoanalysis is critical to the Argentine cultural field is part of the doxa. At the University of California, Berkeley, I once had the opportunity to meet prominent anthropologist Philippe Descola, chair of anthropology at the Collège de France, a position previously held by his mentor Claude Lévi-Strauss. When I told Descola that I was interested in doing research on why psychoanalysis is so prevalent in Buenos Aires, a question that guided my overall interest in anthropology and mental health at the time, he looked at me with a big smile and said emphatically, "Well, then you are going to help resolve a big mystery!"

Is this book the answer to the "mystery"? First, it is important to state that many Argentine scholars from different fields have produced rigorous work explaining how psychoanalysis became part of the cultural milieu of Buenos Aires in particular and Argentina in general. By the time I started my research, it was not a mystery anymore. Maybe it has never been a "mystery," at least not to ordinary Argentines; for them, the ubiquity of psychoanalysis is just common sense. More recently, however, two Argentine scholars began to question the doxic idea that Argentines resort to analysts on a regular basis. Instead, historian Mariano Ben Plotkin and anthropologist Nicolás Viotti (2020) argue that there are "different therapeutic constellations," meaning that some Argentines recur to psychoanalysis or psychology but that there are many other practices of self-care, such as popular religiosity, magic, praying, and yoga. Against the idea of psychoanalysis as the dominant practice of self-care in Argentina, and of the modern and secular nature of Argentina that the prevalence of psychoanalysis would reflect, they emphasize instead the heterogeneity of these therapeutic constellations, which include cases of people who resort to praying before going to therapy—a fact that aligns with the declining, but still dominant, religiosity (above all, Catholicism) of the population as a whole. But the examples they provide, through snowball sampling and interviews, consistently show psychotherapy (psychoanalysis or psychology) as part of these therapeutic constellations, even when its presence seems "peripheral" (such as the case of a woman who does not go to therapy herself, but her close relatives do). This approach opens a productive debate about Argentina's modernity and the role of psychotherapies within wider epistemic repertoires. But it does not affect the fact that the *psi-* disciplines are overwhelmingly present in Argentina, which is apparent when situating this country in a comparative perspective.

That Argentina, and more specifically Buenos Aires, has the highest number of psychologists per capita in the world shows that there is still a high demand for psychoanalysts-psychologists in the country. Also, as chapter 5 of this book discusses in detail, psychoanalysis is ubiquitous: in television and radio shows, podcasts, books, magazines, and even graphic humor. The presence of psychoanalysis in the cultural production of the city is immense, suggesting there is a big professional market for it. In her ethnographic analysis of psychoanalytic practices in the poorest neighborhoods of Buenos Aires, anthropologist María E. Epele (2015) follows psychoanalysts to understand how they work with this vulnerable population. Focusing on listening as a "therapeutic technology" that allows one to connect with unprivileged patients, Epele shows that the "talking cure" also exists in the low-income neighborhoods in the Buenos Aires metropolitan area, via the public health system. The ubiquity of psychoanalysis even in poor neighborhoods underlines the fact that psychoanalysis-psychology is still a strong practice in Buenos Aires.

If we compare the number of practicing psychologists and psychoanalysts in Buenos Aires with other cities around the world, Buenos Aires *ganaría por goleada* (a soccer metaphor: it would win by many goals), as a psychoanalyst told me. Statistician and psychoanalyst Modesto Alonso (2010), who has attempted to produce reliable statistics on psychologists in Argentina, explained the difficulty of coming up with exact numbers. The main problem is that the several psychological associations in Buenos Aires are not obliged to grant a registration (*matrícula*) to its members to practice (unlike in the provinces, where psychologists need to be registered). Also, the metropolitan area of Buenos Aires contains both the city and a large set of counties (*partidos*), and psychologists often live in one jurisdiction but work in another. Anyone seeking to make an accurate count of practicing psychologists and psychoanalysts would need to sift through multiple and incomplete data sources. It is thus impossible to know exactly how many practicing psychologists there are.

Still, Alonso (2010) has an estimate. By calculating the total number of professionals who have graduated as psychologists throughout Argentine history, minus the number registered in the provinces and a reasonable rate of people who died, graduated, or retired, he estimates that in 2015 there were ninety-eight thousand psychologists in Argentina, of whom forty-eight thousand were in the city of Buenos Aires. In other words, the city had 1,572 psychologists for every 100,000 inhabitants or 64 inhabitants per psychologist. As Alonso suggested, even cutting the estimate in half (if we assume an enormous statistical mistake of 100 percent) would give Buenos Aires "around 150 inhabitants per psychologist" or over 700 psychologists per 100,000 inhabitants and 100 psychologists per 100,000 inhabitants in Argentina as a whole. These numbers are

TABLE I.1 Psychologists in the Mental Health Sector (per 100,000 Inhabitants)

Rank	Country	No. of psychologists	Year
1	Argentina	222.6	2016
2	Costa Rica	142	2016
3	Netherlands	123.5	2015
4	Finland	109.5	2017
5	Australia	103	2015
6	Israel	88.09	2016
7	Switzerland	84.14	2015
8	Norway	73.52	2016
9	Germany	49.55	2015
10	Canada	48.74	2017
11	France	48.7	2017
12	Guatemala	46.15	2016
13	Cuba	31.06	2016
14	United States	29.86	2016
15	Poland	16.35	2016

Source: World Health Organization, "Psychologists Working in Mental Health Sector (per 100,000)." Accessed April 25, 2019. https://www.who.int/data/gho/data/indicators/indicator -details/GHO/psychologists-working-in-mental-health-sector-(per-100-000).

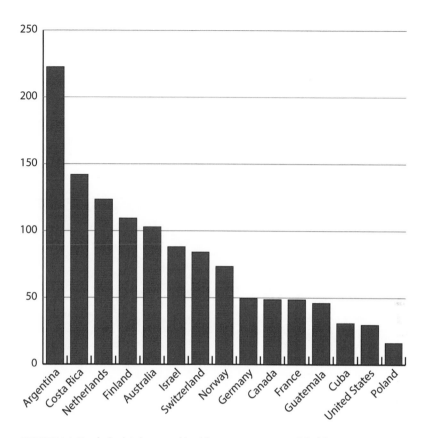

FIGURE I.1 Psychologists in mental health sector, per 100,000 inhabitants. Source: WHO 2015–17.

extremely high, especially when compared with other countries. According to statistics elaborated by the World Health Organization (2021), Argentina is by far the country with the highest number of psychologists working in the mental health sector: 222 per 100,000 inhabitants, far ahead of the next four countries (Costa Rica, the Netherlands, Finland, and Australia), with between 100 and 150 per 100,000. And if we include the city of Buenos Aires in the list of countries (Table 1.2), the numbers are even more astonishing:

The purpose of mentioning these numbers and graphics is not to fetishize data—thanks to the work of many anthropologists and historians, we know that statistics are interpretive constructions (see Adams 2016; Anders 2008; Porter 1996; Tichenor 2020). Instead, I wish to show why, in the imaginary of people around the world, Argentina's (and especially Buenos Aires's) "exceptionality" has been defined by its high number of psychologists (see,

TABLE I.2 International Comparison: City of Buenos Aires, Top Ten Countries, and USA

Rank	Countries	Psychologists per 100K inhabitants	Inhabitants per psychologist	Sources
	Buenos Aires	1,572	63.61	(Alonso, Gago, and Klinar 2015)
	Buenos Aires (conservative est.)	786	127.22	
1	Argentina	222.6	449	(WHO, 2016)
2	Costa Rica	142	704	(WHO 2016)
3	Netherlands	123.5	809	(WHO 2015)
4	Finland	109.5	913	(WHO 2017)
5	Australia	103	970	(WHO 2015)
6	Israel	88.09	1136	(WHO 2016)
7	Switzerland	84.14	1188	(WHO 2015)
8	Norway	73.52	1360	(WHO 2016)
9	Germany	49.55	2018	(WHO 2015)
10	Canada	48.74	2052	(WHO 2017)
11	USA	29.86	3349	(WHO 2016)

among others, Alonso 2010; Balán 1991; Dagfal 2008, 2009; Germán García 2005; Plotkin 2001; Plotkin and Visacovsky 2008; Vezzetti 1983, 1996, 2009; Visacovsky 2002). This number is distinctively, indisputably high, and the presence of so many psychologists affects how people conceptualize the self and understand mental health.

According to a study by Modesto Alonso, Paula Gago, and Doménica Klinar (2018), the predominant theoretical framework for mental health in

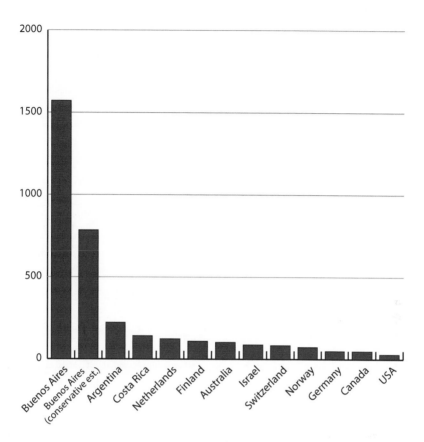

FIGURE I.2 Psychologists per 100,000 inhabitants in City of Buenos Aires, top ten countries, and the United States. Sources: WHO 2021; Alonso, Gago, and Klinar 2015.

Argentina is still psychoanalysis, adopted by 44 percent of psychologists. This is closely followed by cognitive-behavioral practices, employed by 30 percent; integrative approaches by 24 percent; and systemic and "other" approaches by 20 percent. (These percentages add up to more than one hundred because some practitioners adopt more than one framework.)

For a long time, studying psychology in Argentina was synonymous with being a clinical psychologist, and being a psychologist meant being an analyst. As Plotkin and Viotti (2020) argue, things are not static. New social circumstances and processes—fewer people with the time and resources to attend a daily, hour-long psychoanalytic session, as well as the development of rival ideas about mental well-being—are loosening the hegemonic position of psychoanalysis as the most disseminated mental health practice. In my fieldwork I found that neuroscience is the most noticeable emerging trend in Buenos Aires (although this may be different in the provinces). Bookstores are full of neuroscience texts, and authors such as Estanislao Bachrach, a neuroscientist with a doctorate in molecular biology, appear on television to discuss, "from the perspective of the brain," how to be happier and combat stress. But psychotherapies are still very much part of the social life of Buenos Aires, a sort of epistemic filter with which new practices have to coexist. For example, in 2014, Bachrach participated in an hour-long show alongside Gabriel Rolón, arguably the most famous disseminator of psychoanalysis in Argentina today (see chapter 5), in which they discussed how each discipline addresses dissatisfaction. Bachrach's model mirrors neoliberal conceptualizations of the individual self, suggesting that, through discipline, individuals can control environments that people might assume are beyond their control. He explained the "well-established research" on breathing and the brain, insisting that an act as simple as taking three long breaths could generate "thousands of new neurons" capable of helping to resolve the problems at hand. For his part, Rolón insisted on the importance of understanding individuals' personal histories, as well as their connections with others, to begin to understand why suffering occurs. For example, if we get angry in traffic, Rolón believes the most important question is *why*. What causes someone to become angry in certain circumstances? From the other side, Bachrach advocated the search for organic causes and pragmatic solutions, focusing especially on exercises, like taking frequent long breaths, to alleviate discomfort.

I asked Alonso how many people actually seek psychoanalysis in Buenos Aires. His response was blunt: "There is no such figure, because private institutions do not give data. A great deal of the population in treatment is treated privately, in the private practice of a psychologist, or a doctor, or psychotherapist/psychoanalyst, and none of them gives data."[7] There are many possible reasons why practitioners do not report this information. Corroborating what other analysts have told me, Alonso suggested that the most common explanation is that many work *en negro*, informally or under the table, to avoid taxes. But Alonso also described other reasons, from the secretive nature of the therapeutic encounter to more pedestrian ones, such as "rivalries and envies."

Yet the most interesting question regarding *porteños'* relationship to psychoanalysis is why psychoanalytic *listening* came to pervade their cultural practices. Even those who do not go to orthodox analysts get second-hand exposure to psychoanalytic theories by seeing psychologists and psychiatrists at public hospitals and private practices. Psychoanalytic approaches often coexist with other types of treatment within the national health system (see chapter 4). For example, a psychiatrist who works at the Hospital Borda—the public psychiatric hospital for male patients in Buenos Aires—told me, "When you are dealing with a patient that walks like a spider, grunts instead of speaking, and has an untreated skin condition, the first and imminent thing to do is to medicate. Now, once you have stabilized the patient, talk is absolutely key to the patient's treatment. And that's when you go back to thinking about displacement, infancy, trauma, and those things. I think that as a physician you have to work with the story of the patient. We also cure through talking."[8]

For many students of psychology, psychoanalysis is regarded as hegemonic. Yamil, a psychologist trained at the University of Buenos Aires (UBA) who is finishing a PhD in neuroscience in Italy, explained with evident frustration that there were very few elective courses on any branch of psychology other than psychoanalysis (for a discussion of how psychoanalysis has influenced the core curriculum of different mental health specialties, see chapter 4). Sofía, a clinical psychologist who does not consider herself to be a trained analyst and who has worked in private practice since 2015, explained that most of the readings assigned during her training were psychoanalytic texts. She said, "Honestly I cannot understand that someone would doubt the existence of the unconscious. For me, it is as real as water."

This book is about how psychoanalysis permeated different fields and created a culture of psychoanalytic listening. I find this trait unique to Buenos Aires, at least in comparison with Mexico City, my hometown, and the several cities of the United States where I have lived for the past fifteen years (from Manhattan and Philadelphia to the San Francisco Bay area and Atlanta). Undoubtedly, other forms of self-awareness, such as meditation, yoga, and the new religiosity (New Age, evangelicalism), are changing the cartography of practices of self-care, self-knowledge, and self-monitoring (Korman, Viotti, and Garay 2015). Only time will tell whether neuroscience or other methods of self-monitoring and introspection will take the place of psychoanalysis. What is certain is that psychoanalysis has had—and still has—a tremendous influence in Argentina and more broadly in Western cultures of self-reflectiveness. Regardless of one's knowledge of psychoanalytic theory, psychoanalytic notions have become commonsensical. Even people who have not experienced formal analysis believe that events that occurred during infancy have an impact on the later development to adulthood or that human behavior is sometimes the result of unconscious drives and therefore requires sophisticated interpretation. Such ideas, often emerging out of psychoanalysis, have become so ingrained in the doxa that we seldom realize their origins and the remarkable impact that psychoanalytic concepts have had on the way we conceptualize the self. In Argentina, these ideas continue to circulate and are widely accepted.

The decline or outright rejection of psychoanalysis in many scientific fields around the world, particularly in the United States, may obscure the important fact that, historically, psychoanalysis has shared the attention to unconscious practices with other epistemological frameworks. In anthropology, for example, the idea of the unconscious has also proven influential. Independently of Freud's development of his theory of the unconscious, Franz Boas developed, in *The Mind of Primitive Man* (1911 [1938]), a theory of the mind in which customs have unconscious origins that disappear from consciousness.

Boas used the term *secondary rationalizations* to describe the reasons behind an action as ways in which ethnological phenomena become objects of thought (Verdon 2007, 444). This resembles the Freudian use of the term *rationalization* to describe an operation that fulfills functions in the mental life independently of its degree of truth (Freud [1912] 1958). Whereas, for Boas, customs are unconscious in the sense that people misperceive their own behavior, Karl Marx's concept of "false consciousness" describes the systematic misrepresentation of dominant social relations in the consciousness of subordinate classes. Through concepts such as *ideology* and *fetishism*, Marx argues that members of an oppressed class suffer from false consciousness in that their mental representations of the social relations around them systematically conceal or obscure the realities of subordination, exploitation, and domination. Much later, sociologist Pierre Bourdieu (1992, 118) coined the concept of "misrecognition," defined as "the refusal to distinguish the 'objective' truth of 'economic' practices, that is, the law of 'naked self-interest' and egoistic calculation." In his view, social actors fail to recognize social processes because they do not possess the range of dispositions of the habitus of the subjects confronting them. Other epistemes discuss the "concealment" of truth, such as structural analysis, the Frankfurt School, and Louis Althusser's (1996, 125) presentation of the necessity of finding the "structure of the unconscious." Hence, from a variety of perspectives, these models posit that social actors attribute meanings to social phenomena, obscuring the truth behind them. For these theorists, the world hides something deeper behind its representations, something that needs to be discovered.

What is unique to psychoanalysis is its focus on individual subjects as such. While those other frameworks seek to unveil the structures that allow for the reproduction of the practices that mask the truth, psychoanalysis focuses on individuals as unique and irreplaceable beings that have in common their own particular history. This is a very *modern* idea, if we understand modernity as being defined by intersubjectivity as an ontological condition—what Dipankar Gupta (2005, 4) calls iso-ontology, the recognition that other people exist and have different goals and ambitions from our own, differences in turn founded on the "sameness" of human condition, in an ontological sense. This book proposes that by reproducing psychoanalytic listening as a genre, *porteños* perform a modern ideology—that is, one that focuses on intersubjectivity as its point of departure. This ethnography thus shows that the kinds of subjective experiences and linguistic, sonic, and epistemological productions that we usually consider "modern" are not necessarily a colonial import or imposition but a vernacular creation in dialogue with Western traditions.[9]

In the analytic encounter, the analyst anticipates peeling off the *secondary rationalizations* that the analysand brings to the encounter. As a senior female analyst told me, "Not all words, but some, create a form of noise that the analysand brings to the sessions. Especially when they repeat the same story over and over, [the words of the analysand] get in the way of expressing what is really going on; they become the symptom." The analyst's work is thus to look for the *real* significance of the analysand's words by dismantling the secondary rationalizations that the analysand brings to the encounter. Listening plays a crucial role in that the resonance certain words produce serves to anchor the exchange and create the signifying chain that would help to grasp unconscious desires and repressions. In the "wild" form of psychoanalysis that circulates outside of the clinic in Buenos Aires, a similar phenomenon happens. By dismantling the ideas that subjects have about their own actions, everyday practitioners of wild psychoanalysis try to enact exposure of the "real" self and intentions of their subjects. What legitimizes these pedestrian interpretations is that they are inserted into a broader discourse derived from psychoanalysis.

To explore the concept of genres of listening and the circulation of psychoanalytic listening in Buenos Aires, the book is divided into five chapters. The first chapter delves into the theoretical underpinnings of the idea of genres of listening, showing that listening is a structuring and structured act that is therefore capable of assuming discreet forms or *genres*. The next four chapters detail different aspects of the *psychoanalytic* genre of listening in Buenos Aires, explaining how each was constituted and how it circulates.

Chapter 1 presents a conceptual exploration of the different ideas, philosophies, and models that inform the theorization of listening as a genre. Since I am proposing a new concept, this theoretically grounded chapter explains this process in detail. While the book is about the particular genre of psychoanalytic listening, this theoretical examination helps the reader understand, step by step, how genres of listening are constituted in the hopes that the model explored here can be applied to other generic forms of listening. The chapter opens by exploring listening as a semiotic and performative practice. These sections show how, through listening, a process of ordering emerges (listeners always assign a referent, regardless of whether or not they decoded the sound) that facilitates the development of genres capable of framing sound in a particular context at the moment of reception. In this chapter I also discuss the active character of listening by focusing on how listening creates social positions that endow the listener with a social identity (e.g., a doctor listening through the stethoscope, a music expert listening to music), thus generating value.

While showing that listening is a process of ordering, this chapter simultaneously explains why the concept of *genre* is the most useful in describing the form such ordering takes. Engaging with theorists of genre from an array of fields, this chapter enables the reader to understand how my theory of genres of listening differs from and expands upon other theoretical frameworks. Finally, the chapter closes by homing in on the specific case of psychoanalytic listening, exploring how psychoanalysts, including Freud and Lacan, have conceptualized listening inside the clinic, developing what I call the signature formula of the psychoanalytic genre: *When you say X, I hear Y.*

Chapter 2 focuses on the Multi-Family Structured Psychoanalytical Therapeutic (MFSPT) communities, a particular kind of psychoanalysis that includes the participation of entire families, supervised by many psychoanalysts who also participate in the role of analysands. It explains the therapeutic process of this method, in which the stories of the analysands resonate with other participants, thereby creating the structure that organizes each session. While in chapter 1 I explain how forms of listening can be conceptualized as generic, in this chapter I go deeper into psychoanalytic listening; using examples from the MFSPT, I explain in detail what I argue are the four characteristics of psychoanalytic listening as a genre: that it is cumulative; that it is a learned process; that listeners must listen through lived experience (*lo vivencial*); and that the prosodic enunciation—the way in which words "sound"—in many cases trumps the denotation of a statement.

The main focus of chapter 3 is on how this cultivated form of listening based on psychoanalysis trespassed the clinical setting to become a social way of listening in Buenos Aires. Through an ethnographic approach, I explore how lay people replicate psychoanalytic listening through the use of the formula *What you really mean is…*, thereby invoking the idea that the words of their interlocutors hide a message beyond their denotation, which is unknown to the producer of the utterance. Further, when someone seems to know more about your intimate self than you yourself do, ethical concerns emerge. I explore the ethics of listening within a framework in which the self is conceptualized as a social construct rather than as an autonomous individual.

This chapter also explores the ideological component of listening. Listening ideologies are everywhere, and sounds have different meanings, depending on the context and the historical moments in which they are heard. And just as with language, the ideologies that generate diverse sentiments toward certain sounds create hierarchies and differences that have material consequences, as the example of the immigration officer suggested.

Finally, this chapter explores the important idea that, by listening through a psychoanalytic framework, a performance of modernity is enacted. Here I borrow from Gupta's (2005, 1) conceptualization of modernity, which he understands as a specific form of social relations "modified at the most fundamental level by the quality of *intersubjectivity*. A modern society is characterized by intersubjectivity as an ontological condition." Hence, when people in Buenos Aires interpellate their interlocutors' unconscious, the relationship that they are establishing goes beyond their social persona, and they engender a radical form of alterity. The dialogical exchanges that occur during casual interactions bring about a subject position; thus, the performance of modern subjectivity is evident during these encounters.

Chapter 4 is a historical review of the psychoanalytic field in Buenos Aires. What are the specificities of psychoanalysis in this particular setting? How does it differ from, for example, psychoanalysis in the United States? The chapter begins by describing how psychoanalysis was shaped in Buenos Aires by the "mirroring" of Europe, especially France. It explains what many scholars in Argentina have termed *el mundo psi* (the psy-world), a term that relies on the semantic overlap between the three main mental health fields: psychology, psychiatry, and psychoanalysis. I focus on the role of the public university as an important disseminator of psychoanalysis, which, according to several authors (Dagfal 2009; García 2016; Plotkin 2002), became a hegemonic bastion of psychoanalysis and a key driver of its diffusion, relegating other psychological theories and schools to secondary fields. To this day, the main focus of the psychology department at the University of Buenos Aires is psychoanalysis, with readings on Freud, Melanie Klein, Donald Winnicott, Lacan, and other psychoanalysts forming the core of the literature. The public university was also the site where different leftist groups battled over imposing their interpretations of the self and society, such as the Pavlovian school of reflexology, which criticized psychoanalysis by describing it as a bourgeois practice.

The second part of this chapter is devoted to a discussion of the training required to become an analyst, examining two of the main psychoanalytic institutions in Buenos Aires: the Argentine Psychoanalytic Association (APA) and the School of Lacanian Orientation (EOL in its Spanish acronym). I focus specifically on how listening is openly discussed in each program as one of the main traits of psychoanalysis.

Chapter 5 continues to focus on psychoanalysis as a listening genre but explores its circulation in its textual form as well, through different media outlets and cultural representations. The aim is to show how lay audiences in Buenos Aires are exposed to psychoanalysis as a framework of interpretation and how listening as a practice gets reproduced in these media. I center the discussion on three examples that represent psychoanalysis in different ways: graphic humor, television shows, and advertisements. The chapter begins by noting that the interpretive framework of psychoanalysis spread beyond the clinical sphere almost from its inception. A noticeable place of diffusion has been the university, where prominent analysts (and nonanalysts) have given seminars and used psychoanalysis to explain an array of social phenomena. In Argentina, as Plotkin (2002) has demonstrated, the public university played a quintessential role in the later dissemination of psychoanalysis.

My emphasis on listening does not entail a dismissal of the visual-textual paradigm. In the final part of chapter 5, two main concepts accompany my analysis of the circulation of psychoanalysis in the media: *mediatization*, the link between institutional practices and processes of communication and commoditization (Agha 2011), and *communicability*, the way in which discourses spread through ideological channels (Briggs and Hallin 2007). Mediatization serves the purpose of explaining how texts circulate and how they acquire material value. Communicability helps us understand how producers and disseminators of texts are ideologically positioned and how these positions are not fixed; indeed, in the case of psychoanalysis, these distinctions become porous. I analyze the media representation of psychoanalysis using these two frameworks to follow the semiotic chains that permit me to trace what parts of psychoanalysis are embedded in other discourses. A good example can be found in the dissemination of gendered ideologies through psychoanalytic discourses. Specifically, I analyze the figure of "the mother" through the invocation of the Oedipus complex, as well as depictions of mother-son relationships in advertisements and graphic humor that construct a particular form of femininity that is usually accompanied by negative traits. These two concepts allow me to locate the specific moments in which psychoanalysis and its ideological components are invoked.

*   *   *

This book makes a contribution to anthropological theory at the intersection of linguistic and medical-psychological anthropology, sound studies, and Argentine cultural history. More specifically, it enters into conversation with a growing body of ethnographic literature that focuses on sensorial forms as a way of approaching culture beyond the "textual paradigm." This book is an ethnographic study of *the act of listening* as such, independently from its social determinations (e.g., ethnicity, gender, class relations) or technological mediations (from cassettes to new media). It thereby seeks to develop a new theoretical framework for understanding listening as a social fact.

This book demonstrates that listening creates and sustains social relations. It also suggests these social relations reproduce a form of listening that defies the here and now of sound production, a process embodied in the concept of resonance. Building upon semiotics, philosopher Mark Johnson (2007, ix) has suggested that meaning "is not just a matter of concepts and propositions, but also reaches down into the images, sensorimotor schemas, feelings, qualities, and emotions that constitute our meaningful encounter with the world." Following Johnson, listening in the psychoanalytic field creates meaning that is an embodied experience in which reason is not always involved. The fact that words *sound* in particular ways allows for a form of communication that is experienced rather than rationally discussed. Thus, genres of listening emerge through practice (Hanks 1996). This book is an attempt to describe a form of listening that is distinctive and thus generic. It is an attempt to find the normativity within aural perception, a difficult task for a sensory capacity that is individually experienced and not always rational. I focus on the performative aspect of this generic form by analyzing interactions where people listen but also discuss listening: most important are the responses that surface in the dialogic encounters that a psychoanalytic listening produces, often expressed in the formula *When you say x, I hear y*. The latter is a form of reported speech that points to how the listeners are listening, even if such knowledge is always only a partial picture, given the limitations of studying reception. Even so, one can be "touched" by the discourse (or silence) of the other and resonate together.

As musician and cultural theorist Scott Wilson notes, "One could say that one only hears what one already knows, one always hears an echo, but at the same time the music that animates and disturbs us always hints at something else, something strange and unknown" (Dessal 2017). Sounds are impregnated with semiotic content, and the meaning we assign to them is the product of the relation of an active body encountering and structuring the world. This book is a window to a world traversed by listening, to *that which is not said* but is still known.

1   For a Theory of Genres of Listening

Our human interest in the person to whose confession we listen remains alive because we do not only hear his words, but also what is said and left unsaid between and beyond the words. We do not only listen, we also look at the person, observe him, become aware of peculiarities of his gestures, of his posture, of the movement of his body and of his facial expression.

Theodor Reik, *Fragment of a Great Confession* **(1949)**

To listen is an effort. And just to hear is no merit. A duck hears also.
Attributed to Igor Stravinsky

In the summer of 2018, during a dinner party at the house of my friend Ramiro, the conversation turned to psychoanalysis in Argentina. Ramiro has undergone analysis himself and is aware of some of the literature regarding the so-called *cultura psi*, or psychoanalytic culture in Argentina. I asked Ramiro, who was born and raised in Buenos Aires, if he thought discourses about psychoanalysis circulate outside of the closed relationship between analyst and analysand (e.g., patient), beyond the clinic into the public discourse. He responded that he believed it to be a practice confined to the clinic and exclusive to the elite and middle-class spheres. But at one moment during our conversation, he seemed to remember something. He then told me the following story:

Well, now that I think about it, last summer in Buenos Aires, I was coming back from having dinner with my brother, and the taxi driver kept trying to make small talk. At one point he asked me if I had kids. I said, "Yes, Leo and Fede." He then asked me how old they were. I told him, "Leo is eleven and Fede is fifteen." At that point we were on a stoplight and the taxi driver—a man in his fifties—turned to the back seat where I was sitting and asked me, "Why did you mention the name of your youngest son first?" It was such a strange question, so I mumbled, "I don't know, because eleven goes before fifteen?" To which he responded, "Yes, but Fede was born before Leo, right?"

Ramiro told me that the exchange left him feeling uneasy and sad. He kept wondering whether he actually had a favorite son—the question he had *heard* when the taxi driver asked why he mentioned Leo's name before Fede's. After a long pause, he laughed and said, "I don't know why I listened to the taxi driver, but the question still resonates in my head." He then reconsidered my question and agreed that psychoanalytic discourses might indeed have extended outside of the clinic and beyond elite and middle-class soirees.

Ramiro's exchange with the taxi driver is very common. Many *porteños* (as the inhabitants of Buenos Aires are called) I interviewed or interacted with during my years of fieldwork in Buenos Aires had the experience of being interpreted by others who seemingly "were able to hear things that they themselves were incapable of hearing," as Natalia, an Argentine musician who has been psychoanalyzed throughout her life, told me. In Natalia's view, *porteños* have been exposed to psychoanalysis by under-going analysis themselves, by reading the permanent flow of articles on psychoanalysis published in newspapers, magazines, and media outlets, or by watching television shows that discuss analytic encounters. Through these experiences, she thought, they "learned how to interpret through a psychoanalytic framework." This creates a "kind of a *cultura psi* that it is very specific to Buenos Aires," as a renowned psychoanalyst told me.

Although most people in Buenos Aires accept the interpellation, there are some instances when *porteños* think that these interpretations—which, they agree, circulate in many social contexts—can become "overinterpreta-tions," as Tute, a famous graphic humorist who has drawn many cartoons depicting analytic encounters, told me in an interview. For Tute, as for others, interpretations of one's intimate self should be confined to the clini-cal setting or to close friendships, not undertaken by strangers in casual en-counters. This ambivalence was also expressed by Carlos, a neuroscientist who complained that, in Buenos Aires, "everyone thinks they are psychologists, and as such, they try to interpret your life as if they were a card reader," suggesting that, because of the widespread circulation and popularization of psi culture, people's appropriation of psychology becomes *as fanatical as* card reading.

Even though Carlos disparaged *cultura psi*, during my fieldwork I encountered more people who were interested in deciphering possible buried meanings, and in hearing interpretations of their psyches, than critics. As Ernesto, an expat *porteño* living in Europe, told me, "The only good thing about this damned country [Argentina] is that people are interested in listening to what you have to say." Ernesto, like many other Argentines, finds that there is a sociability in Buenos Aires that allows for the exchange of personal stories, even when there is no close familiarity with the interlocutors. In their view, personal tales are shared with strangers to find solutions to life's predicaments.

Beyond the ethical discussion about whether it is acceptable for a stranger to unearth potentially hidden meanings beneath people's statements during casual verbal interactions (see chapter 3), the questions posed by Ramiro's exchange with the taxi driver deserves closer attention. What does it mean to listen to something that was not said? The taxi driver never asked Ramiro whether he had a favorite son. What were the taxi driver and Ramiro *listening* to in each other's statements? Clearly, both heard something beyond the mere denotations of their words, prompting the taxi driver to ask why Ramiro chose that particular order when mentioning his son's names and, in turn, compelling Ramiro to *hear* that he was being accused of having a favorite son. Such questions raise a further query about listening practices: How do we, as social actors, listen? My research in Buenos Aires led me to identify the circulation of a specific form of listening that goes beyond the denotation of utterances to one that infers meanings from the resonance of other people's experiences and communicates those resonances back to the speaker. This form of listening emanates from psychoanalysis and has permeated many social arenas. It is so ubiquitous that I analyze it here as a particular genre of listening. The basic premise of this genre can be schematized in the formula *When you say x, I hear y*. In Ramiro's example, both interlocutors heard "something else" in each other's statements, opening the door to the emergence of particular ideologies and forms of interaction that emerge from listening "in a particular way."

Defining this form of listening as a genre provides a structure to identify its specific theoretical lineages and its ability to circulate through social practices. It also offers important implications regarding listening practices, particularly relating to the implicit ideological biases that circulate within specific social contexts, and especially through listening forms. When I was developing the idea of genres of listening, psychoanalyst Salman Akhtar published the book *Psychoanalytic Listening* (2013), wherein he explains the methods analysts use to listen to analysands, including objective, subjective, empathetic, and intersubjective listening (see chapter 2).[1] This book is not only about the specific techniques that psychoanalysts apply, which Akhtar studies convincingly, but about something broader. Through an ethnographic approach to a form of listening based on the psychoanalytic framework that social actors in Buenos Aires deploy inside and outside of the clinic, I propose to conceptualize Akhtar's specifically clinical forms of listening, as well as other forms encountered in my ethnography, as a genre of listening.

The chapters that follow document how psychoanalytic listening as a genre and its associated listening ideologies are reproduced in professional and clinical contexts, as well as in an array of other social contexts outside of the clinic. Before discussing these issues, this chapter lays out three central concepts that are necessary for understanding both the theoretical underpinnings of the concept of listening genres and the ethnographic approach to one genre in particular, psychoanalytic listening, in its concrete implications, circulation, and reproduction in Buenos Aires. To do so, this chapter delves into questions of listening and meaning making by understanding the semiotics of listening and its performative reach. It continues by analyzing the concept of genre and why it is a useful approach to understand the ubiquities of psychoanalytic listening in Buenos Aires. The chapter ends by presenting a genealogy of listening as it has been defined by Freud and his disciples and considers how some of Freud's intuitions gave rise to the concept of *resonance* later developed by Lacan, which constitutes the core element of psychoanalytic listening as a genre.

THE SEMIOTICS OF LISTENING

To understand Ramiro's exchange with the taxi driver as involving a particular listening practice that can be defined as a genre—following the structure *When you say x, I hear y*—it is important to understand the semiotics of listening and its importance in creating directionality, or how *listening orders and orients our attention*.

Sounds carry information about the world, and when one listens to sounds, communication takes place. This has been well documented in terms of speech sounds, though other nonspeech sounds such as music, machine-produced sounds, and natural sounds can communicate information as well (Darwin 2008; Menon and Levitin 2005; Werker and Fennell 2004). In principle, each acoustic event can be perceived as a sign carrier through which information about the world is communicated. How listeners interpret sound is dependent on the context and on the indexical connections the listener has established with specific referents—that is, the decoding of sounds are dependent on different variants, such as belonging to a particular social group or knowing a particular language. But sounds without a conventionalized referent are open to different interpretations, with the potential to point to distinct ideologies or worldviews.

A good example demonstrating how this process of creating meanings from nonconventional sounds unfolds appears in Edgar Allan Poe's famous story "The Murders in the Rue Morgue." In Poe's story, Auguste Dupin, a fallen French aristocrat with a remarkable capacity for analytic reasoning, solves the brutal murders of two women. In solving the mystery, the hero is faced with a confounding set of aural evidence: while the murders were taking place, numerous witnesses heard two suspects, one speaking in a gruff tone and the second in a shrill voice. All of the witnesses agree that the first was a French man, but the language of the second was difficult to identify. The witnesses—the listeners—are of five different nationalities: Italian, English, Spanish, Dutch, and French. Each witness is sure that it was not the voice of one of their own countrymen; instead, they describe hearing a different language (Spanish, French, German, English, and Russian, respectively). This sharp discrepancy in the language that the witnesses heard ultimately leads Dupin to conclude that the voice could not be human. The killer is revealed to be an orangutan, and the mystery is solved.

The drama of Poe's plot arises from the perception of sounds that are neither linguistic utterances nor musical compositions and therefore lack the systematicness inherent in symbolic systems. Within a symbolic system, if a hearer cannot recognize the meaning of particular signs, their meaning can most likely be inferred through context (see, among others, Cicourel 1992; Duranti and Goodwin 1992; Gumperz and Hymes 1972; Schegloff 1987). This means that unintelligible sounds are given meaning depending on where, when, and by whom they are produced. But when there is no systematicness, as in the sounds produced by the unrecognizable shrill voice in Poe's story, the hearer will most likely invoke a sound that resembles something familiar. This is because in order to be able to codify a sound, the hearer must have previously been exposed to the sound, by witnessing its production firsthand, by reproducing the action that produced the sound, or by internalizing conventional knowledge that links this particular sound to a specific action (e.g., the sound produced by a hammer pounding against a nail). Sounds thus become comprehensible and are transformed into signs, even in the absence of a referent.[2]

In Buenos Aires, as in most places, the words that people use to communicate in casual conversations have conventionalized, fixed meanings. Yet, like the listeners in Poe's story, in some exchanges they treat the words of their interlocutors as unknown and mysterious. Aural signs are not obvious or objective but constructed and contextual. The peculiarity of Buenos Aires is that what prompts these interpretations is the assumption that words have meanings beyond their denotation, a proposition that comes from psychoanalysis and the belief in unconscious practices.

Hence, listening never takes place in a void; it is shaped by other kinds of sensory experiences. In a 1955 experiment, the French composer Pierre Schaeffer (1966) sought to isolate listening from other forms of sensorial perception. He created what he described as an "acousmatic" situation in which listeners were forced to rely on hearing alone to make sense of sound (91). After blindfolding listeners, Schaeffer reproduced sounds and asked the listeners to decode them. He concluded that listeners' temporary blindness prompted them to move their attention away from the physical object responsible for sound and toward the content of the perception itself, redirecting their awareness to hearing alone. Through this sensorily reductive procedure, Schaeffer concluded that "often surprised, often uncertain, we discover that much of what we thought we were hearing, was in reality only seen, and explained, by the context" (93).

In "The Murders in the Rue Morgue," Poe offers a similar example in which the source of a sound is unseen. Unable to see the scene, the witnesses are forced to rely on sound alone—in this case voices—to understand what is happening inside the house at Rue Morgue. Unlike in an acousmatic scenario, however, the context—two screaming women in danger, plus two voices in conversation—allows the listeners to transform the unknown sound into signs: different languages. Poe's tale shows that outside of the artifice of the acousmatic setting, we create signs (real or imagined) every time we hear something. Indeed, as David Toop (2010, 8) notes, we become unnerved when we cannot identify the source of a sound: "Sound must be trusted, cannot be trusted, so has power. When sound that should be present seems to be absent, this is frightening." As a result, in everyday experience, listeners are always looking for meaning; sounds are always attached to a sound image, and there is always a semiotic process at work, whether we are conscious of it or not. In Buenos Aires, the semiotics of listening takes the form of a hermeneutic approach to language, where words have meaning beyond their denotation.

The degree to which the act of listening creates meaning is visible in the example of so-called mondegreens. A mondegreen is the mishearing or misinterpretation of a nearly homophonic phrase in a way that gives it a new meaning. These misinterpretations are common when listening to the lyrics of music or verbal poetry, although they can occur in any other context. Sylvia Wright (1954) proposed the term *mondegreens* as she revisited a childhood memory of listening to the ballad "The Earl of Murray." These are the lyrics Wright thought she heard:

> Ye Highlands and Ye Lowlands
> Oh where *hae* you been?
> They *hae* slain the Earl of Murray,
> And *the Lady Mondegreen.*

The original verse reads:

> Ye Highlands and Ye Lowlands
> Oh where *have* you been?
> They *have* slain Earl Murray,
> And *they've laid him on the green.*

As the listener, Wright took what was, to her, an unintelligible set of sounds and reinterpreted them as "Lady Mondegreen." In doing so, she subtly shifted the meaning of the original utterance. As literary critic Steven Connor (2009) notes, such mishearings stand in direct opposition to verbal confusion or "slips of the tongue." The latter are momentary relaxations of self-monitoring, whereas mondegreens transform random noise into meaning, thereby moving from the direction of nonsense to sense (Connor 2009). As Poe's example shows, mishearing seems to represent human intolerance toward pure meaningless phenomena. Here, once again, listening entails a process of *ordering*, of putting things into place.

The ordering impulse in listening is essential to understanding genres of listening. The process by which such ordering takes on a generic quality becomes clear when we look at how the same sound is decoded differently when listened to by different hearers. Take, for example, the musical or medical realms in which each sound, whether a singular note or a sound inside the body, is attached to a particular referent that is fixed. In order to understand these sounds, the ear has to be trained in what French film theorist and composer Michel Chion (2012) calls semantic listening.[3] As hearers situated within a general public, we can all understand the nature of the sound, but the specialized meaning is something that only a few master.

This mastery has a material reality. For example, when I hear the beats of my heart, I recognize them as such because they have been codified not as a random sound that comes from inside my body but as a particular sound that the heart emits when a human (or animal) is alive. This sound has been transformed into a sign. By contrast, when a doctor listens to my heart with a stethoscope, the concepts attached to the sound image or signifier are very different.[4]

The doctor is able to hear signs that the patient is unable to decipher because the doctor has learned to decode a specific genre of listening. Particular sound images will have different concepts attached to them, depending on the individual who *listens in a particular way*. Doctors listen differently because they have labored or built a skill to listen in this fashion. Listening is something that hearers learn to do, and it depends on a kind of *pragmatics*—the production of meaning in context.[5] Social actors listen *pragmatically* as well as *intentionally*.[6] Whether we are talking about the taxi driver in Ramiro's example, the doctor with a stethoscope, mondegreens, or the witnesses in Poe's tale, hearers are listening with a purpose; people are constantly looking for meanings, and the outcome of their interpretations transforms various social dimensions. As Stravinsky says in the epigraph that begins this chapter, listening "is an effort." And this "effort" points to the constitution of social positions and identities. While fluid, the boundaries of these social positions and identities in turn shape the culturally situated listening practices that I identify as genres of listening.

PERFORMATIVE LISTENING

While sounds are unpredictable, coming and going with no apparent control, listening involves intentional positioning vis-à-vis a given sound, and the codification and interpretation of that sound are an act of consciousness.[7] Studies have postulated that hearing and listening are not passive modes of reception; rather, the listener/hearer is an individual agent (see Carter 2004; Connor 2004a; Hirschkind 2004, 2006; Sterne 2012). As an embodied listener, one is able to position oneself in particular ways in relation to symbolic sounds. In consequence, particular sound images are constituted differently depending on the location, the social actors involved, and the production of sound itself; they rely on the distinct *context* in which the action of listening takes place, developing specific characteristics that differ greatly from one context to another.[8] Accordingly, while listening is an act of interpretation, it also entails occupying a particular social space, a way of being in the world.[9]

A remarkable example of this paradigm is found in Steven Feld's concept of acoustemology (1982). Combining acoustics and epistemology, acoustemology "asks what is knowable, and how it becomes known, through sounding and listening" (Feld 2017, 84). Rather than focusing on the physical components of sounds' materiality, acoustemology focuses instead on the plane of the audible to inquire into sound as simultaneously social and material, exploring the experiential nexus of sonic sensation.

In his book *The Ethical Soundscape*, anthropologist Charles Hirschkind (2006, 56) explains how the widespread practice of listening to Islamic sermon cassette tapes in Egypt is a way of acquiring "knowledge and sensibilities that help one to live and act ethically in a rapidly changing social and political world." Listening to these tapes is a social practice, and no matter where they are being played (inside a cab, in somebody's home), the personal disposition—or what I would call context—that shapes people's listening to the sermons is based purely on the act of listening. The cassettes are not musical but speech oriented, containing words that ultimately transform the listener. Similar to the concept of resonance in psychoanalysis, the words uttered in the cassettes do not dictate behavior because they are attached to a particular semantic reference. Rather, transformation happens through the anticipation and the disposition that the body establishes to allow for listening "through the heart." The source of this transformation comes through the disposition toward acquiring ethical behavior. It is as if the Egyptians who listen to these Islamic sermon-tapes "turn on" a particular ear—that is, they inhabit a specific genre of listening.[10]

The lay listeners in Buenos Aires have developed their own listening practice resonating with the referents of the words but not accepting them as face value. Instead, through their dialogical exchanges, a translation emerges, creating a form of symbolic exchange that creates new narratives but also social positionings indexing the lay listener as a translator.

Thus, how listeners position themselves vis-à-vis received sound becomes a key marker of differing social identities. The tolling of bells from churches in nineteenth-century Europe defined the very being of the proletariat by segmenting their labor and leisure time. At the same time, churchgoers relied on the ringing of bells to comply with the call for ecclesiastical duties (see Corbin 1998). In both instances, listening not only directed behavior; it also indexed the listener as a worker, or as a worshiper. There is a social role performed by listening.

The same phenomenon is replicated with the mastery of a particular genre of listening (as in the case of the doctor listening to a patient's heartbeat). For example, skilled listeners of musical performance who can recognize even a tiny mistake or the most insignificant change in tone or style index themselves as inhabiting a particular social persona: a music expert. Sound experts (e.g., mechanics, physicians, instrument tuners) occupy a specific social role by virtue of their ability to listen within a particular framework of expertise.

In the context of speech, philosopher J. L. Austin (1962) coined the term *performative utterances* to describe situations where the act of speaking goes beyond simply reporting on or describing reality. Austin partitioned speech acts into *locutionary* (referring to the ostensible meaning of an utterance: a statement), *illocutionary* (where the utterance prompts an action: a request or a command), and *perlocutionary* (referring to speech activities that give rise to consequences: a promise). The perlocutionary act sets an expected outcome that any illocutionary act may or may not perform. For example, when a friend promises to return the book that I lent her within a couple of days, the sense of expectancy that I experience will linger until she returns the book to me. Her words of promise convey a perlocutionary effect that will continue until the promise is fulfilled.

The perlocutionary effect of the utterance of a particular statement or a word (e.g., "Stop!"), comprises both the subject who uttered a particular directive (the illocution) and the listener. When we say that listening has the capacity to direct behavior, the directive is sometimes evident and automatic, as in the case of the bells ringing from churches that call forth a particular action. But the consequences or outcomes of the perlocution of listening can linger and manifest much later, or during an extended period of time. This is the case for "ethical listening," which generates the lasting effect of pious behavior. When one listens to an Islamic sermon, it is not the semantic content of a statement (as in the case of a promise, a greeting, or a directive) that prompts an action. Instead, it is the prosody or the component of praying, or the activation of a memory, that can in turn trigger a particular behavior. In short, it is the *resonance* of words and rhythm that have the potential to continue to produce an effect even many hours (or days) after the subject has heard the sermon. As in Ramiro's example, the uneasy feeling that the conversation with the taxi driver generated and that continued to emerge exemplifies how the perlocutionary temporality of listening defies the here and now of sound production and is key to the constitution of psychoanalysis as a genre of listening (see chapter 2).

Taken together, listening to "that which was not said"—in Ramiro's words to the taxi driver, in the sounds of music while one is blindfolded, in a heartbeat heard through a stethoscope, or in the sounds of a murderous ape in Poe's story—constitutes particular ways of apprehending the world that also involve taking a particular position through the performative act of listening. Listening to music, listening to the body through a stethoscope, and listening to sermons are also social practices. They could be described as *situated listening* with specific characteristics that pertain to each sphere. In each case, listening is a unique act with a particular path that can be observed and analyzed (see Becker 2010). These modes of listening also possess *boundaries* that define them, creating genres of listening.[11]

WHY GENRES?

Just as textual genres have distinctive characteristics (contextualization cues, intertextuality, and pragmatics, among many others), genres of listening have their own characteristics that allow us to understand the constitution of a variety of complex social relations. There is a substantial literature on the formation and propagation of textual, verbal, and musical genres, ranging from the study of poetic structure to music composition, practice theory, and literary theory, to name just a few areas of investigation.[12] The abundance of studies that focus on conceptualizing genres is motivated by the fact that genres have the capacity to create context and social relations, bringing an array of ideologies, orders of knowledge, and horizons together in practice (Hanks 1993). Each genre has structural and compositional dimensions that organize the thematic content and style of particular works. Operating prior to the interactional settings in which they are inserted, these constraints create "relatively stable types" (Bakhtin 1986, 60). The result is a co-occurrence of formal features and social structures.[13] What this means is that as listeners, we recognize words or sounds through rules defined at a grammatical level; simultaneously, that grammatical structure itself must be replicated in our social world. For example, when the taxi driver told Ramiro that "Fede was born before Leo," the formula (at grammatical level) *When you say x, I hear y* surfaced because the taxi driver dismissed Ramiro's own explanation of his statement—namely, that "eleven goes before fifteen." If Ramiro did not *hear* that the taxi driver was asking something else, then this listening genre would not have emerged. The listening genre *When you say x, I hear y* surfaced only when Ramiro "entered" a dialogical exchange by applying a psychoanalytic framework; the "meaning" of the taxi driver's comment thus emerged at the moment of reception. Consequently, the psychoanalytic listening genre that emerges with the formula *When you say x, I hear y* is followed by a constant social response (thus the co-occurrence). In this case, listening beyond the denotation and focusing on possible alternate meanings emerge from the *resonance* that the taxi driver produced in Ramiro through his questioning.

How genres of listening accomplish this function is part of an ongoing discussion across different fields. For those of us interested in reception, genres can be constituted by particular operations of reading/reception determined by the interpretation of the reader, who focuses on some features of the text (in its broader sense) while overlooking others—this is, the reader creates the genre *at* the moment of reading/reception.[14] This approach postulates that receiving and producing are in a constant dialogical relation in which the receiver is not passive but rather an active producer of meaning. In Ramiro's conversation with the taxi driver, the genre emerged at the moment of reception—that is, when the taxi driver "heard something else" in Ramiro's words, although it was preceded by a particular "listening culture" in which both participate, based in psychoanalysis.

Sounds embedded into a particular context become genres when there is a co-occurrence (a structure or a pattern at the level of syntax, phonetics. and morphology) that is the internalization of norms and the knowledge of when and how to apply these norms to everyday situations. In this process we see a dialectic between the structural and the social.[15]

Consequently, genres do not emerge in a vacuum; they are shaped by a set of "normative basic patterns" that help delineate the process of reception.[16] These patterns encompass the social norms and the historical situation of a given time and place and also situate the genre in relation to others. This means that genres are historically flexible and can be understood differently depending on the dialogical relationship established within a particular historical/cultural context.

Genres are historically constituted, and they reflect an overarching normativity. In the case of listening genres, this means that such genres emerge out of already existent *listening discourses*. Listeners do not receive sound in a vacuum but rather classify sounds in relationship to preexisting listening texts. In Ramiro's exchange with the taxi driver, both have been exposed to psychoanalytic methodology where "free associations," or freely occurring ideas that emerge after someone has uttered a sentence, have a meaning beyond their denotation. They are listening to each other's statements in a particular historical context (Buenos Aires in 2017) and through a disciplinary lens ("psychoanalysis" in a broad sense) that makes the exchange intelligible.

Thus, genres are useful units of analysis because they link particular formal units (e.g., phonetic, lexical, and grammatical) to thematic ones. In the case of psychoanalytic listening as a genre, it is the formula *When you say x, I hear y* that provides the structural component of the genre. The taxi driver embedded Ramiro's words into a psychoanalytic framework because he had been exposed to other thematic episodes (i.e., conversations where a hermeneutic interpretation trumped the denotation). Put in formal terms, a genre emerges only when the construction and maintenance of the significance and indexical associations enable a description of the genre as a social, culture-specific phenomenon, in relation to which expressions can be produced and interpreted (Agha 2007; Agha and Frog 2015; Briggs and Bauman 1992). That Ramiro accepted the interpellation shows that he is part of the *cultura psi* of Buenos Aires, as explained by the senior psychoanalysts I interviewed.[17]

Accordingly, genres structure relations between the speaker, listener, and other participants during spoken communication (Bakhtin 1986). They preexist any particular interaction, even as they are adopted and combined in speech situations (Goffman 1964). Generic types orient speakers and listeners toward a specific conceptual horizon, determined by "the concrete situation of the speech communication, the personal composition of its participants" (Bakhtin 1986, 78), and what Bauman (2006, 2012) calls the already established "orders of knowledge" that precede the interaction. These orders of knowledge are reproduced, as in Ramiro's example, as a tacit framework inhabited by both the taxi driver and Ramiro.

Genres are thus defined as *kinds of discourse* (including listening) that are the outcome of historically specific acts that "derive their thematic organization from the interplay between systems of social value, linguistic convention, and the world portrayed" (Hanks 1987, 671). As a result, the listener's personal history and social agreements inform a particular social situation, become embedded, and create specific genres of listening.

The genres most studied by linguistic scholars are speech genres, seen as a precondition for meaningful communication, because they organize our speech in almost the same way as grammatical forms do, conveying expectations of content, style, and structure that help to shape any verbal exchange, from the simplest conversational rejoinder to the most complex scientific statement (Bakhtin 1986, 90). If we transpose the idea that speech genres point to a specific conceptual horizon during interaction from reading to listening practices, we will find that generic types *order* reception (as the mondegreens or Poe's orangutan shows). Genres of listening differentially tune or guide the ear to attend to some aspects of an utterance—or sound—while not attending to others. *Genres create context and frameworks of relevance that shape the listener's orientation at the moment of reception.*

Understanding the listening formula *When you say X, I hear Y* in Buenos Aires as a genre of listening allows us to focus on a particular sociability that is based on a listening practice and on the resonances that language creates in each other's psyches. It helps us to trace and understand how psychoanalytic discourses are disseminated in and permeate throughout *porteño* culture.

The particularities of Ramiro's exchange with the taxi driver exemplify that just as there are many ways of speaking, there are many possible ways of listening. When a mechanic listens to the sound of a broken car, it is not the same as a music lover listening to Wagner's *The Ring of the Nibelung* opera or a doctor listening to a patient's heart through the stethoscope. Moreover, these types of listening can further diverge depending on qualities of the listener. Musicologists, for instance, may be listening *for* the musical form of a particular music piece, focusing on musical structure, syntax, style, and history, through either architectonic or synoptic listening, drawing from their knowledge of musical structure (Kivy 2001), while neophytes who listen to the same musical piece may experience instead a physical and emotional change (such as goose bumps or tears) but without a concern for musical structure.

I contend that each particular way of listening in these examples is a listening genre. A listening genre is a *framework of relevance* that surfaces at the moment of reception and orients the apprehension of sound. Sound reception is neither neutral nor automatic and always involves a particular type of ideological and practice intervention. By focusing through a particular frame, the listener creates a context or, more precisely, a *contextual configuration of reception* that provides a unique interpretive lens. Listening genres—like speech genres—are types produced at the moment of reception (Bauman 1992; Bauman and Briggs 1990; Hanks 1987) and are also social in that they present a "cultural horizon" (Hanks 1996) by helping to elucidate how the listener "tunes" the ear into a particular frequency and thus, as much as ways of speaking (Hymes 1974), create structures of relevance that provide directionality.

In this book, I scrutinize psychoanalytic listening as a genre defined through the analysis of *overtly occurring discourse*. As Ramiro's example shows, this genre of listening emerges through the *responses during the dialogic encounters* that a psychoanalytic listening produces. The formula *When you say X, I hear Y* is a form of reported speech that points to how the listener positions the self vis-à-vis a particular statement. Ramiro heard that he loved one of his sons more than the other, whereas the taxi driver conceivably heard a hesitancy or a change of tone in Ramiro's voice, which seemingly triggered in his own psyche a memory or a bodily sensation that awakened through the resonance of Ramiro's words, compelling him to inquire further into Ramiro's answer. As Reik's statement in the epigraph of this chapter suggests, we as listeners also listen to the hesitancies, the silences, the "in-between lines"; thus, listening is an embodied experience containing different cognitive modalities.

GENEALOGIES OF PSYCHOANALYTIC LISTENING

To demonstrate how genres of listening emerge, I now turn to the central subject of this book, psychoanalytic listening, a listening genre that permeates social life in the city of Buenos Aires, Argentina, where I conducted fieldwork over a period of six years. As exemplified in Ramiro's exchange with the taxi driver, in Buenos Aires there is a displacement of the *performativity of speaking* in favor of a *performativity of listening*. Although linguistic practices are an intrinsic part of the exchange, the argument is that the taxi driver is dismissing the denotation in favor of focusing—listening—to "that which Ramiro did not say," by resonating with his words.

What are the contours of the genre of psychoanalytic listening? In the clinical setting, psychoanalysts are invested in being acutely aware of their own ways of listening and speaking, and they attend to analysands (i.e., the patient) through a specific interpretive lens (thus the performativity of listening practices). Typically, this means that psychoanalysts go far beyond what a patient says to infer what is meant, even though it may remain unsaid. Spoken words are placed in a relation of relevance to a patient's unspoken (and perhaps unrecognized) motives and feelings. This generates the signature statement of the genre *When you say X, I hear Y*. The regularities of this genre allow the analyst to move from what is said to what is inferentially heard.[18]

Eduardo Mandelbaum, a senior psychoanalyst with more than fifty years of clinical practice experience, told me in an interview, "Being trained as an analyst and having worked for so many years in both my personal practice and 'the Multi' [multifamily psychoanalytic sessions; see chapter 2], it's hard to turn off the psychoanalytic ear. Everywhere you go you start to analyze what people are saying. It's like a curse!" As an analyst with many years of experience listening to different analysands, Mandelbaum developed a *psychoanalytic ear*, one that refuses to be contained within the space of the clinic.

Even though listening is one of the key elements in the psychoanalytic encounter (i.e., an analysand speaks and a psychoanalyst listens, and vice versa), most of the studies of psychoanalysis that focus on listening are concerned either with listening to the internal voices produced by the punitive superego or with the process of fantasy creation through the repression of desire (see Freud [1923] 1995; Isakower 1939). A number of psychoanalysts have directly theorized listening between analyst and analysand. Among them were Sigmund Freud; the Viennese American psychiatrist Otto Isakower; Theodor Reik, a friend and disciple of Freud, with many connections in Argentina; and Jacques Lacan, another theorist with a large following in Argentina. Additionally, a number of recent scholars, most notably Salman Akhtar (2013), have continued to study and systematize the phenomenon of psychoanalytic listening (Connor 1997, 2004a, 2009; Wilberg 2004). Reconstructing the genealogy of this theoretical effort is necessary to understand psychoanalytical listening as a genre of listening, both from a theoretical perspective "internal" to psychoanalysis and from an ethnographic perspective situated in Buenos Aires.

The "Third Ear"

While analyzing the sense of "guilt" in *The Ego and the Id*, Freud ([1923] 1995, 654) remarked on the role of auditory traces in the constitution of fantasies: "It is as impossible for the super-ego as for the ego to disclaim its origin from things heard; for it is a part of the ego and remains accessible to consciousness by way of these word-presentation . . . but the *cathetic energy* does not reach these contents of the super-ego from auditory perception (instruction or reading) but from sources of the id."[19]

Here Freud explains a particular kind of listening, constituted during childhood and in dialogue with the superego, which involves the internalization of parental voices. "First and foremost," notes Freud ([1923] 1995, 780), "there is the incorporation of the former parental agency as a super-ego . . . [and] identifications with the two parents of the later period and with other influential figures." Internalizing the parental voice creates verbal residues derived from auditory perceptions that the child is not yet capable of understanding as such. The unconscious process of internalizing these auditory insights will eventually constitute the superego, which many times is punitive and regulatory. Thus, the superego is depicted as an "internal voice" that will both reprimand us for our disobedience and encourage us in the pursuit of impossible tasks, while the ego is left to suffer the consequences of these contradictory imperatives (654–55, 780–85).

Following Freud's proposition on the constitution of the superego as an internal voice, Otto Isakower, in his article "On the Exceptional Position of the Auditory Sphere" (1939), analyzed this idea into a more direct reflection on the physical and psychic process of hearing. Isakower concluded that "the auditory sphere," which encompasses both the auditory dimension and the bodily sense of equilibrium and orientation, is of critical importance for the formation of the unconscious.[20] Making a curious comparison between the constitution of the superego and that of the crustacean *Palaemon* (figure 1.1), he explained that the otolith apparatus (a structure in the inner ear responsible for balance, movement, and sound detection in higher aquatic and terrestrial vertebrates and for a sense of gravity in lower animals) does not serve the function of hearing in the *Palaemon* but instead enables "the perception of movement and position of the body relative to its environment and orientation in space" (340). In order to be able to orient itself, this crustacean fills the canal of the otolith apparatus with sand or any material that is close by. In other words, the crustacean incorporates external elements into its organ to be able to orient itself, and the characteristics of the elements it incorporates (rock, sand, magnetic debris, etc.) shape its awareness and perception of the external environment. For Isakower, something similar happens with the formation of the unconscious: the external "resonance" of the outer world, which is yet to be decoded by an infant, enters the auditory sphere, making an unconscious imprint that will shape the

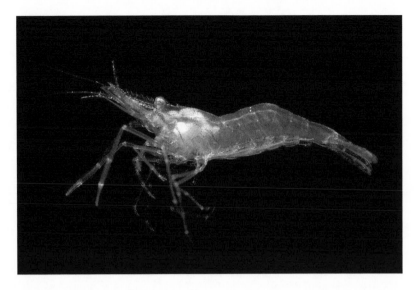

FIGURE 1.1 *Palaemon macrodactylus* Rathbun, 1902. Live color. Photography of the body in lateral view. Photo by Nahuel Farias. In Spivak et al. 2019.

infant's behavior. The superego is thus constituted as the "psychical organ of equilibrium" (344), the apparatus that regulates and controls behavior. It is in the capacity of linguistically ordering the structure of the auditory perception that the child begins to form an inner voice, and for Isakower, this is what constitutes the "ego-apparatus in man" (345).

This theory about the auditory sphere as incorporating more than one cognitive modality (i.e., audition and equilibrium) constitutes a particular way of understanding listening.[21] Within this framework, listening becomes nothing less than the most valuable sensorial dimension for the constitution of one's self. As Isakower explains, the visual system of a newborn infant takes some time to develop. In the first week of life, babies do not see much detail. Their first view of the world is indistinct and only in shades of gray, and it takes several months for the child's vision to develop fully. In contrast, the auditory system of a newborn is fully developed.[22]

These early theorists of the discipline of psychoanalysis ultimately understood listening as a dialogue within the psyche. But how this theory of listening translates in the psychoanalytic encounter is a different analytic problem altogether. Understanding the connection between a sound image and a concept in a psychoanalytic exchange—a session between an analysand and an analyst—is a difficult task. In his books *Listening with the Third Ear* (1948) and *Voices from the Inaudible* (1964), Theodor Reik described how psychoanalysis developed its own way of listening or what he calls a "third ear." According to Reik (1948, 144), the main peculiarity of this genre of listening is that it surpasses the conscious dimension: "Psychoanalysis is not so much a heart-to-heart talk as a drive-to-drive talk, an inaudible but highly expressive dialogue." The psychoanalyst learns to collect this material, which is not conscious but which has to become conscious. The suggestion is that when an analysand speaks to an analyst, certain utterances lose their semantic referents, and the analyst's task is to *listen* to how "one mind speaks to another beyond words and in silence" (144). Reik continues, "It can be demonstrated that the analyst, like his patient, knows things without knowing that he knows them. The voice that speaks in him speaks low, but he who listens with the third ear hears also what is expressed almost noiselessly, what is said, *pianissimo.* There are instances in which things a person has said in psychoanalysis are consciously not even heard by the analyst [*When you say x, I hear y*] but nonetheless understood or interpreted" (145).

To illustrate this process, Reik recounts the story of a female patient he had been treating for some time. At the end of their fifth meeting, he noticed that this patient did not look at herself in the mirror when putting on her coat and hat. Reik realized this conduct was unusual and began to wonder why he had not noticed it before.[23] His conclusion was that, through all the previous sessions, he had unconsciously begun to hear things beyond what was explicitly said. Reik's sudden realization that his patient never looked at herself in the mirror was the result of this auditory accumulation, which finally—unconsciously—revealed itself as he noticed this single trait. Reik's inability to notice his patient's habit of not looking in the mirror became a sign of something he was not able to understand before. In his recollection of the story, Reik suggests that he had likely noticed this action before but recognized its significance only "when the unconscious became visible" (147). This is because, for Reik, psychoanalytic listening is neither a conscious thought process nor a logical operation but "an unconscious—I might almost say instinctive—reaction that takes place within" (147). As in the metaphor of the crustacean *Palaemon,* the analyst internalizes—takes in—information of all kinds that will later develop in the demarcation of a specific path. When declaring that a psychoanalyst should be able to hear the "inner voice" of the patient's unconscious, Reik is referring to this phenomenon. While not necessarily focusing only on the restrictive inner voice of the superego, the aurality a psychoanalyst seeks to decode pertains to the unconscious world. For Freud ([1923] 1995, 630), psychoanalysis "cannot situate the essence of the psychical in consciousness, but is obliged to regard consciousness as a quality of the psychical." Thus, the duty of the analyst is to find this auditory space inside the psyche of the analysand, and by doing so, the analyst constitutes a specific psychoanalytic listening genre.

The approaches and literature of such theorists as Reik, Freud, Lacan, and Isakower were central in the curriculum for psychoanalytic training in Argentina. It is no coincidence that the individual most often identified as the founding father of psychoanalysis in Argentina, the Spanish-born psychoanalyst Ángel Garma, was Reik's close disciple and analysand. Therefore, generations of psychoanalysis in Argentina inherited and recirculated this specific approach to listening.

In the therapeutical settings I visited, as well as in my own theoretical analysis based on the clinical practice that my informants shared with me, of all the key concepts related to psychoanalytical listening, one reappeared constantly, explicitly, and tacitly: that of *resonance*.

Resonance

The concept of language as transindividual—as something passing from one individual to another—is of paramount importance for understanding psychoanalytic listening as a genre. Foundational to the emergence of psychoanalytic listening is a process resembling what psychoanalysts call resonance. Freud postulated that resonance makes an imprint in the infant's psyche. Isakower later developed this idea further, and his interpretation was amplified and circulated by Lacan and his followers in dialogue with their reading of the Swiss founder of modern linguistics, Ferdinand de Saussure.

In "The Function and Field of Speech and Language in Psychoanalysis," Lacan ([1966] 2006) outlines the idea that the unconscious is structured like a language—not just any kind of language, but rather one full of parapraxes, condensation, and the evocative intricacies of dream work. He writes, "The unconscious is that part of concrete discourse qua transindividual, which is not at the subject's disposal in reestablishing the continuity of his conscious discourse" (258). According to Lacan, speech is transindividual, meaning it moves from one psyche to another and is divided into two classes. The first, which Freud called secondary processes, involves those linguistic utterances that are at the disposal of the speaking subjects (and are preconscious and conscious)—that is to say, verbal acts that the subject understands as autonomous when using them to communicate something. The second belongs to the class of primary processes and is unconscious; it contains those utterances that obtrude against the will of the speaking subject. Accordingly, the human self appears split into two agencies: one potentially or actually conscious and seemingly autonomous, the other unconscious and only "symptomatically irruptive" (Bär 1974, 476).

Lacan introduced the idea that the unconscious is structured as a language to distance himself from a pseudobiological model derived from nineteenth-century physics (see James 1890; Schwarz and Pfister 2016). In his view, linguistics could provide a more exact analysis of the psychoanalytic encounter. In particular, he depicted the role of the therapist as that of a *translator* (similar to what lay listeners do by interpreting the speech of others) between conscious and unconscious systems of meaning, meanings that themselves emerge in the clinical encounter between the analyst and analysand.

Central to Lacan's early theory of language is de Saussure's observation that the linguistic system is constituted by signifiers that stand in relation to something (x) that is signified, this relationship being arbitrarily assigned by a particular code. Lacan ([1966] 2006) decided to invert this relationship by proposing that something (x) which is signified is itself another signifier. Consequently, signifiers relate to each other forming sequences in a *signifying chain*, which "gives an approximate idea: links by which a necklace firmly hooks onto a link of another necklace made of links" (418). Lacan focused on the subjective signification that people create throughout their individual stories in which particular words become "nodes" for a particular salient and polyphonic chain of signifiers. Thereby, the primary task of the analyst is the "achievement of a state of resonance" (126) with the polyphony of the patient's language, which, in turn, may permit a recognition and explication of nodal points in the patient's discourse when they occur. In describing the process of resonance in Lacan, analyst Samuel Ysseling (1970, 108) observed, "Analysis does not intend so much to control the speaking, but rather to let oneself be dominated and controlled by a word to which one must correspond and listen"—that is, resonance. By employing their own associations in resonance with the patients', analysts join in the quest for that which is signified at a nodal point. Lacan contends that this activity can permit and facilitate the analysand to speak fully by bringing those words in their signifying relationship to one another into speech, which constitutes "the essential structure of his own fundamental subjectivity" (Gorney 1978, 255). The importance of the concept of resonance is not that it leads to interpretation on the part of the analyst, but rather that it permits the analyst to speak evocatively, therein facilitating an enrichment in the polyphony of the discourse of the other. In chapter 3 I identify this form of listening as a learned process that can be cultivated and, as Eduardo Mandelbaum noted, is capable of being deployed in contexts well beyond the clinic.

The ramifications of this approach are rich, and they speak to an array of disciplines. The idea of the deferment of signification as a form of listening can also be found in philosopher Jean-Luc Nancy's *Listening* (2009). Nancy asks whether listening can be conceptualized as a resonant act that does not relate to an understanding but to sense itself: "perhaps it is necessary that sense not be content to make sense (or to be logos), but that it wants also to resound" (5). Sensing is conceived through the act of listening (re-sounding) as the "experience of truth."[24] Contrary to the theorizations previously discussed, Nancy's conceptualization of listening does not necessitate reason; he inverts the relationship between hearing and listening by conceptualizing hearing as responsible for neutralizing understanding and listening as the corporeal "reverberant echoing of the resonant" (9).[25] Resonance is represented as pure phenomenon, as a sort of Dasein. He shares with Lacan (and ethnomusicologist Steven Feld) the idea that listening is not necessarily sonorous, especially when listening to oneself through the transindividual self.[26] But Lacan is still looking for some kind of logos by finding the "nodes" in the signifying chain that will eventually help the analyst and the analysand give meaning to the analysand's suffering. Yet this interpretation is unconscious, embodied knowledge that resonates in the polyphonic relationship with the analysand. Both models present the idea that resonance surpasses the sonic realm. To listen is to resonate, and this resonance lingers and may—or may not—find a signifier.

The concept of resonance developed by Freud, his students, philosophers, and scholars interested in the formation of the psyche remains the core of psychoanalytic listening: it implicates a codification that does not necessarily involve an act of consciousness, yet it needs to reach consciousness for interpretation through the resonance of the analysand's and analyst's listening. Thus, the imprints on the psyche during infancy will inform the analysand's subjectivity, creating nodes, as Lacan points out, with the enunciation of particular words that analysts will be able to uncover once they "resonate" with the analysand's subjectivity.

In Ramiro's example, both he and the taxi driver were listening to denotation but let themselves resonate with each other's words. In doing so, they created referents that were beyond the mere sense of the words they exchanged. This is precisely how resonance works and why it is transindividual. Ramiro and the taxi driver embodied a genre of listening where consciousness is not located solely in an individual body (through an empiricist framework) nor by means of pure intellectualism but, rather, is a listening formed in a dynamic process of interaction between the resonances produced in each other.

Psychoanalytic listening, as a genre, is to listen through the intersubjective dialogue of analysands and "resonate" with them. This surpasses the here and now of the verbal interaction through the perlocutionary effect produced by listening in the clinical setting. The fact that Ramiro continued to "feel bad" about the encounter with the taxi driver exemplifies how psychoanalytic listening as a genre can "linger" (the perlocutionary force of listening) and find a referent or not.

Resonance is thus a central feature of psychoanalytic listening as a genre—and in psychoanalytic theory, resonance is conceptualized as a central feature of listening in general. But the frameworks through which resonance occurs and that organize the listener's interpretations are specific, contextual, and in some cases determined by concrete ideologies. This book critically "tunes into" resonance in Buenos Aires. Each of the particular ways of listening in the examples I have provided in this chapter—from doctors listening to heartbeats, to the implications of church bells and the effects of Islamic cassette sermons, to the multiple theories of sound in psychoanalytic theory and in linguistics—inform my concept *genre of listening*. The theoretical cartography I have outlined in this chapter is crucial to understanding the genre of listening shared by Ramiro and his taxi driver, as well as countless others whose voices fill my analysis of how this genre of listening unfolds and functions.

Throughout the rest of the book, I illuminate the multiple textures that intersect to form and codify psychoanalytic listening as a genre of listening in Argentina. Psychoanalytic listening has moved beyond the clinic and emerges as a key genre of listening that permeates social interaction in Buenos Aires in significant social ways. In the following chapters I discuss the methodological impossibility of listening for someone else and analyze genres of listening through the examination of *how subjects talk about listening*. It is through the dialogic encounters that incidents of "hearing beyond what someone is saying" reflect the dense history and continued presence of psi culture today.

2   The Music in the Words

It suffices to listen to poetry . . . or a polyphony to be heard and for it to become clear that all discourse is aligned along the several staves of a musical score.
Jacques Lacan, Écrits ([1966] 2006)

A [music] masterpiece always moves, by definition, in the manner of a ghost.
Jacques Derrida, Specters of Marx (2012)

Valeria, a single mother of two young boys, was extremely attentive to what Hugo was saying. Hugo, a sixty-five-year-old man who had recently lost his wife to an autoimmune disease, was explaining that the worst part of living alone had been to confront his own misery by listening to a mental dialogue that won't give him peace. He explained that those voices never appeared when Carla, his late wife, was alive: "These voices I hear are pointing to every single problem or bad decision I have made; they are deafening."[1] After he finished talking, Valeria asked for the microphone and said, "I think, Hugo, that these voices that you are now beginning to hear were there all along. You just weren't listening, but they conditioned your life. Now that you are alone, you are forced to listen and confront yourself. But don't feel bad. You are given the opportunity to listen and try to make peace with yourself. Listening to you makes me realize the importance of paying attention. To stop and listen. If we sharpen our ears, we will be able to listen to ourselves and, with a little bit of luck, change."[2]

After Valeria's intervention, María Elisa Mitre, one of the coordinators of the meeting, asked Hugo if he could recount the exact words the voices were saying. Hugo responded, "I don't know... that I don't do things right, that I didn't achieve many goals that I set for myself... but sometimes it's more like sounds than a voice."[3] This prompted Mitre to intervene again by saying, "This is what I call experiential memory (*memoria vivencial*), violent sounds without representation or words."[4]

This sui generis psychoanalytic session took place within the framework of Multi-Family Structured Psychoanalytical Therapy (MFSPT), a group form of psychoanalytic therapy, at Centro DITEM (Diagnóstico, Investigación y Tratamiento de Enfermedades Mentales) (Center for Diagnosis, Research, and Treatment of Mental Diseases) on Thames Street in the trendy neighborhood of Palermo in Buenos Aires. This psychoanalytic method was pioneered by Jorgé García Badaracco and today is regularly practiced at different sites in and around the city, as well as in several other countries. While psychoanalysis is usually conducted in one-on-one, private meetings between an analyst and an analysand that are closed to third-party observation, these group sessions provide a rare opportunity for documenting in clinical contexts many of the features of the genre of psychoanalytic listening that have now permeated the city well beyond the clinic.

At bottom, psychoanalytic listening has become a social fact today in Buenos Aires as a result of the strong historical presence of the practice and theory of psychoanalysis within the city, notably in its educational institutions and public hospitals. The per capita rate of psychoanalysts in the city appears to be among the highest in the world, and the listening practices in the clinic have circulated widely outside those settings into basic areas of social interaction and cultural production. But to explore how this form of listening emerged in the city and acquired a transformative social force, it is helpful to first explain the structure of psychoanalytic listening within the clinical setting.

Because psychoanalytic encounters are normally private, it is often impossible to record or have access to the interactions between the analyst and the analysand. Consequently, public group sessions of psychoanalysis of the MFSPT provide opportunities to observe important parts of the psychoanalytic process. In Buenos Aires, two useful places to observe this kind of psychoanalytic encounter have been the Asociación Psicoanalítica Argentina (APA, Argentine Psychoanalytic Association) and Centro DITEM, sites where MFSPT is practiced and the public can attend.[5]

The group model of the multifamily psychoanalytic session is atypical within the clinical practice of psychoanalysis. Psychoanalysis originally emerged as a highly ritualized interaction between analysand and analyst, the session being private and not to be disrupted by any external force (for instance, my psychoanalyst did not allow me to record our own private sessions because it would bring something external that could potentially disturb the flow of unconscious impulses). Inside this setting, an analysand will talk, mostly without interruption, with an attentive listener who is trying to make sense of the flow of speech. The analysand is considered the object of interpretation by the other participant, the psychoanalyst (although analysands listen to themselves also). In this encounter, there is the potential participation of four interactants: the analyst, the analysand, and their psychic doppelgängers.[6] This notion, that subjects are constituted not only by their own "self" but by a complex system of interacting psychic entities and processes—instances that Freud called the conscious, preconscious, and unconscious, as well as the three agencies of id, ego, and superego—is at odds with the idea of a unitary subject postulated by classical philosophy, from Plato to Kant and Descartes. These philosophers conveyed the idea that human beings have an essence—variously called the soul or self— that gives subjects a unified form (see, among others, Descartes [1637] 2006; Marshall 2010; Tschemplik 2008). But the practice of psychoanalysis pushes back against this notion. When describing the function of dreamwork, for example, Freud ([1900] 1953, 580–81) wrote in *The Interpretation of Dreams*, "Thus a dreamer in relation to his dream-wishes can only be compared to an amalgamation of *two separate people* who are linked by some important common element" (emphasis added). Here Freud articulated the central psychoanalytic notion that unconscious motivations are key drivers of our behavior.

This idea of a decentered subject is the basis of psychoanalysis in all its different variants, and consequently it forms the basis of psychoanalysis in Buenos Aires today, in both the broader psychoanalytic professional organizations and the group settings of MFSPT, such as at Centro DITEM and public mental health hospitals in the city. Generally speaking, Freud's methodology is based on the notion that human behavior is determined by drives and that these drives are mostly unconscious. They are constituted during particular events that occur in early childhood and are then repressed, creating such ailments as neurosis and anxiety (and in some cases more serious conditions, such as psychotic outbreaks), obscuring the "real" cause of the analysand's symptoms (Freud [1915] 1963). Through the analytic encounter, this repressed force comes to light, free association appears, and the suffering analysand, now able to articulate the source of the symptom, can better understand and live with it. In a successful encounter, the analyst is able to bring the normally backgrounded doppelgänger into the foreground. The guiding assumption is that knowledge (whether conscious or not) emancipates us from suffering, even if some symptoms may persist. Thus, psychoanalysis does not always look for a cure (although this claim is debated among different schools of psychoanalysis) but is in search of some kind of "truth" that would allow analysands to understand something of their inner selves (see Miller's introduction in Lacan 1988).[7]

For this process to happen, there must be *transference* between the analysand and the analyst. As Freud described it, transference is understood to be based on "the psychological mechanisms of displacement: a set of intense feeling is diverted from the person to whom they belong and instead is directed towards some other person, in this instance, the psychoanalyst" (Frosh 2002, 88). *Countertransference* occurs when the repressed feelings are experienced by analysts when they are with a patient (e.g., the feeling of annoyance or fatigue awakened when being in the presence of an analysand). Lacan has a different take on transference. For him, the affective component of transference belongs to the realm of the imaginary, since it entails a "belief" on the part of analysands, disguised as a sentimental disposition (e.g., a love or hate relationship toward the analyst), that the analyst will "solve" the secret meaning of their words; Lacan deems this belief a form of resistance to analysis.[8] But in his later writings, Lacan (2015) argues that transference belongs, in fact, to the territory of the symbolic, borrowing from anthropology's notion of exchange: an exchange of signs that transforms both speaker and listener. Transference is thus, in its different conceptualizations, the developing relationship between patient and analyst as it transforms over the course of an analytic session. Listening plays an important role in this process.

Argentine psychoanalysts have also written extensively about this subject, including those working in Buenos Aires among the communities and psychoanalytic clinics where I conducted fieldwork for this book. One recent study, *Las Voces del Silencio* (2016), written by María Elisa Mitre, offers a good example of how transference works and the role that listening plays in the phenomenon. Mitre is a renowned Argentine psychoanalyst and the founder and director of Centro DITEM. She is also a disciple of Jorge García Badaracco, the original theorist behind the MFSPT. Her relationship with García Badaracco was originally that of analyst/analysand, but later she became his closest pupil, and they worked together at Hospital Borda, one of the largest public mental health hospitals in Buenos Aires, as well as at Centro DITEM.

Mitre's ideas about transference can be seen in the beginning pages of *Las Voces del Silencio* as she recounts the story of a difficult patient she calls Andrés. A successful businessman, Andrés becomes particularly violent when people describe him as a good person. During multifamily psychoanalytic sessions, various analysands comment on his sweet and overall good disposition, but these compliments seem to awaken in him an unkind and bad character. Mitre believes Andrés has internalized the authoritative and cruel character of his father and enacts this persona to prevent the "real" Andrés from coming out. During an individual session with Mitre, Andrés accuses her of failing to help him manage his suffering while repeatedly telling her that the tone of her voice irritates him. Mitre finally responds, "Stop please. It feels as if you are stabbing me in the stomach. I cannot stand your aggression anymore."[9] After a long silence, Andrés looks Mitre in the eye and starts crying inconsolably, like a little boy. Mitre and Andrés embrace each other, and Mitre at last can *feel* the real Andrés coming out.

Mitre emphasizes the importance of this encounter: "In a way, I was able to tell Andrés, from my *true self*, ultimately de-identified from the presences that kept me hostage over many years, what I was never able to tell my parents. I also had the opportunity to realize that when I was a child, I never knew how to defend myself from abusive situations. I think that that *experiential scene*, of which we were both protagonists, produced a psychic change in both of us."[10]

The transferential relationship that emerges in this example brings to light the psychic doppelgängers that each participant carried to the session. The aggressiveness manifested by Andrés represents the affective state that Lacan found to be an obstacle to analysis. Because Andrés hopes that Mitre will help ease his pain, he positions this relationship in the realm of the imaginary. But when Mitre responds from her own unconscious, a symbolic exchange takes place, altering both participants.

When I asked Mitre about this encounter, she mentioned that listening was key to the transformation they both had undergone. As she put it, "We need to listen from *lo vivencial* (the experiential). Otherwise, one only develops an intellectual understanding of the symptoms. But that won't help with suffering. One has to listen from within, from the actual lived experience. And that is what Andrés and I experienced. Andrés and I were listening beyond the words, although words matter."[11] When I asked if she could explain how to listen in such a fashion, she responded that the clinic teaches one to find an attunement to the real self of the analysand, transference being key to this process. She added that moments of listening had accumulated over time and became integrated into a whole, deeper understanding that evening. "In many cases," she continued, "it doesn't matter what you say but how you say it."

I found that there are four key elements of psychoanalytic listening, each of which is largely exemplified in Mitre's experience working with Andrés. First, it is *cumulative*—meaning that it has a particular temporality different from the here and now of mere sound production. Second, it is a learned process; in other words, it can be *cultivated*. Third, we need to listen from *lo vivencial* and not through the characters we have constructed throughout our lives. Fourth, the *prosodic* enunciation—namely, the way in which words are pronounced—in some cases trumps the denotational content of a statement, or its semantic meaning.

In Buenos Aires, this approach to understanding and meaning is hardly confined to the psychoanalytic clinic. Today, one can see this method of listening and understanding in a wide variety of social contexts, including television shows, casual conversations, theater, news, and many other cultural expressions.

Mitre's encounter with Andrés invites us to approach psychoanalytic listening as a dialogical exchange, not only in terms of a clinical technique in the hands of the analyst but more broadly as a form of listening shared by all participants in analytic interactions.

This chapter looks closely at the MFSPT communities to understand psychoanalysis in face-to-face interactions and discuss the four elements of psychoanalytic listening that I am proposing. Understanding the characteristics of psychoanalytic listening helps us understand the circulation and impact of this generic form of listening outside the clinic, in the wider social interactions in Buenos Aires.

PSYCHOANALYTIC LISTENING AMONG THE MFSPT COMMUNITIES

The MFSPT was established in Buenos Aires in 1962 and later was exported to Italy, Spain, Uruguay, and Brazil (Markez 2010). As the opening vignette indicates, it is a multitudinous group that uses the psychoanalytic framework. This peculiar form of psychoanalysis, and its dynamics of intimacy and exchange through transference, takes place not in a one-on-one setting but in a big room filled with many analysands and their families and as many as ten or more analysts.

The man behind the idea and design of this therapeutic group, Dr. Jorge García Badaracco, was a prominent Argentinean psychiatrist and psychoanalyst. After finishing his medical degree with a specialization in psychiatry in 1947, García Badaracco went to Paris in 1950, where he studied with some of the most prominent psychiatrists and psychoanalysts of the time, including Henri Ey and Paul Guiraud. He was enrolled in Lacan's seminars from 1951 to 1953 and later became an accepted member of the Paris Psychoanalytic Association. Upon his return to Argentina in 1956, he worked as a professor of neuropsychiatry.[12] He subsequently served as director of the neuropsychiatry division at José T. Borda Public Hospital in Buenos Aires, one of the two major public mental health hospitals, where mostly male patients are admitted (the other, Neuropsychiatric Hospital Barulio A. Moyano, admits only women). In 1972 he became the director of the Mental Health Department of the Argentine National University (UBA), and from 1980 to 1984 he was the president of the APA. After the inception of the MFSPT in 1962, García Badaracco dedicated his efforts to forming and participating in these groups inside the public hospital but also at the APA in the Barrio Norte neighborhood and later at Mitre's Centro DITEM.

García Badaracco died shortly before I began my research in Buenos Aires in 2010. But the influence of his ideas at the organization was still very strong, and I interviewed many of his disciples. The theoretical and clinical innovation proposed by García Badaracco through the MFSPT provides an opportunity to access ethnographically the key elements of psychoanalytic listening in a way that clarifies it as a listening genre.

A History of the MFSPT

In the 1960s, as psychoanalysis was expanding its presence in the university and public health systems, García Badaracco and his colleagues designed the initial MFSPT sessions for psychotic patients—in particular, patients who had been in mental health institutions for years and with whom psychiatrists and others found it difficult to establish a dialogue. But once they were jointly meeting with other patients and families, these so-called difficult patients were able to engage in conversations about what was problematic for them and, in some cases, began to improve, sometimes immensely (García Badaracco 2000).

During the early years of the program, the meetings at MFSPT began casually at Hospital Borda, in what García Badaracco (1992, 52) called an *encuadre espontáneo* (spontaneous framework), as he emphasized the importance of "being available" to patients and watching for the moment when the conditions to create a group became possible. This was drastically different from the classic analysand-analyst contract, where a session always had a set time, date, duration, and commitment to attend. In multifamily sessions, the spontaneous framework is at the base of the therapeutic relation, and while patients and family members are encouraged to attend, no one is required to. In the 1970s, however, the MFSPT sessions became more regulated, with a specific time and place where the sessions were to occur.

Borrowing from Donald Jackson (1960, 1964), an American psychiatrist and pioneer in the field of family therapies, García Badaracco employs the term *homeostasis* to refer to the family tendency to equilibrium. Change in one member of a family produces deep structural changes, as other family members try to reach homeostasis again. This can generate networks of pathological interdependency among the family members, who tend to reproduce and perpetuate the problem. García Badaracco (2000, 40) highlights the interrelationship between mental health patients and their families as a dialectic that constructs and maintains the mental problem, noting that "this creates the 'power of the pathogen' between one over the other, between the patient and the so-called healthy family member." According to García Badaracco, it is inside the family that one can elucidate the gestation of the problem and thus be able to control it. For García Badaracco everything is relational, an idea he learned from the British psychiatrist Maxwell Jones (1968), who explored the idea of the "therapeutic community" as a democratization of the relationship between mental health patients, nurses, and psychiatrists who together build a network of support for the patient. García Badaracco's contribution was to include the families of the patients in this network and to do so simultaneously with other families and other patients. But for many patients, especially the "difficult ones," a family therapy session does not always yield results, since the family is already alienated. It can take a long time to disentangle the complex webs of misunderstandings, blame, rancor, and multifarious pathological dynamics that develop inside families. According to García Badaracco, this is where MFSPT sessions come into play: in the context of *listening to* other family interactions, it becomes much easier to observe the negative influence patients might have on their own family members. Consequently, García Badaracco (2000, 67) proposes to focus on what he calls virtual sanity, which he describes as the ability "to go *beyond listening* and respect, tolerate and redirect the 'gaze of the other' to parts that no one has gone to before, those parts that have to do with the human existence" of the patient (emphasis added). It is through the virtual image of the sane person that this therapy becomes effective, thanks to the rehumanization of the patient.

This teleological projection is exemplified in García Badaracco's book *Psicoanálisis Multifamiliar* (2000). He describes being in the middle of a multifamily session inside the Hospital Borda when suddenly one of the patients appeared, completely naked. His first reaction was to call the nurse to make sure the man would get properly dressed. But after feeling the impact on the rest of the group, he decided to stay quiet, even though everyone was expecting him to say something:

> I started to think that the patient had just brought up something really valuable that [he] was unable to share with others. If I didn't have the capacity to see the humanity in the patient, I would have called the nurse telling him that "he was crazy" and needed to put on some clothes. There was no doubt that he "was crazy" to any psychiatrists who would have treated him as a schizophrenic. But I felt that he was bringing an experience of abandonment, of helplessness, that could only be expressed in the way he acted. And through this act, he was able to bring up a feeling of solidarity among all [those] present. Each one of them began to feel that there was something about that in them, about the nakedness, the helplessness, the abandonment. A little later, the patient left and came back to the group dressed up, and through the solidarity created, we were able to work on this subject. (86)

This example illuminates many aspects of MFSPT dynamics. That García Badaracco was able to "see" the humanity (or what he calls the virtual sanity) in the act of the patient distinguishes him from his fellow psychiatrists, who would likely have a markedly different response to such a patient.

This humanistic dimension characterizes the work inside the MFSPT. García Badaracco was known for fighting like no one before in Argentina against the "incurability of the psychotics," as Mitre told me. The reason he "dedicated fifty years to the formation and dissemination of the MFSPT is because he was able to witness first-hand the benefits, improvements and cure of psychotic patients he worked with" (Markez 2009, 86).[13] According to García Badaracco, by being exposed in the presence of a large group, patients experience a "release" that has two sides. They have a platform where they can "act crazy and be contained" and thus liberate and expose an oppressive feeling (García Badaracco 2000, 36). But this release also moves something inside the other participants. A sort of communion is enacted through the resonance of the silences, the gazes, and the words that are produced inside the MFSPT group.

This communion is translated into transference inside the MFSPT. There, "what has been said from others, can be *heard* differently and connect with something deep and particular *inside the hearer*" (García Badaracco 2000, 31; emphasis added). This process is similar to what Lacan defined as *resonance*, which surfaces in a particular moment and resounds with the shock wave emitted by something that happened "over there," creating a myriad of experiential possibilities (Gorney 1978). In the same way, the story of the patient in the MFSPT produces a resonance effect and opens up possibilities for change.

At one level, the structure of the MFSTP is very democratic. Every participant is able to contribute to the well-being of the patient. Yet insofar as psychotherapists bring their own interpretations and contributions to the group, García Badaracco underscores their importance as coordinators. Through their collective expertise, they can guide the group and listen to different aspects of the conversation that others may have missed: "The role of the coordinator is to be able to detect the transference aspects that keep emerging and be capable of bringing them back for analysis," as Diana, a senior analyst at Centro DITEM, told me. Still, these roles are sometimes blurry, and different social configurations are enacted throughout the sessions (for example, when analysts tell a participant to stop talking). But overall, the interactions inside the MFSTP are expressed horizontally rather than vertically.

After the MFSPT groups began to extend beyond the hospital walls and formed at the APA and other places in the 1990s, they started to attract and work with neurotic patients as well. The group at the APA and Centro DITEM, where I attended MFSPT sessions, included a combination of medicated patients who suffered psychotic episodes and neurotic patients. At Hospital San Isidro, where I also attended sessions, the group was much smaller, and most of the people in attendance were self-identified as neurotic or suffered from a particular addiction. Most of those who attended the MFSPT were undergoing personal analysis, and some also had psychiatric appointments, often with the analysts who served as moderators inside the group. The MFSPT served to reinforce and contain the participants, but it was usually accompanied by other forms of psychotherapy.

In order to grasp the specificities of psychoanalysis as a listening genre, not from García Badaracco's theories and recollections but from the MFSPT encounters themselves, we need first to describe their spatial and dialogic settings. The analysis of the MFSPT is important for understanding psychoanalytic listening as a genre because the *resonance* produced in this setting is a quintessential component of psychoanalytic listening. Understanding how it emerges helps elucidate many ways in which it has left the clinic and become a social way of listening.

The MFSPT Setting

I attended these sessions on multiple occasions and in several places. From 2010 to 2012, I attended weekly MFSPT sessions at the APA and additional sessions at Hospital San Isidro, a public hospital located in a wealthy suburb of Buenos Aires. In 2018 I also began attending MFSPT sessions at Centro DITEM. All three places shared the same structural features of García Badaracco's methods.

At APA meetings, the sessions were conducted inside a big room, a kind of auditorium, with a carpeted floor, long drapes covering the windows, and chairs facing a stage at the very end of the room. The room could easily accommodate over a hundred people and was big enough to require a microphone so that participants could be heard. The sessions I attended had around eighty-five people in attendance, of whom twelve to seventeen (the numbers fluctuated with every session) were psychoanalysts from the APA and other psychoanalytic organizations.[14] The psychoanalysts were spread out in the front rows, except for five who sat on chairs on the stage. Those who were not psychoanalysts were either analysands or people who simply wanted to talk. There were also approximately fifteen students from the Ángel Garma Institute who came to "observe and learn," as one of them told me.[15] The age, gender, and socioeconomic backgrounds of analysands were mixed, though none were children. There were people with university degrees, "blue-collar" workers, housewives, and professionals of different kinds. Most came by themselves, but others were accompanied by a family member, usually a spouse, a son or daughter, or a parent. Their common denominator was that they had experienced some kind of emotional distress, and they came to this room to try to ease their suffering.

The meetings were open to the general public and happened every Tuesday night, from eight to ten o'clock. I was allowed to record the sessions.[16] The psychoanalysts, who are known and respected in the field, do not charge for the sessions; as one told me, "We feel passionate about the work we do during these sessions," and therefore they ask for no remuneration. Anyone walking by could go up to the second floor at the APA on a Tuesday night and participate; there were no restrictions.

These sessions stopped being offered at the APA in 2016 and later were moved to Centro DITEM, where I continued attending in 2018. The spatial disposition at Centro DITEM is different from that at the APA. Instead of a room with a stage, the room here contains up to one hundred chairs in concentric circles. At the center is a marble table where a recording device is placed. There are fewer analysts (from four to seven), and they sit in the very first circle. The attendees are a mix of regular analysands and people from the psychoanalytic community (students, practitioners, and former analysands).

In both institutions the sessions followed more or less the same process. People begin to gather in the room at ten minutes before eight o'clock. The "regulars" greet each other and chitchat about mundane things, such as the weather, the clothes they are wearing, and their family members. The attendees who are not extroverted, or who have not attended many sessions, sit by themselves and wait for the session to begin. Psychoanalysts are the last to arrive, and it is common for some to arrive a little late. At about ten or fifteen minutes past the hour, one of the psychoanalysts sitting on the stage with a microphone starts the session by asking for quiet. After a few minutes of silence, an audience member raises a hand; after receiving a microphone, this person introduces themselves, always beginning with the first name (e.g., "Hello, my name is Emilia, and I want to tell you . . ."), followed by a verbal performance of a personal story involving different registers and temporalities, changes in footing, and a number of different contextual frameworks that provide a particular narrative situating the analysand as a historical subject.[17]

The duration of these interventions varies greatly, depending on the person speaking. This is often an occasion for conflict to erupt, as can happen when the speaker wants to keep talking but is interrupted by an analyst or fellow attendee. But the rationale behind the stopping or interruption of a verbal performance is not always clear. Most times, interruptions seem to happen when an analysand's speech becomes repetitive, when an analysand is inconsiderate about the time framework (many other people may want to talk), or especially when there does not seem to be a rapport between the analysand, the general public, and the psychoanalysts (e.g., when the analysand keeps talking without acknowledging questions and other interventions).

Depending on different factors—for instance, if there is an emotional outburst and the person suffering the breakdown is given more time to speak—there will be between five and a dozen interventions of analysands. (The maximum number I witnessed was twelve.) Once a couple of analysands perform their stories, a psychoanalyst begins to ask questions, gives a general reflection about García Badaracco's approach to the problem, or just refers to issues that were brought up during the performance. Usually other psychoanalysts intervene, at which point another person in the audience will raise a hand and the cycle begins again (these cycles get interrupted when conflict arises).[18]

At the end of the session there is a closing reflection, and the "theme" of the session is chosen. Topics such as solitude, rancor, and family appear as the guiding axes of the sessions. Long and complicated exchanges between some of the participants become a solid and unified narrative.[19] Following the logic of the MFSPT, one story leads to another, which still relates to the first, and the cycle continues. The analysts consider this the advantage of this therapy, as a unified discourse emerges through the polyphony of voices and positionalities. Once the session is over, people stay and talk with each other for a while, the analysts mingle with the audience and give some hugs, and little by little the room empties until all the analysands are gone.

Then the analysts reassemble to discuss some of their observations regarding particular analysands, share other comments, and reflect on the overall dynamics of the evening. I sat in on very few of these sessions. Despite occasional episodes of venting (I found it striking to hear such comments as "*¡Está más loca que una cabra!*" [She's crazier than a goat!] in reference to a particular patient), the overall tone is generally respectful, and the postsession meeting provides a place to exchange information about individual clinical sessions of analysands and their overall performance.

LISTENING INSIDE THE MFSPT

While the psychoanalytic encounters at the MFSPT meetings are unorthodox, they follow most of the ideas and procedures that occur inside private practice, providing access to the main tenets of psychoanalytic listening inside the clinical setting.

Several authors in addition to Freud and Lacan have developed their own nomenclature for understanding psychoanalytic listening. In 2013, psychoanalyst Salman Akhtar proposed in *Psychoanalytic Listening: Methods, Limits, and Innovations* four components of psychoanalytic listening from the point of view of the analyst. The first one, *objective listening*, consists of paying attention to *what* the patient is saying and *how* the patient says it: focusing on slips of the tongue, emphases, and hesitations within a story, the analyst relies on "his intellectual capacity, however silently [it] may operate during his clinical work" (Akhtar 2013, 7). More than resounding with the analysand's words, objective listening entails an intellectual effort on the part of the analyst to discern the underlying discourse the analysand brings to the session. The second component he calls *subjective listening*, relying upon the analysts' subjectivity in their attempts to understand what the analysand is trying to communicate. The analyst's unconscious, when properly attuned, is able to pick up what the patient's unconscious is transmitting. Thus, subjective listening relies on intuition rather than intellectual analysis. The third component, *emphatic listening*, is the one by which the analyst actively seeks to resonate with the patient's experience. In order to empathize, the analyst "introjects this object transiently, and projects the introject again into the object. This alone enables him in the end to square a perception from without and one from within" (9). Lastly, *intersubjective listening* is an interpersonal view based on the premise that the self is nothing but a collection of "reflective appraisals." In this view, the analyst's perception of the patient's thoughts, feelings, or fantasies is always shaped by the analyst's subjectivity. Therefore, the patient's psychology is itself coconstructed (13).

Akhtar's book is mainly directed to aspiring analysts and colleagues and therefore has a propaedeutic purpose: it seeks to structure the process of listening in the clinic. The four characteristics I found at the MFSPT complement Akhtar's components. In particular, emphatic listening resembles *lo vivencial*, where what counts is the resonance that the unconscious doppelgängers form. But there is a fundamental difference between Akhtar's categorizations and mine, and it is that the form of listening learned, cultivated, and performed inside the MFSPT is enacted not only by the analysts but by the analysands as well. Since the MFSPT is a multitudinous psychoanalytic encounter, everyone learns to listen and has the right to interpretation. Instead of being an erudite form of listening belonging only to the analysts formally trained in the discipline, the listening practiced in the

MFSPT is "democratic": everyone participates and learns from it. Although the MFSPT sessions are based on differentiated roles and clinical expertise, all the participants practice psychoanalytic listening. In this context, and due to four specific dimensions I analyze below, the genre becomes a horizontal and multidirectional practice and therefore can circulate widely beyond the clinic. Now let us unpack each of these components through concrete examples from the meetings at MFSPT.

Temporality

As Mitre's encounter with Andrés illustrates, there is in psychoanalytic listening a specific temporality, one that defies the here and now of sound production: a cumulative quality of listening over time. That the memory of her parents' voices emerged during Andrés's performance shows a sonic line that traveled through different time frames. The following case exemplifies this phenomenon even more deeply.

On November 16, 2010, the meeting's focus was a story that Adela told to the group. Adela had been a frequent attendee for a year and a half and tended to talk for long periods of time, repeating what seemed to be the same story. She saw herself as the victim of misunderstanding and abuse— misdiagnosed by previous psychiatrists who labeled her a "crazy person," thus alienating her from family and friends.[20] When speaking, she was very aggressive toward both the analysts and the attendees and used "a tone of superiority," as one of the attendees described it. Throughout the delivery of her story she emphasized that she had not done anything wrong, that she was just a victim. This lack of "taking responsibility for her actions," as one analyst stated, created in the group some animosity toward her. Analysts often felt the need to interrupt her, but she invariably tried to continue speaking, which irritated many who were present. I must admit that Adela's constant repetition of her story could be tiring, and on more than one occasion her interventions made me uneasy.

But in this particular instance, Adela's story opened the door to a variety of reflections about why she kept repeating the same account. Unlike in other sessions, most of the comments were positive and encouraging. For example, one man in his mid-twenties requested the microphone and said, "My name is Juan, and I have been coming to the meetings for more or less a year, and I never talked before. It is sad to listen to the lady's [Adela] story. She obviously wants to tell us something, *if we could only hear what she wants to say, what she means,* but the lady keeps repeating the same story without producing any effect."[21] After Juan's comment, one of the senior psychoanalysts responded, "Juan, first, I am surprised by the 'Adela always repeats the same thing, and it does not produce any effect.' She got you talking today! [General laughter] For the first time! Great! Something happened so that her insistent discourse finally found an answer. Because you thought, 'I have to say something.' So, she is not so wrong insisting *to be listened to,* because at the end, *someone would listen to her.*"[22]

After having attended the MFSPT sessions for a year, Juan finally felt compelled to speak, moved, as he said, by his desire to understand the unconscious meaning behind Adela's story. Juan did not aim to have what Adela was *saying* clarified or conceptualized, represented or reformulated in the analyst's words; rather, he wanted to *listen* to the inaudible voices of Adela's aural residues. Listening in this context is a bodily experience rather than a mere reception of sounds. It implicates a codification that does not involve an act of consciousness, yet it needs to reach consciousness for interpretation.

By focusing on the unspoken intentionality of Adela's story, Juan was already *listening* in a particular mode: he was looking for meaning that had not been uttered, that was to be found somehow outside of the conscious realm of utterances. He was enacting psychoanalytic listening as a generic type: listening not as something one passively submits to but as a particular kind of action itself. The relevance structure that anchored the directionality of this encounter was embedded in the frame that Juan brought by suspending the denotation and referential qualities of Adela's speech.

There is always a particular *temporality* attached to this listening genre. The amount of time required to "listen" and to be able to make sense of it varies from case to case. The intervention of the senior analyst underlines this point: "something happened so that her insistent discourse finally found an answer." Following the logic of psychoanalytic listening, what happened to Juan is that something "resonated" inside him, and even though he could not make conscious sense of it, he was able to listen to Adela within Freud's conceptualization of aural residues (see Freud [1923] 1995; Isakower 1939) or Reik's (1948, 1964) idea of the "third ear." He might have waited another year to speak, or he could have spoken earlier. The temporality involved in this listening genre is unpredictable. As with Mitre's example or Hugo's sudden perception of sounds and voices, the temporality of listening is aleatory. The time involved in the unconscious recollection of stories as well as the subject's "inner voice" is unpredictable. At some point, the accumulation of all these aural residues will reveal something.

In purely physical terms, listening occurs in the here and now after a sound is produced. After a sound is made, sound waves are "reflected and attenuated when they hit the pinna, and these changes provide additional information that will help the brain determine the direction from which the sounds came" (*Oxford Dictionary* 2010). Then the ear canal is responsible for the amplification of sounds. But psychoanalytic listening is cumulative (as is anthropological listening). Sound images will acquire a resonance that echoes inside one's self and will be triggered by something that surpasses the conscious dimension: in Mitre's example through Andrés's sadistic performance and in Hugo's case through the loss of his wife. This listening genre is not linear. While it develops in time, it possesses its own temporality.

Cultivation

Psychoanalytic listening entails a long cultivation process. In this way, it is different from listening genres that are ephemeral and unintentional. For example, when one listens to a passing sound, a piece of music, or a lament, a frame of reference might abruptly surface through the embedding of the sound into a particular setting (Goffman 1964). The relevance structure that emerges when one listens to ephemeral and spontaneous sounds does not require a specific pedagogy.

Other genres of listening require explicit training, especially when listening *for* a particular sign—for example, a mechanic learns how to interpret sounds produced by cars. Yet another category of listening requires listeners to be exposed over time to a genre of which they are not necessarily conscious but which still makes an imprint on their psyche. This *cultivation* is a key element in the genre of psychoanalytic listening. Take, for example, Roberto, an avid attendee in his late sixties who had been coming to the MFSPT sessions for ten years and had developed a close relationship with Jorge García Badaracco. Following a discussion about misunderstandings within families, Roberto explained that he always used to get involved and give unsolicited opinions every time his daughter had a conversation with her mother. But then something happened: "*There was a moment in which I could listen*, and I could see that I was wrong, and that I have been wrong for a long, long time. I was wrong because the truth is that *I could not listen*. And here [at the MFSPT], *I was taught how* [to listen]. Because when one is taken by a sentiment, one cannot think straight or listen. And that is a phrase that one has to take home."[23] Roberto's example describes the cultivation of psychoanalytic listening as a moment of revelation. There was an instant when he was suddenly able to listen, and through this acquired competence, he was able to understand his past mistakes and make amends. This learning process follows a personal trajectory and cannot be measured. Again, a particular temporality becomes present. The moment of revelation that Roberto experienced is related to the emergence of a particular frame of reference that gives directionality to a situation that he was previously unable to codify. This moment was spontaneous and unexpected, but it required a long process of listening practice to reach proficiency.

In spaces where there is a form of "social listening," as in the case of the MFSPT, there emerges what Judith Becker (2010) calls a specific "habitus of listening," which produces a concrete "culture of listeners." Becker's analysis focuses on what she calls the "Pentecostal arousal," a phenomenon in Pentecostal churches where music becomes the vehicle for creating an emotional apotheosis. Music's ability to awaken a particular sensibility in a sudden moment is due to the cultivation of a particular genre.

While the listening that Roberto experiences and the sudden "awakening" of a Pentecostal follower do not belong to the same experiential phenomenon, they are similar in that the listening occurs unexpectedly. They are both immersed within a situated listening framework where there is a pedagogy of listening, and through this acquired capacity, transformation occurs. If we extrapolate Becker's conceptualization to the MFSPT sessions, as a place where a particular listening habitus is formed—through the sensibilities and dispositions of attendees—we can substantiate the claim that listening develops in practice (Hanks 1987).

It is important to note the distinctions between habitus and genres of listening—particularly when looking at Buenos Aires and, more broadly, Argentina, where the concept of genre helps to clarify key processes in the wider circulation of psychoanalytic listening. Defined at the level of practice, "genres mediate between event types and modes of participation: the totalization and segmentability that distinguish *events* as units from *action* as an ongoing process depend on the same genre types which govern the engagements of participants" (Hanks 1996, 161). This means that, in addition to their thematic orientation, texts (whether oral, written, or aural) are also oriented toward the *action contexts* in which they are produced, distributed, and received. In this formulation, textual genres are seen as both resulting from historically specific acts and instantiating action; thus genres are shaped by context and create context at the same time. Something similar happens with listening. Listening genres, to the same degree as textual genres, orient action. And this action is both motivated and created by modes of listening as practice and the internal structure that organizes the specific practice.

Roberto's is an active listening, a kind that entails action and that happens inside a specific institution with specific characteristics, similar to the Pentecostal example. But while the idea of a listening habitus is useful for analyzing the pedagogy of developing a particular listening ear, the listening *genre* is more pertinent here. Unlike the concept of habitus, the concept of genre does not necessitate a dialectical relationship with the notion of field. Whereas linguistic phenomena are never universally available and tend to be produced, circulated, and accumulated asymmetrically, in a world of power relations and commodification of linguistic (listening) resources (see Bourdieu 1977; Gal 1989; Irvine 1989; Silverstein 1979; Woolard 1985a), our listening is not determined by our position in an objective and asymmetric field. It is true that forms of capital are created through listening (e.g., the doctor listening through the stethoscope establishes power relationships that are emphasized throughout the whole auscultation process), but listening, in fact, allows for a more inclusive framework in which asymmetries and political economies are insufficient to account for the emergence of specific genres (e.g., passionate and compassionate listening). Thus, habitus always entails competition of resources, something that the democratization of listening that emerges inside the MFSPT does not create. The distinction between habitus and genre is important because psychoanalytic listening as a genre circulates outside of the clinical setting because it is not coercive and is flexible.

The question of how to cultivate psychoanalytic listening has been posed by many psychoanalysts. Both Lacan and Freud wrote extensively about the pedagogy of psychoanalysis, in which the subject's own experience of analysis functions as the most essential learning tool for the development of an analytic ear (Freud [1913] 1958; Lacan 1998). The novelty proposed by García Badaracco was to make newcomers part of a *community of practice*. At the MFSPT, the participation of all the partakers of the meetings is necessary and contributes to the healing of the patient. In order to cultivate psychoanalytic listening as a genre, it is imperative that the listener is not only exposed to the genre but participates in it. The MFSPT is precisely constructed by coparticipation.

The format of the MFSPT is democratic in that all participants have the right to speak and voice their opinion regardless of their credentials. The voice of anyone can trigger in other attendees something that would transform their emotional being. As Roberto explained, he was "suddenly able to listen." This "sudden" acquisition of a listening genre was possible, in part, because he had been exposed to psychoanalytic listening for many years by being part of this specific community of practice. He was part of what Jean Lave and Etienne Wenger (1991) refer to as the "legitimate peripheral participation," by which learners participate in communities of practitioners and the learning process is relational and participatory, since the stories brought by the analysands, the analysts' interpretations, and the comments of other participants make possible the habituation of the ear to this particular genre. How these stories contribute to listening psychoanalytically is dependent on the particularities, or "situation," as Lave and Wenger put it, of the learning experience.[24]

Within psychoanalytic listening, before one is able to *listen*, there is a process parallel to Charles Peirce's categories of Firstness and Secondness— and, much later, Thirdness. Peirce's (1998, 2.228) broad definition of a sign is useful because it extends beyond words: he defines a sign as "something which stands to somebody for something on some respect or capacity." It addresses somebody, creating in the mind of that person an equivalent sign, or perhaps a more developed sign. More simply, a sign evokes something for someone. A sign points to an object and, at the same time, it brings to the interpreter's mind another sign (the "interpretant") that translates and mediates the original one (Peirce 1998). This is the structure of semiosis, or the making of meaning, of which sign, object, and interpretant are three necessary parts. Without one of the parts, semiosis does not take place— the triad is not reducible to pairs of dyads.

Peirce's typology of Firstness, Secondness, and Thirdness, which describe degrees of mediation and reflexivity, is essential to semiosis. Firstness is a condition of unmediated, unreflexive access—experiences without reaction, causes without effect (Peirce 1998, 1.305). Secondness is a condition of mediated but not yet reflexive access—experiences and the reaction they evoke, causes and the effects they provoke, but not yet a reflection on the reaction or effect. Thirdness, finally, is a condition of mediated, reflexive access: thirds are experience, reaction, and the reflection upon that reaction. They are cause, effect, and the extension of that effect to the form of habit or convention or law (1.303–1.312).

This typology is relevant to psychoanalytic listening. Firstness is a conception of being in its wholeness or completeness, with no boundaries or parts and no cause or effect (1.305). It is the quality of pure, latent potentiality. Therefore, it belongs to the realm of possibility and is experienced within a kind of timelessness. It corresponds to emotional experience. Like Goffman's "situation," Firstness is pure potentiality. Once the setting is embedded, Thirdness appears.

Because the temporality of psychoanalytic listening as a genre is arbitrary—it can happen at any moment in time, as the example of Adela and Juan shows, or Roberto's "sudden" listening—there is a constant suspension of interpretation, in a space between Firstness and Secondness, until it gets embedded (into an interpretation). But the embeddedness is not necessarily codifiable. Juan's example illustrates how even when he *listened* to something that compelled him to speak (according to the analyst's interpretation), he still did not have a definite idea of what he listened to. It was clear, though, that he was listening inside a psychoanalytic framework, dismissing the denotation and referential meaning of Adela's words. When I state that this listening is suspended between Firstness and Secondness, that is because Thirdness, or interpretation, is missing (at least in Juan's case). Once there is a code of understanding, interpretation finally can happen. In the meantime, the chains of signifiers described by Lacan represent this suspension between Firstness and Secondness.

The purpose of bringing Peirce's typology to psychoanalytic listening is to show how in this particular listening genre the intentionality of the listener is suspended. The cultivation of psychoanalytic listening consists in being able to be suspended within these categories.

Participants in the MFSPT place a strong emphasis on the emergence of a particular word as being able to define the course of the whole meeting. This view resembles both Lacan's idea of resonance, by which certain words "touch" analysands in a particular way without their knowing it, and Freud's ([1909] 1953, 23) idea of "floating attention," where analysts suppress all critical activity, "suspend . . . judgment and give . . . impartial attention to everything there is to observe." Freud also recommended, as an optimal attentional stance or state of mind, the absence of reason or of deliberate attempts to select, concentrate, or understand and an even and impartial attention to all that occurs within the field of awareness. As the examples discussed demonstrate, attention is not the defining quality of listening in the psychoanalytic realm. This listening genre involves suspending attention and simply being open to resonate with the world around us. The resonance that generates inside the MFSPT produces signs that are heard and felt but lack a specific referent.

Lo Vivencial (The Others in Us)

Psychoanalytic listening is a genre that includes a particular temporality and a particular pedagogy or disposition. Its interpretation awaits codification, being suspended until it is embedded into a setting. For the scholar interested in the study of language in interaction, this listening genre poses many analytical challenges, since the analyst is supposed to listen to something that is not uttered and that does not coincide with the convention already established of particular signs; instead, analysts should listen to the "inner voice" that they reproduce in their inner speech through the cultivation of a "third ear," as Theodor Reik would suggest.

Listening psychoanalytically poses additional analytical problems because it is not only the analysand who is listening without codification; the analyst is attempting to listen to the "discourse of the other," as Lacan (1977, 86) indicates. And in the case of the MFSPT, *all* the participants are listening as well. Everyone involved listens to something different, even if sometimes there is agreement on what was listened to, once it has already been contextually situated. In other words, the ear has already been *tuned* so that the context has already been defined; thus, the "aboutness" of the genre has been established, and it has been embedded into a setting. The following example illustrates this process.

Lucía, a young professional in her early thirties who comes from a well-to-do family, had often described in previous meetings the bad relationship she had with her mother, who did not seem to validate Lucía's life choices and constantly criticized her actions. This created animosity between them, which in turn generated constant fights:

> The truth is that I don't really know what to say. Every time I go to my mother's house, the only things I keep hearing are complaints. She doesn't like my clothes; she gets mad because I didn't call her on time.... The other day she even told me that I am gaining weight. In the end, through her eyes I don't do anything right! But the only thing that I do is work and work, I pay my bills with my own money. But I don't know, sometimes I think that I don't do things right. The other day at work—because I cannot stop thinking about all my problems—I submitted a budget for the remodeling of a hotel in downtown, and it had many errors in it. You cannot imagine the embarrassment that I felt! What is the client going to think? That if I am unable to count, there's no way I will be able to remodel and participate in their project!

I haven't heard from them . . . but of course! Most likely they don't want to know anything about me ever again.[25]

Lucía was crying when a female psychoanalyst interrupted her: "Lucía . . . I, I feel compelled to interrupt you because, because . . . I need you to come back. *The person who is speaking is not you; it is your mother speaking, and I need to listen to you, not her.* You realize this, don't you? You disappear from the story, and we only listen to your mother speaking."[26] On the day that Lucía made this intervention, the MFSPT conference room was packed. Eighty-one persons were present, one of the highest concentrations I witnessed during the time I attended the sessions. We all witnessed her moving performance. To my surprise, no one challenged the idea that Lucía was somehow possessed by her mother's voice: everyone seemed to agree with this scenario. After the female analyst finished talking, another attendee—an analysand—further expressed this idea by saying, "You know, Lucía, I think that Dr. M. is perceiving something right. I also cannot recognize you in what you are saying. And this is not always the case; many times when you participate, it is very clear that you are the one speaking. But today, I don't know, *it doesn't seem that the person that I'm listening to is you.*"[27]

What does it mean that Lucía is not speaking, but instead it is her mother? What does it mean to *listen to* the mother speak?

To answer these questions, we need to consider a listening community, in this case the MFSPT, that encompasses a group of subjects who, at different levels, are familiar with the basic ideas of psychoanalysis and are inside a psychoanalytic institution. The theory of psychoanalysis places great emphasis on the idea of the unconscious. The idea of a decentered subject capable of invoking her psychic doppelgänger epitomizes what many psychoanalysts identify as the struggle of self-alienation inherent in the process of becoming a subject and achieving social identity (see Faurholt 2009). This alienation can represent itself as a form of alterity, a term generally defined as "otherness," which implies the complexities of self and other on the formation of identity. In Lacan's theory of "radical otherness," alterity emerges through language. The subject is not merely an "I" or the ego; it is the "speaking being" who becomes the subject. Through the symbolic order of language, the subject consolidates and comes forth. Subjects do not merely "know" themselves. Rather, they represent what is known through language. They are created by the unconscious and language—two factors that, according to Lacan, set limits but also offer possibilities (Lacan [1966] 2006, 197–268).

In Lucía's example, the alterity is presented as a form of ventriloquism where her mother speaks for her. As a result of the cultivation of psycho-analytic listening, the participants of the MFSPT are able to identify the "otherness" in Lucía's narrative. In this setting, the context is already set; the voice of Lucía's mother as an embodied force is validated and accepted because there is a convention that sustains this practice: that in psychoanalytic theory the subject is divided and spoken through and can bring up different voices through the Other inside the analysand.

As we saw when discussing its temporality, psychoanalytic listening as a genre is a sort of "residual listening" that surpasses the here-and-now production of sound. This has a profound connection with the question of how "others" appear in someone's talk. In his theory of the novel, Mikhail Bakhtin (1981, 61) postulates that there are no "free" utterances, meaning that all "images of language are inseparable from images of various world views and from the living beings who are their agents—people who think, talk, and act in a setting that is socially and historically concrete." Speakers are not unified entities, and their words are not transparent expressions of subjective experience (see Keane 2001) but rather are informed by a multiplicity of voices, or polyphony, and the different social personae they inhabit (Bakhtin 1981, 61).

Psychoanalytic listening aims to find the different voices that Bakhtin discusses. The "residual" trace of previous "listenings" accumulates in the listener, who then starts to create a coherent narrative. The auditory residue is formed by different soundscapes and sources, ranging from the actual voices of the people surrounding us to nonreferential sounds coming from the external world, as well as our own inner voice. These multiple sound images do not necessarily have referents attached to them: the listener registers them unconsciously inside the psyche. The sound images finally acquire meaning—surface the conscious world—when they get connected to a larger interpretive frame (Goffman 1974), and this frame is *experienced* rather than denoted. As in the case of polyphony in verbal and nonverbal texts, psychoanalytic listening is always informed by a multiplicity of sound images that the analyst and the analysand are trying to retrieve. In the residual sound is a coexistence of ideas of the present and the past, as well as different ideological constructs.

In psychoanalytic listening, multiple voices shape the interpretive frame and threaten to take over the agent's own voice. In Lucía's case, the speaker's words are directly influenced by her mother's own ideas about her. This experience, Bakhtin (1986, 89) tells us, can be characterized to some degree as "the process of *assimilation*—more or less creative—of others' words," making all utterances "filled with others' words, varying degrees of otherness or varying degrees of 'our-own-ness.'... These words of others carry with them their own expression, their own evaluative tone, which we assimilate, rework, and re-accentuate." In Bakhtin's framework, any word uttered is "interindividual" because everything that is expressed is located outside the speaker: "The author (speaker) has his own inalienable right to the word, but *the listener has his rights*, and those whose voices are heard in the word before the author comes upon it also have their rights (121–22; emphasis added)—for after all, there are no words that belong to no one." Lucía brought her mother's voice to the setting. According to the analyst, she appropriated these words and began to enact the stories that the mother told, something that I, as a listener outside of this community of listeners, was not able to register. The listener also has a right of interpretation, which may or may not coincide with the speaker's denotative utterance. When a speaker utters a word, that word is already immersed in a particular frame of interpretation; listening therefore becomes crucial for the understanding of the direction that the interpretation is taking.

After the female analyst interrupted Lucía, audience and analysts alike sought to console Lucía. Everyone seemed to have "listened" that she was performing her mother's words and that when she could "see the real Lucía" her sorrows would come to an end. Nobody in the audience questioned the idea that she was speaking her mother's words. Everyone inside the MFSPT was listening in the same way because there was a context already in place that focused on a particular way of conceiving subjectivity.

This phenomenon—to perform the speech of another person—has unique theoretical ramifications when considered from the perspective of listening genres. It is different from *entextualization* (inserting a text into a different context) and closer, to a certain degree, to *replication*, since it tries to portray the textual as opposed to contextual aspects of original discourse (see Urban 1996). But Lucía's case is closer to Derrida's idea of the decentered subject, formed in the performative reverberation of language itself: "Voice can betray the body to which it is lent, it can make it ventriloquize as if the body were no longer anything more than the actor or the double of another voice, of the voice of the other, even of an innumerable, incalculable polyphony. A voice may give birth and—there you are, *voilà*—to another body" (Derrida 1984, 79). This capacity of language to create particular subjectivities has been amply studied, especially in feminist theory (see Butler 1993, 1997; Butler, Guillory, and Thomas 2000). From these studies it is clear that an identity is not the source of more secondary actions such as speech; rather, identities can be described as being caused by performative actions (Butler 1993). In these studies, speech (and writing) has been the center of the performative experience.

But Lucía's example is different: the transformation happened through listening. It is by *listening psychoanalytically*, listening inside a specific genre, that Lucía's mother is brought into the MFSPT. Not everyone inside the MFSPT session may have listened in the same way, and the analyst certainly directed the attention to this particular aural interpretation. But even if just a few listeners listened, not necessarily to the voice of the mother but, as one of the participants put it, "as if she [Lucía] was not the one speaking," there was a particular listening context that the listeners were reproducing by tuning the ear to the psychoanalytic frequency. As in Becker's discussion of the Pentecostal arousal, the people reproducing and enacting a particular context at the MFSPT create a particular context in which such interpretations are possible, a context that is part of socially and culturally wider forms of listening in Argentina well beyond the clinical setting.

Prosodic Enunciation

The fourth key element that makes up the genre of psychoanalytic listening is prosodic enunciation: "the music in the words," or how words *sound* (and *resound*), rather than their denotational meanings.

Two different moments at the Centro DITEM during the summer of 2018 provide a helpful illustration of how this works within the genre of psychoanalytic listening. In early July, the soccer World Cup was taking place, and Argentina's national *fútbol* team had not performed as expected. They had lost to France in the playoff and were out of the competition, and people were disenchanted and angry. In the streets of Buenos Aires, the advertisement posters found all over the city depicting a smiling Lionel Messi—Argentina's captain and global *fútbol* star—contrasted sharply with the overwhelming discontent of *porteños*. The rain was getting more intense when I arrived at Centro DITEM. As usual, everyone was greeting each other. But this time, instead of the usual cheerful disposition, a somber cloud lingered. Many expressed their frustration with Argentina's national team. They needed a culprit and the scapegoat was Messi, whom everyone was criticizing and blaming for their loss. This was also, of course, a convenient excuse to speak negatively of Argentina, something one frequently encounters in Buenos Aires—when talking to taxi drivers, waiters, professors, or even just friends and acquaintances, inevitably at one point someone has something bad to say about the Argentine government, institutions, or "the culture." Centro DITEM was no exception, and now the dashed hopes of winning the World Cup helped confirm suspicions that everything in the country was indeed corrupt.

That evening in the hallway, before entering the big room to begin the MFSPT session, I heard a male senior analyst talking to a disillusioned attendee who was complaining about the Argentine Football Association and its corrupt management. The analyst interrupted: "Yes, yes, we all like to blame something else for our misfortunes instead of looking at oneself. That's what we try to do here, to look inside and stop the music player."[28] This was neither the first nor the last time that a metaphor related to music was used at Centro DITEM. In fact, the concept of music is used to denote a sort of interference or noise that forbids the natural flow of ideas and affective states. Statements such as "*¡Otra vez con esa canción!*" (Again, with that song!), voiced when analysts perceive that the analysand is not speaking from *lo vivencial*, are common. At the same time, as a senior analyst at Centro DITEM explained to me when discussing her methodology, the metaphor of music can uncover important features inside an analysand's speech. Echoing Mitre's earlier comment, she said, "When talking to our patients, what is more important to us is not what they say but *how they say it*. We focus on the music in the words."[29]

How a message is delivered is important for the therapeutic encounter. According to Summerson Carr and Yvonne Smith's (2014, 99) analysis of Motivational Interview (MI), professionals trained to conduct these interviews are asked to shift "their attention from semantic content to the poetic form of the therapeutic message." Through their specific analysis of pause and silence, the authors suggest that the aesthetic management of the style and delivery of this particular register helps patients in different capacities: they may speak more or feel that they have some control over the interaction. Similarly, at Centro DITEM, the focus is on the resonances that the "music in the words" generates in the listener; thus, as in the MI interview, the poetics of the interaction is more valuable than the denotation, and both have therapeutic usefulness in helping the therapist have some control over the interaction and helping patients focus on particular aspects of their speech patterns.

Music in this setting is conceptualized in a twofold manner: as an interference and as an indexical pathway that the skilled listener can decode by focusing on the quality of sound rather than on a fixed semantic meaning. The latter conceptualization resembles the notion of resonance that Lacan developed throughout his work. In Lacanian psychoanalysis—as the opening quote of this chapter suggests—to harmonize with the analysand's speech, the analyst must take into account the different "staves" or resonances by focusing on the signifiers the analysand produces. Decoding words as music allows the analyst to suspend the denotation in favor of a hermeneutic interpretation.

Another example—this one from early August 2018 at Centro DITEM, a few weeks after the night when everyone was complaining about Messi—further illustrates how prosodic enunciation is present in the psychoanalytic encounter. On this occasion, a man named Gonzalo looked extremely sad. His hands were tangled in a nervous fist, and he barely looked at the audience. He began his story by explaining that he was approaching retirement, and he expressed concern about the cost of his son's treatment once money became scarce. His son, Carlos, had been diagnosed as a "difficult patient." He had experienced intermittent psychotic episodes throughout his life and needed constant care. Gonzalo also revealed that his business, a small car repair shop, was not doing well, as the economic crisis looming over Argentina was significantly affecting both his clients and the business's overall performance. He discussed the political climate in Argentina and what he considered the government's lack of commitment to its citizens: "I am fed up with governments that don't do anything for us. One works all day trying as best as one can to provide for the family. Prices change every day, and I don't know how I am going to be able to keep the business running, sustain my family, and Carlos's treatment. At night I don't sleep thinking about all the responsibilities I have that I'm not sure I'll be able to continue to fulfill. Every night thinking of all that's coming, and I'm becoming old."[30] Gonzalo was eager to continue his story when a senior psychiatrist and analyst interrupted him: "Gonzalo, Gonzalo, we heard that music many times before. Why don't you tell us how you really feel? Leave that melody that is not letting you say what you are really experiencing."[31] Gonzalo nodded and began to describe how sad and impotent he felt. He was afraid to even think about not working. What would he do if the routine he had performed for over thirty years vanished? He was used to work and did not understand life without structure. He was terrified: "The truth is that I am very scared. I don't know how to do anything except work. It anguishes me to think what is going to happen to me when I retire. I don't know if I'm going to be able to recognize myself in that new character. I see myself helpless."[32] He began to sob.

Marcelo, an older male analysand who had been coming to the sessions for many years, interjected: "Listening to Gonzalo reminds me of the importance of learning to listen and learning to stop the music. That melody that Diana [the analyst who interrupted Gonzalo] pointed to was hiding the real fear that he is experiencing. It is not really about money; it is about having a new identity, and I can relate to that feeling very well. I retired seven years ago, and I still follow the same routine that I did when I was working. It's hard to become someone new."[33]

The most common definition of music is "organized sound" (Novak and Sakakeeny 2015, 112). As many scholars have noted (see Adorno [1938] 1978; Attali 1985; Becker 1986), this definition raises many questions, particularly the issue of who decides what constitutes order and what distinguishes sound from noise. Does "disorganized" sound then constitute noise? Ethnomusicologists have emphasized that the concept of noise is essentially relational, entailing a metadiscourse of sound that is socially defined (Novak and Sakakeeny 2015, 126). The boundaries between sound and noise are thus social interpretations.

Inside the MFSPT, music and speech overlap. There, the concept of music, as Gonzalo's example shows, is considered an interference—a kind of disorganized sound—that conceals the real motives and feelings behind Gonzalo's impulse to speak. The trained listener, as Marcelo suggests, is able to detect the interference, thereby helping analysands to find the right "tune" to let them understand the "real" source of their problems. Here again, one encounters the idea that the emancipatory act of uncovering serves to alleviate the experience of suffering. The denotation takes a second step in favor of the tone, of the music, of how things are said.

The overtly prescriptive directionality of the linguistic content that the analyst asked Gonzalo to perform is a common practice inside the MFSPT. Talk about talk—pointing to specific linguistic ideologies through metalinguistic and metapragmatic assertions and directives (see Carr 2010b; Silverstein 1979; Woolard 1985b)—is fairly common inside this space. Talk is considered the "royal road to the unconscious," as one analyst told me, paraphrasing Lacan's (1977, 45) famous quote.[34] But listening seems equally important. In this setting, analysts direct analysands to share their emotional states rather than talk about their money woes, their fear of eviction, legal troubles, or any form of material uncertainty. When the "material" narratives appear, the analysts intervene by interrupting the analysand's flow of speech with interjections such as "Again with that song, Marina?" "Rocío, we all know that discourse already; can you talk about what's really going on?" "I think, Rubén, that the noise that emerges with the story that you tell yourself all day long is not allowing the real Rubén to come out." "Rosa, why don't you tell us how you feel? We want to listen to the real Rosa."[35] When these interjections happen, the analysands respond in different ways. Usually, the ones who have been attending the sessions for some time, such as Gonzalo, immediately change the narrative and perform the story that has been elicited. In other cases, especially with newer or intermittent participants, there is indignation—some would leave the room slamming the door, while others would let everyone know that is the precise reason why they want to stop coming to the sessions, and others silently cry.

In her excellent study of treatment programs for addicted women, Summerson Carr (2010b) explains that language is key to these women to demonstrate that they are on the road of recovery. Through what she calls the "ideology of inner reference" (IIR), addicted women are required to perform a linguistic script where "healthy language" functions as a general assessment of their overall health. The IIR implies that "healthy" language refers to preexisting phenomena, and the phenomena to which it refers are internal to speakers. What this means is that the women are inside a clinical discipline that "demands a totally unmediated language, one that appears to transparently refer to and reveal the inner thoughts, feelings, and memories of its speakers" (11).

While there is definitely a prescriptive directive in moments inside the MFSPT when speakers are encouraged to talk about their inner states (e.g., "Tell us how you really feel"), there is also a sharp contrast with the addiction treatment programs presented in Carr's book. In MFSPT sessions, there is no purity in the stories the analysands are required to produce. The word *real* may appear as eliciting an unmediated discourse where the *true* self emerges, but it is the transferential relationship between the analyst and analysand that makes possible the emergence of their doppelgängers. So, by definition, in the psychoanalytic encounter there is no "true self," as Lucía's example shows, but a divided subject who is trying to put many pieces together. Once again, it is not about the speech itself but about how the analysands are saying it and how the analysands and analysts are listening. For Lacan, the Real is an impossibility because it emerges as that which is outside language and resists symbolization. It is untainted experience, which an analysand and an analyst can only glimpse through moments of attunement.[36]

Inside the MFSPT, listening is more a phenomenological experience than a prescriptivist process of purification. When I asked a senior analyst why she and her colleagues would interrupt some analysands and not others with comparable stories (isn't there always music in the words?), she responded that because speaking nonstop is a form of evasion: "stopping the automatic recording and listening to what you are saying and what your words awakened in others is an important therapeutic tool." She also mentioned the need to stop narcissistic performances.

In his essay "The Instance of the Letter in the Unconscious, or Reason since Freud," Lacan ([1966] 2006, 412–41) refers to *scansion*, a method (or practice) of determining and graphically representing the metrical pattern of a line in a poem. It relies on the existence of meter, whose structure it brings to light through the action of scanning. Scanning reveals a hidden rhythm, allowing one to hear a tempo, at first indiscernible but working silently without saying its name. For analyst and literary scholar Isabelle Alfandary (2017, 368), "scansion enables the tuning into the text of the unconscious." The music in the words is thus what enables a psychoanalytic performance, where listening to the staves of the music in the speech of the analysand is key to bringing to light the psychic doppelgänger. Inside the MFSPT, both analysands and analysts get attuned to the pattern of the music that resonates within their psyches. There is an imperceptible tempo that guides the meeting that, at the end of each session, becomes a clear melody.

*   *   *

As the examples presented in this chapter demonstrate, an interesting aspect observed in the MFSPT is that the participants openly discuss listening practices: they explicitly comment about listening. This includes a conscious emphasis on the importance of listening for the healing/well-being of the analysand, as well as for the reproduction of the MFSPT sessions (the person attends to be able to listen and to be listened to). The importance of focusing on a metalistening level is considerable because through the conscious acknowledgment of the role that listening plays, attendees provide direct evidence of their interpretive structures, where the interpretive frames the speakers share derive in large measure from their metalinguistic common sense, and the process of producing frameworks in actual use incorporates a significant metalinguistic component. In other words, what is performed metalinguistically is the culturally specific "competence," or knowledge, that renders the context of the performance accessible to an individual who belongs to a particular group. The overt focus on listening in this chapter's examples provides evidence that inside the MFSPT sessions are shared schemes of discursive but also aural knowledge that can be understood only inside this particular listening genre.

Yet this is only one aspect. The cultivation of this elusive listening genre, since it defies time, entails the suspension of interpretation, being in an almost liminal state, trapped between Firstness and Secondness. The next chapter will discuss how psychoanalytic listening spilled out of the clinical setting and became woven into the fabric of everyday experience. The focus is mainly on the circulation of psychoanalytic representations in conversations outside the clinical setting in everyday life interactions.

3   "What You Really Mean Is..."

Listening to "That Which Is Not Said"

To say who I am (who thinks, who wishes, who fantasizes in me)
is no longer in my power.
Mikkel Borch-Jacobsen, *The Freudian Subject* (1988)

After all, there are no words that belong to no one.
M. M. Bakhtin, *Speech Genres and Other Late Essays* (1986)

In the early fall of 2018, Buenos Aires was consumed by disruption as enraged labor organizers led protests across the city against government austerity measures. These protests were part of a wave of popular anger that erupted after President Mauricio Macri decreased public spending and pensions earlier that year. These actions by Macri depressed both wages and the employment rate amid very high inflation, to the benefit of concentrated local and global financial interests. As the protests spread, the government tried to suppress the unrest, even briefly incarcerating Juan Grabois, a charismatic social organizer and founder of the Movimiento de Trabajadores Excluídos (Movement of Excluded Workers).

On September 24, 2018, the Central de Trabajadores de la Argentina (Argentine Workers' Central Union), one of the three union conglomerates in the country, led a march that ended at the iconic Plaza de Mayo, Buenos Aires's main square and the symbolic center of the country. During the protest, Sergio

Palazzo, the general secretary of the Asociación Bancaria—the union of bank employees—directed a message to the crowds: "This is where the austerity of Mauricio Macri ends." He spoke of the threats that Macri's government had made about imprisoning even more social organizers and union leaders. Then he added: "They are not seeking to imprison leaders. *That might be perhaps a Lacanian object of desire, as we say here. In reality, what they are seeking is* to imprison the politics of inclusion and participation, the politics of inclusion developed by the popular governments" (Portal de Noticias 2018; emphasis added).[1] That a union leader quoted Lacan did not go unnoticed. Four days after this incident, writer and literary critic Martín Kohan (2018) published a note in the newspaper *Perfil* that opened with a question: "Where is Slavoj Zizek when he is most needed? We need to call him right away, we need to find him wherever he is." He went on: "Who else but [Zizek] can find out what is the implication that a union leader, specifically Sergio Palazzo, a bank employee, had quoted—as he did—Jacques Lacan right in the act at Plaza de Mayo? He quoted Lacan, really. He invoked his conceptualization of the object of desire; he talked to a working mass that listened to him at the foot of the podium."[2] Speculating on Palazzo's reasons for bringing up Lacan in a speech before a workers' march, Kohan first suggests that Palazzo sought to distinguish the order of *symbolic* capital from that of *sheer* capital, submitting that even Palazzo—a worker—might be knowledgeable about an abstruse philosopher. Palazzo's use of the deictic *here* ("That might be perhaps a Lacanian object of desire, as we say here") could be interpreted as meaning here in Argentina or here among the workers. Kohan proposes that bringing up such a sophisticated framework was Palazzo's way of demonstrating the relative ignorance of Macri and his government compared to the workers. Later Kohan wonders whether Palazzo was calling attention to the authorities of the University of Buenos Aires School of Psychology and their recent attacks on students and professors who were demanding better salaries and a healthier operational budget.[3] Invoking Lacan at a workers' strike could be interpreted as "a clear gesture from the workers' realm to the realm of knowledge so that those from the realm of knowledge could recognize themselves as workers."[4] Kohan closes by dismissing these purely speculative interpretations and returning to his original plea for Slavoj Žižek.

A psychoanalyst and political cartoonist named Marcelo Rudaeff, better known as Rudy, also commented on Palazzo's reference to Lacan. In a humorous note published on September 29 in *Página 12*, a leftist newspaper known for its severe criticism of Macri's government, Rudy harshly criticized what he described as a failed "love affair" between Mauricio Macri and Christine Lagarde, the former president of the International Monetary Fund (Rudaeff 2018). He then interpreted the incident at Plaza de Mayo: "Perhaps (and this is a serious [interpretation] and with all due respect) he [Palazzo] perceived, or intuitively saw that in the face of the delirious certainty (another Lacanian expression with which the *mauritocrático* narcissism wants to mark us), in the face of the neglect of reality and common sense by which they affirm that inflation decreases when life becomes more expensive, or that it is good to lose your job . . . psychoanalysis is—why not?—a tool of resistance, one more path that allows us to get out of this strange storm called neoliberalism."[5] Admittedly, a union leader bringing up Lacan at a workers' march is an interesting phenomenon in its own right. It is hard to think of any other country where something like this could happen. But my interest in Palazzo's discourse and the later interpretations of his words by renowned writers goes beyond the seemingly ludicrous nature of this episode. I present this episode because of what Palazzo is actually doing by quoting Lacan: he is interpreting through a psychoanalytic framework what he considers to be the government's "real" intentions. Palazzo is translating to the crowds the real motives behind the words—namely, that the rhetoric of incarcerating workers' leaders is a metaphor for eliminating social inclusion. He is performing a sort of expertise that can be compared to the one analysts and analysands execute inside the MFSPT or the one-on-one clinic.

By performing *When you say X, I hear Y*, Palazzo is enacting a psychoanalytic listening genre. He is telling the crowd: I hear that the government is threatening to send us to prison, but the true meaning of their words, what they really mean, is that they want to destroy social services.

It does not stop there. In writing about the speech, Kohan and Rudy continue to replicate psychoanalytic listening by trying to uncover the *real* meaning of Palazzo's words. The subtext is that there must be an intention, a hidden message waiting to be discovered. Though at first it may appear that this is a discussion between people initiated in psychoanalytic theory, the very heterogeneity of Palazzo's audience suggests that psychoanalytic listening in Buenos Aires has permeated a range of social spheres and has become a social way of listening among many different sectors of the population, surpassing class and gender classifications.

This chapter describes how psychoanalytic listening as a genre has extended beyond the borders of the clinical setting and become a way of listening in day-to-day interaction. To see how this has occurred, it is necessary to understand how the key addressivity form ("I think that you mean something else . . . " [*When you say x, I hear y*]), used during casual inter-actions and in many social settings, functions. An addressivity form is a term coined by Bakhtin (1986) when trying to explain the dialogic nature of language. Language, he tells us, is always oriented toward a listener, who will not only respond to an utterance after it is made but also shape the ut-terance while it is being made (see Morson 2006, 55). For example, a listener who responds "What you really mean is . . . " points to how the speaker is actually *listening* to the other person, a formulation that implies a reorder-ing of who is the producer of the utterance.

Psychoanalytic listening is heteroglossic because it is constituted by multiple voices, but these voices are structured differently from voices in or-dinary speech. For instance, when Palazzo claims to hear "something else" or "that which is not said" in President Macri's words, he is attributing aspects of the president's utterance to different sources: the self, the doppelgänger, repressed desires, and so on. This is similar to the way that the analysts and participants at the MFSPT heard Lucía's mother's voice (see chapter 2).

The voices in ordinary speech are organized this way:

I = current self
Others = can be quoted but normally are signaled as such
Doppelgänger = held in abeyance

In psychoanalytic listening, they are reorganized like this:

I = doppelgänger
Others = are voiced unconsciously
Self = all of the above

In nonpsychoanalytic listening—ordinary speech—the hearer takes the *I* as the sole producer of the utterance. But in the formula *When you say x, I hear y*, the *I* who produced the utterance is relegated, and the listener directs their full focus to the doppelgänger. If a listener uses this new hierarchiza-tion between I/doppelgänger, other/self, to understand a person's words, the listener is employing the genre of psychoanalytic listening. The addressivity form *What you really mean is* thus plays the role of a *shifter*—a term whose meaning cannot be determined without referring to the message that is being communicated between a sender and a receiver. For example, the words *I, you, here,* and *now* can be understood only in the context in which they have been uttered—making explicit how the listener is *listening*.

Today, throughout Buenos Aires, personal identities, conceptions of citizenship, and construction of the political are consistently rooted not only in the performativity associated with speaking but also—and crucially—in this particular form of listening based on psychoanalysis. Such listening is social—produced by a collectivity of individuals and performed in all sorts of interactions surpassing class, age, and gender categorizations. In this way, the genre of psychoanalytic listening has become what Marcel Mauss (1966) calls a social fact, which he defined as an activity that has consequences throughout society, in the economic, legal, political, and religious spheres (for example, the Argentine Pope Francis said in an interview that during the country's 1976–83 dictatorship he resorted to psychoanalysis [Piangiani 2017]). These listening practices provide crucial insight in creating and sustaining social relations in the country, affecting how media and cultural production, identities, and the political are formulated.

PSYCHOANALYSIS OUTSIDE THE CLINIC

In Buenos Aires, discussions of psychoanalysis, of one's own therapy, and of ¿Cómo va el divan? (How's the couch going?) are common. Many people in Buenos Aires use psychoanalytic terms to talk about common situations. For example, they often use the word *hysteric* to refer to women or men who do not commit to anything (especially to emotional relationships); the word *phobia* expresses dislike for any situation; the term *psychosomatic* is ascribed to specific bodily ailments; and *Me psicopatió* (They "psychopathized" me) describes a situation when another does something bad and blames you.

Not only do people use psychoanalytic jargon; they tell stories about it. During my fieldwork in Buenos Aires I casually overheard many examples of this—from the taxi driver who tells you that he is going to analysis because he "likes women too much" but doesn't want to put at risk his long-term relationship with his wife; to the sad woman at a convenience store who, when asked by the owner of the store why she looks so sad, responds, "I just came out from therapy" (to which the store owner replies, with absolute familiarity, "Who said knowing yourself was easy?"); to random conversations at the subway and bus stations. Everywhere, it seemed, friends or relatives freely discussed their own or someone else's analytic situation in public.

However, as Palazzo's use of *When you say x, I hear y* to understand the president's speech demonstrates, psychoanalysis circulates in Argentina in ways that go beyond the use of clinical jargon or stories of one's own or others' analytic experiences. In a wide range of social contexts in Buenos Aires, people of different ages, genders, and professions consistently reproduce psychoanalytic listening outside the clinical setting by making use of lay psychoanalytic interpretation. For instance, in the fall of 2011, I was riding in a taxi cab with another woman who entered into a revealing exchange with the driver. The woman (w) was in her early thirties, and the taxi driver (TD) was in his fifties. Both were born and raised in Buenos Aires. During the ride, the taxi driver drove past a group of children dressed in beige and light blue. After the woman looked at the children, the following exchange ensued:

> **W:** I really dislike that combination of colors, especially light blue. I don't think anybody looks good in that color.
> *[w: No me gusta nada esa combinación de colores, especialmente el celeste. No creo que le quede bien a nadie.]*
> **TD:** What's the matter? *I hear a lot of animosity in your words.* Does your mother wear that color often?
> *[TD: ¿Qué pasa? Escucho un montón de mala onda en tus palabras. ¿Tu vieja usa ese color seguido?]*
> **W:** What are you talking about?
> *[w: ¿Qué decís?]*
> **TD:** *I think that you mean something else,* but you don't dare say it. No one hates a color without a reason.
> *[TD: Y yo creo que querés decir otra cosa, pero no te animás a decirlo. Nadie odia un color así sin razón.]*
> **W:** No, not my mother... but now that you mention it... I will have to think about it.
> *[w: No, mi vieja no... pero ahora que lo decís... voy a tener que pensarlo.]*[6]

Asked if he had formal training as an analyst, the taxi driver responded, "I think more than thirteen years of therapy makes you understand how these things work. But to answer your question: no, I have never been trained as an analyst."

This sort of interaction is extraordinarily common in Buenos Aires, and so is the response to queries about an individual's psychoanalytic credentials. Frequently this question is answered through a reference to the number of years that an individual has undergone therapy. Some explain their psychoanalytic interpretations by claiming, without elaboration, a "commonsensical" relation between an utterance and its "real meaning," while others reveal that a close friend or family member is a therapist, and consequently they are exposed to the particularities of this listening genre.

When people such as the taxi driver and Palazzo use the formulation *What you really mean is*, they are making explicit how they are listening. But they are not only reproducing a psychoanalytic genre (the rehierarchization of the total utterance)—they are also pointing to different *ideological* dimensions. These include an explicit ideology of knowledge (i.e., indexing the taxi driver and Palazzo as knowledgeable about something others do not perceive), a belief in unconscious practices, a disregard for semantic content in favor of a hermeneutic approach, and faith in a "true" (perhaps unmediated) self (see Ricoeur 1975 for his discussion of hermeneutics of suspicion).

The implication is that interpretation of verbal utterances can "uncover" aspects of the most intimate self, and that this interpretation can be performed by anyone who listens closely. The tacit subtext suggests that *you are unable to understand the real motives of your actions and feelings, so a translation is needed.* When someone says, "What you really mean is," a social situation is immediately transformed (Goffman 1964) into a setting that grounds the exchange psychoanalytically, where many ideologies emerge. Consequently, in Buenos Aires a form of sociability is enacted through listening practices, moving from the performativity of speaking to a performativity of listening.

The prevalence of psychoanalytic listening as a genre of listening in Argentina has important implications for how key areas of social organization are enacted and maintained. This includes the way people formulate knowledge and assign authority, index themselves as political subjects, and engage in conversations across class, gender, and racial divisions. Psychoanalytic listening draws heavily on philosophical and theoretical constructs of the modern self, which inform the way people engage broader social, personal, and political arenas. Recognizing the way these ideologies are deployed through listening is essential for grasping how listening contributes to their reproduction and dissemination. To help the reader understand these arguments, I will now provide a basic overview of what listening ideologies are, along with some examples of how they have been discussed by scholars in other contexts.

In linguistic anthropology, the concept of *linguistic ideology* points to a person's ability, through their knowledge of communication practices in a local context, to evaluate any given speech utterance within that specific context. This knowledge is both pragmatic and self-reflexive. As pointed out by Susan Gal (1998, 322), "linguistic ideology is a guide to speakers for how they should understand the metapragmatic cues that relate linguistic signals to their context of use and that provide information about the 'what is going on here' of interaction." From its inception, the "ethnography of communication" has been concerned with language ideology as the cultural system of ideas, beliefs, and social values about language use. Current writings on linguistic ideology, focusing on the linkages among linguistic forms, semiotic codes, and power and social relations, reject the notion that linguistic ideology is a singular and politically neutral cultural construction. Instead, a number of scholars argue that multiple differing ideologies construct alternate, even opposing, realities within a culture (Briggs 1988). Language ideologies are the mediating link between social forms and forms of talk (Hanks 1996). As a result, the choice of a speech form (i.e., polite language, informal speech, scientific language, slang, etc.) has political implications on the basis of speakers' commonsensical convictions about what a language is and what the use of language is assumed to imply. As Asif Agha (2007, 145) puts it: "They [speakers] hint at the existence of cultural models of speech—a metapragmatic classification of discourse types—linking speech repertoires to typification of actor, relationship and conduct." Therefore, if linguistic ideologies encompass both social interaction and linguistic forms, it is because they can be understood as verbalized, thematized discussions and as the implicit understandings and unspoken assumptions embedded and reproduced in the structure of institutions and their everyday practices (Gal 1998, 319).

In the same way that linguistic ideologies point to a particular framework of action, interpretation, and subjectivity, "aural ideologies" or "listening ideologies" also provide a clarifying lens for how action, interpretation, and subjectivity operate within social interactions. Historically, the ideological dimension of listening has been generally conceptualized in terms of the content and the social prestige of what is being listened to (see Emmison 2003; Peterson 1992a, 1992b; Savage and Gayo 2011). The most extensive studies have focused on music, since the classificatory ideologies of music (e.g., highbrow vs. lowbrow) opens a debate about how consumers of music use cultural taste to reinforce symbolic boundaries between themselves and categories of people they dislike (Bourdieu 1977, 1986, 1993; Bryson 1997). These studies emphasize shared networks of signification that are constituted in the appreciation of music. Hence, the ideological construct is somehow "external" to the actual listening. The ideological sphere of listening is located *in the associations*, not in the act of listening per se. These associations are shaped by dominant aesthetic and social expectations that are themselves historically structured and are constantly changing, creating particular kinds of audiences (see Savage and Gayo 2011; Warde, Wright, and Gayo 2008). Accordingly, the cultural history of listening to particular kinds of music, as well as its ideological dimension, encompasses changing aesthetic responses in relationship to public behavior. Studies of music consumption thus conceptualize the constitution of a social subject in relation to the choices a person makes about listening to particular symbolic sounds.[7]

However, if we focus only on the relationship between sounds linked to particular groups of people, we miss elements that are key to understanding listening ideologies *in the act* of listening. To undercover aural ideologies, we need to focus on the *metalevel* of listening. How do subjects listen? What are the evaluations that listeners construct? Do sounds have the same meanings for everyone? An array of ideological conceptualizations comes into play when we perceive sound, especially when the sound source is not visible (Kane 2016). Listening—like any other mode of perception—is historically structured (Foucault 1972, 1988), and by focusing on the way social actors apprehend sound, we can begin to understand how listening ideologies are shaped.

Listening and sounds are historically dependent and reflect different paradigms depending on context. For example, in *Listening in Paris: A Cultural History*, James Johnson (1995, 2) explains that in travelers' descriptions and concertgoers' accounts of the Paris Opera in the eighteenth century, the audience was "at times loud and at other merely sociable, but seldom deeply attentive." Concertgoers talked throughout the performances, paying little attention to the music. It was not until a hundred years later, through a long process of subtle transformation, that the relationship between concertgoers and music changed; people stopped talking, and the audience began to *listen* to the music. The notorious shift in listening practices (or auditory ideologies) between the eighteenth and nineteenth centuries in Paris was a result of changing popular comprehension of new aesthetic styles that, according to Johnson, are "at the same time structural and personal" (4).

Johnson points to the fact that any public response to sounds—including silence—is social: "public expression, although freely chosen, is drawn from a finite number of behaviors and styles of discourse shaped by the culture" (3). At the same time, the expression of these modes of reception does not exist objectively. Their significance resides in *the particular moment of reception.*

The dialectical relationship between the structural and the personal aspects of reception resonates with the concept of "meaning" in language, which makes sense only in light of the social and psychological conditions under which a particular linguistic code is used (Basso and Selby 1976; Ochs 1979). Meaning is shaped by various factors, including the age, sex, and social class of speakers and hearers. It is shaped by the style of speaking, the events or activities in which language is being used, the institutional roles of participants in the interaction, and the organization or flow of information in the prior discourse. This relationship is known to be bidirectional: "language shapes contexts as much as context shapes language" (Duranti and Goodwin 1992, 77). In the case of the Paris Opera in the eighteenth century, we can say that *reception shaped contexts as much as context shaped reception.* In other words, the reality of the sign, whether linguistic or auditory, is wholly a matter determined by communication (see Voloshinov 1973). It is in the intricacies of this dialectic that linguistic and aural ideologies come into being, since both concern how the structure of language or sounds, the use of language and listening practices, and the beliefs about language and sounds are necessarily interconnected and constitutive of each other. Johnson's analysis of the transformations of the Paris Opera exemplifies how a social space's ideology and practice of listening can develop into a new regime of silence, attention, and focus. As this example suggests, listening is an extraordinary force for constituting social space and directing behavior.

Looking at these kinds of ideological constructs in the context of psychoanalytic listening brings to light a number of important ways that such ideologies circulate through listening in Buenos Aires and Argentina. But although listening ideologies have not been specifically termed as such previously, auditory ideologies are everywhere, and other scholars have directly taken up many important examples of how listening ideologies operate through a number of important frameworks. As R. Murray Schafer (2003, 25) writes, since "we have no ear lids," "we are condemned to listen." Every time we listen, we are consciously or unconsciously making assumptions and judgments and sometimes having fastidious ideas about the ranges of sounds we consider "good" or interruptive. The sounds we are constantly assessing are themselves impregnated with semiotic meaning. Scholars have identified numerous important examples of these kinds of listening ideologies, along with their impact within specific social contexts.

In his historical analysis of the constitution of meanings and sounds in antebellum America, Mark Smith (2003, 2001) describes how some regional soundscapes helped to define social relations. He (2001, 139) explains how the elites of both northern and southern states associated certain sounds with the notion of progress: "defined by nascent capitalists and boosters, sound heralded progress and, as such, it was sound, not noise." These were mainly industrial sounds that, far from being signified as noise, were considered signs of growth and development (e.g., the sound of the first railroads). In contrast, the quietness of the countryside was synonymous with recession and backwardness. In this context, when Native Americans were expelled from their land, the elites' policy was to "settle them in a *quiet home*" (G. C. Munro, cited in Smith 2003, 141; emphasis added). In antebellum America these different sounds acquired meanings that reflected the desires, the fears, and the discomfort of the period. As in the example from the Paris Opera, these are instances of reflexivity of listening, which entails a strong ideological component.

However, aural ideologies associated with these kinds of sounds were hardly static, and the same sounds that were considered harbingers of progress and economic growth in the eighteenth and early nineteenth centuries acquired a totally different value in the late nineteenth and early twentieth centuries. As Kerin Bijsterveld (2001) explains in "The Diabolical Symphony of the Mechanical Age," the sounds of the city and the mechanical revolution that in antebellum America were considered "good" sounds were resignified in Europe as noise by the turn of the century. As social classifications transformed, those who showed no sensitivity to noise were considered "insensible to arguments, ideas, poetry and art—in sum, to mental impressions of all kinds, due to the tough and rude texture of the brains," as philosopher Arthur Schopenhauer suggested in an article published in 1851 (cited in Bijsterveld 2001, 45). Schopenhauer was not alone in his dislike for external noise—the intellectual elite at the turn of the century in Europe agreed that a "noise etiquette" should be implemented. They worried that they could not concentrate and contemplate beauty due to the "many torments to which our delicate organs [the ear] are exposed" (Bijsterveld 2001, 45). New typologies of people emerged, separating the "brute" and uneducated, who were unable to distinguish noise from other types of sounds, from the refined and delicate, who could not appreciate beauty under the "torments" produced by excessive sounds.

What is remarkable about these debates is the emergence of subjects who heard things differently and thus belonged to different social strata. In each example, we can grasp a specific listening ideology that indexes particular social actors to certain practices that are ideologically constructed. Among these practices, gender also emerges as a notable feature. Bijsterveld notices that the people who pushed for noise reduction at the turn of the nineteenth century in Europe were at times classified as feminine and weak. This fed a gendered narrative, where the ability to tolerate sounds was masculine and powerful, in contrast to the womanly inability to abide harsh noise (Bijsterveld 2001, 56). (For a discussion of how specific notions of gender are implicated in the circulation of psychoanalytic discourses and are reproduced by the genre of psychoanalytic listening, specifically constructions of the mother, see chapter 5.)

Beyond the issues discussed in this book, however, gendered subjectivities are productive sites for understanding the importance of sound and listening within all social contexts. In the brilliant research by Miyako Inoue (2006) into the constitution of a modern Japanese female subjectivity, the practice of listening and other corporeal sites of subject formation (e.g., other senses, such as seeing and smelling) emerge as socially constructed and historically emergent. Inoue pays particular attention to the gendered constitution of the female character in Japan, focusing on how Japanese schoolgirl speech became a signifier related to modernization. In her account, the female voice, previously largely unheard, began to have semiotic meaning from approximately 1887 to the end of World War II. The female voice slowly transformed from background noise into the form of a linguistic genre: "schoolgirl talk," which was dubbed "vulgar," "sugary and shallow," and problematic in the view of male Japanese intellectuals at the turn of the century (156–59). Inoue takes on Michael Silverstein's (1979) examination of linguistic ideology and explains that these auditory practices are embedded inside an already customary language ideology that established what constituted a language and what did not. In her analysis, Inoue focuses her attention on the metapragmatic ideology that emerges in male intellectual descriptions of schoolgirl talk so as to demonstrate that these intellectuals are listening ideologically. Inoue presents examples where schoolgirl talk emerges as an imagined *auditory ideology* that existed more in the minds of elite Japanese intellectuals than in the mouths of girls. But the auditory ideology is sufficiently real that it enables people to hear this imaginary talk. Particular sounds created a noteworthy discomfort in the listener and were later classified as schoolgirl talk. This process was possible, according to Inoue, because the female voice was already embedded in a specific linguistic ideology with clear boundaries and expectations about what it should be or sound like.

Although in Argentina the concept of race is less central than in other social contexts, such as the United States, race is a powerful lens for understanding how specific ideologies and social biases circulate within listening practices. For example, recent scholarship has focused on the concept of *raciolinguistics*, exploring the role that language plays in shaping ideas about race, and vice versa (see Alim, Rickford, and Ball 2016; Flores and Rosa 2015). In these investigations, the listener becomes the arbiter of defining who is a racialized-sounding subject (Flores and Rosa 2015). The politics of listening practices create particular subjects as "sounding like a race," while others sound "neutral," thus creating unequal subjects (Rosa 2019). In *The Sonic Color Line* (2016), Jennifer Lynn Stoever analyzes what she considers to be white-constructed ideas of "sounding Other." These ideas encompass accents, slang, and dialects, which she claims have "flattened the complex range of sounds actually produced by people of color, marking the sonic color line's main contour" (11). Thus, the racialized body occupies not only a physical form but a sonic space—an imagined space where, for example, sounding "eloquent" or "articulate" becomes a synonym of sounding white (Alim and Smitherman 2012).

The examples provided by Inoue and by raciolinguistics scholarship help us understand that listening ideologies are, to a large degree, imagined. There is nothing "real" about the discourses that link certain types of people to certain listening practices—these are but beliefs and projections that indicate a way in which subjects understand the world.

In Argentina, when people tune the ear into a "psychoanalytic genre of listening" (such as Ramiro and the taxi driver discussed in chapter 1 or the woman speaking to the taxi driver discussed earlier in this chapter), they bring to life a set of beliefs that index the listener as inhabiting a particular epistemology. They take up a specific ideology of knowledge, marking the listener as knowledgeable about something the speaker is unable to recognize. The ideologies of believing in unconscious practices favor a hermeneutic approach to signification, signaling the possibility of having a "real" intimate self, unknown to the speaker but seemingly up for interpretation. In psychoanalytic listening there is an additional ideological bias that is rooted in radical modern subjectivities, which undergird this genre of listening and have a profound impact on people's understanding of specific social, personal, and political constructions.

Unlike the examples above, where the ideological component of listening underscores connections between the production of certain sounds and a social classification (e.g., if you don't mind listening to rough noises, you must be an unsophisticated brute), the listening ideology of psychoanalytic listening (*What you really mean is*) does not necessarily rely on specific social class biases. In cases where racial, gendered, and class hierarchies are established by extralinguistic features, the listener creates relationships linking sounds or phonetic variations to kinds of people based on their social position. In such situations, it matters whether the listener is a man or a woman, wealthy, white or occupies another social position. But in the ideology produced by listening psychoanalytically, the relationship between the listener and the listened is not determined by such extradiscursive factors. Instead, what matters is the capacity for listening and interpreting. Rather than bestowing a social position (other than that of being interpreted), psychoanalytic listening creates a particular scenario, a setting, a possibility.

Certainly, there are hierarchical structures that favor some analytic interpretations over others. Someone with a degree in psychology has an institutional voice with more credibility when interpreting the actions or discourses of a specific subject. But as the two stories about taxi drivers show, anyone with an appropriate "ear" has the potential to listen to unconscious practices. Thus, there seems to be a horizontal circulation of interpretations wherein the subject decides whether or not to accept the interpellation.

When it comes to using the formula *What you really mean is*, social position is not part of the equation in Buenos Aires. I witnessed male and female, younger and older, middle-class and wealthy people performing this listening practice. In doing so, they performed an indexical transposition— that is, taking an indexical sign from one field and embedding it in a new field (for example, when I say *I*, but I am quoting someone else's speech, I have transposed the first-person pronoun from the deictic field to the narrative field). *Porteños* perform an indexical transposition of the present dyad into the psychoanalytic dyad, which rehierarchizes the *I-you, here-now* relationship. This is so prevalent in Buenos Aires that people rarely react negatively to the interpretation. It is part of their communicative practices, even though in other contexts it can be interpreted as a violent act: as one of my United States mentors told me, "it sounds dystopic, like a mocking inversion of empathy into intrusion."

Listening to the voice of the Other implies advocating for the Other. Listening thus implies a form of care. If we understand the subject as an atomized unit, the *What you really mean is* addressivity form would most likely be perceived as an intrusion. But if we take at face value Freud's idea that the psyche is extended and cannot truly know of its own existence, we can understand subjectivity not as one individual but as a continuum of "resonances." The listener who translates the words of others into seemingly unconnected interpretations is helping the subject find the "nodes" that anchor the chain of signifiers. Thus, the listener's interpretations could be read as an act of generosity, as repair.[8] As Bakhtin (1986, 121–22) writes, "The author (speaker) has his own inalienable right to the word, but *the listener* has his rights, and those whose voices are *heard* in the word before the author comes upon *it also have their rights*" (emphasis added). "[A]fter all, there are no words that belong to no one" (124).

PSYCHOANALYTIC LISTENING AND MODERNITY

Contemporary Argentine listening practices tie into larger sociopolitical forces, both regionally and globally, and intersect with important historical lineages of power and identity. Psychoanalytic listening is a profoundly modern form of listening—in the sense that it comprises a modern subjectivity that is constituted in relation to an alterity—where the Other is not an accidental by-product but a necessary condition for the modern self (B. R. Anderson [1983] 2006; Certeau 1984, 1988; Chakrabarty 2000; Deleuze and Guattari 1988; Gupta 2005; Horrocks 2001; Inoue 2006). In this view, the modern individual, whose political life is lived in citizenship, is also supposed to have an interiorized "private" self that pours out through different outlets, such as diaries, autobiographies, memoirs, and other literary or artistic forms. Inside this episteme, the analyst's office becomes the epitome of the expression of the private self. For example, Dipesh Chakrabarty (2000, 35) pointed directly to psychoanalysis as a "genre that helps express the modern self." The main idea is that there is an *internal life that is unique* and is not to be found in the expression of a social position. The modern subject represents the self as irreplaceable, personal, intimate, and not transferable.[9]

In this literature, then, psychoanalysis is depicted as a modern enterprise because it helps to uncover the intimate self. The relations that are formed are "intersubjective" (Gupta 2005). If we transpose the particular way in which modernity has been defined to the circulation of psychoanalysis outside the clinical setting in Buenos Aires, we can say that through listening psychoanalytically, the listener not only refers to the ideologies already discussed but also performs a modern subjectivity based primarily on the idea of unconscious practices. This means that in Buenos Aires there is a public culture constructed on the basis of a radically modern ideology—psychoanalysis—and this culture is created through listening practices that circulate on an everyday basis.

To the extent that this holds true—that psychoanalysis is a modern practice—listening psychoanalytically may seem to contradict some of the Enlightenment epistemologies that conceptualize listening as non-modern and the visual as modern (Gouk 2004; Jay 1993). In the wake of the "communication revolution" that took place through the emergence of the printing press, it has become commonplace to assert that the early modern West shifted from a predominantly aural to a primarily visual culture (B. R. Anderson [1983] 2006; McLuhan 1962).[10] The emergence of positivistic frames of interpretation based on observable facts to determine the veracity of particular phenomena also emphasized the visual, relegating other sensorial expressions to secondary importance (Gouk 1999, 2004; Schmidt 2000; B. Smith 1999).

The ear, on the contrary, has been historically connected with the past, with religious practices, stories of possessions, and other storytelling, and with a connection with the so-called natural and sensible world, among other representations (see Certeau 2000). Psychoanalytic focus, which for many years was placed as "the talking cure," presents a model of listening that defies linear conceptualizations of time and implies a codification of signs that are referential but whose reference is concealed. Most importantly, through this framework one listens to the inner and perhaps "true" self (Lacan [1966] 2006). Psychoanalysis created a new form of subjective experience that gave birth to the idea of a divided subject, unique and exceptional, pointing to how the modern self is conceptualized. Thus, by being mostly a listening practice, psychoanalysis is a modern enterprise.

In Buenos Aires, listening is based on a radically modern form—psychoanalysis—which is, by definition, intrinsically modern (modern in the sense of alterity, on the idea of separation of the private and public self and the uniqueness of one's self). When listeners tune their ears into the psychoanalytic listening genre outside the clinical setting, they are performing a modern subjectivity wherein ideologies about a private and unique self become evident.

Reported Speech as the Creation of Alterity

To see how the genre of psychoanalytic listening reproduces specific modern subjectivities in Argentina, it's useful to look at the way this genre of listening helps create alterity. By turning the ear into a psychoanalytic genre, and thus performing a modern subjectivity, we conceptualize a very particular form of *reported speech*, or how speakers represent the speech of others, as well as their own (Bakhtin 1981; Voloshinov 1973). This form does not report directly or indirectly a speech but creates a whole new narrative centered on translating unconscious practices. The following example illustrates this point.

Inside a coffee shop are four friends, three men and one woman: Carlos (C), age forty; Darío (D), age thirty-five; and Andrés (A) and Lorena (L), both thirty-nine. They are discussing a positive review that appeared in the national newspaper *Clarín* of a book recently published by Darío. (I was also present but did not participate in the conversation.)

1 **C:** Hey, it says here that you are thirty-nine years old, but you are not thirty-nine.
   [*c: Ey, acá dice que tenés 39 años, pero vos no tenés 39.*]
2 **D:** No.
   [*D: No.*]
3 **L:** How old are you?
   [*L: ¿Cuántos años tenés?*]
4 **D:** Well, my analyst says that I am fifteen years old; this guy says that I am thirty-nine, and my document says that I am thirty-five. So I don't know. [*laughs*]
   [*D: Y, mi analista dice que tengo 15 años; este tipo dice que tengo 39, y en mi documento dice que tengo 35. Así que ¿qué se yo?*]
5 **A:** At least your analyst says that you are fifteen. Mine says that I am eleven! [*laughs*]
   [*A: Por lo menos tu analista dice que tenés 15, el mio dice que tengo ¡11!*]

6 **D:** The next time that Andrea [the analyst] tells me, "Darío, it seems as if I am listening to my son Manu when I am listening to you."— C'mon, the kid is around fifteen years old!—I am going to send her this note. [*laughs*]

   [**D:** *La próxima vez que Andrea me diga: "Darío, me parece que estoy oyendo a mi hijo Manu cuando te escucho a vos."—¡No me jodas, el pibe tiene como 15 años!—Le voy a mandar esta nota.*]

7 **A:** No, what your analyst is telling you is that she thinks of you as her child, so she is not available to fuck. [*laughs*]

   [**A:** *No, lo que tu analista te está diciendo es que te ve como a su hijo, así que no te la podés garchar.*]

8 **D:** What a big moron you are! Andrea is my mother's age!

   [**D:** *¡Pero qué pedazo de pelotudo! ¡Andrea es de la edad de mi vieja!*]

9 **C:** Oops, here comes the [Oedipus] complex. [*laughs*]

   [**C:** *Uy, ahí se sale el complejo.*]

10 **A:** Congratulations, dude! You are great!

   [**A:** *¡Felicidades chabón! ¡Sos re-grosso!*]

11 **C:** She [the analyst] was generous. I would have guessed three years, max. [*laughs*]

   [**C:** *Y fue generosa, yo te daría 3 años como mucho.*]

A significant way in which "self" and "other" are differentiated is through the exploration of reported speech. Valentine Voloshinov (1973, 116–19) conceptualized reported speech in three ways: *direct,* when the speaker repeats the same statement with no apparent change; *indirect,* when the speaker paraphrases the statement; and *quasi-direct,* when the speaker presents the statement through a third-person narrative formulation—that is, from the point of view of the narrator in a novel.[11] The formulation *What you really mean is...* suggests yet another form of reported speech.

Reported speech, in any of its forms, is very useful for the analysis of how alterity is brought to light as well as of listening genres. It points to *how* listeners listen to each other's words. When we use indirect discourse, we do not just apply a grammatical rule. Instead, we need to analyze and respond to the reported utterance and identify the dialogic relationship within which it operates. As Bakhtin suggests in the opening quote of this chapter, the word cannot be assigned to a single speaker.

When people in Buenos Aires use the addressivity form *What you really mean is,* they are reporting the speech of the other person's utterance. This appropriation of one speaker's discourse by another, who may then employ

it to oppose the original intention (either directly or obliquely), is fundamental in psychoanalytic listening. It also points to the way that psychoanalytical listening helps reproduce key aspects of the conceptualization of
the modern self in very quotidian social contexts.

In the opening line of the exchange in the coffee shop, Carlos indirectly
reports what he read in the newspaper: "it says here that you are thirty-
nine years old." The deictic word *here* behaves much like a demonstrative
that, in conjunction with the physical gesture that Carlos is performing by
pointing to the newspaper article, is used not only to identify the source of
the narrative but to indicate the referent's spatial and temporal location. It
also generates a collective orientation in the conversation to the newspaper text. In this case, the quotation is happening in the present. Likewise,
in line 4, Darío is reporting three different sources (three quotations): "my
analyst says that I am fifteen years old; this guy says that I am thirty-nine;
and my document says that I am thirty-five."

Unlike in Carlos's quotation, Darío's first quotation (of his analysis) lacks
the deictic *here* and thus does not provide a specific time frame. Since the
analyst is not present at the moment this exchange happened, the implication is that Darío is indirectly quoting what the therapist told him some-
time in the past. Darío's second quotation (in reference to the literary critic)
introduces another deictic: *this*. In this case, the deictic not only helps to
contextualize the source of the utterance but reduces the scope of interpretation to a particular individual and in a particular time frame, since he,
like Carlos, is pointing directly to the newspaper. This is a classic example
of transposition; there is a metonymy: pointing at the newspaper and referring to an author (a deferred ostention between counterparts). In both cases,
Darío is bringing two absent social actors into the present context.

In line 6 of the conversation, there is a direct form of quotation when
Darío straightforwardly quotes his analyst ("The next time that Andrea tells
me: 'Darío, it seems as if I am listening to my son Manu when I am listening
to you'"). In this instance, Darío does not claim authorship for a part of his
utterance, which he ascribes to another speaker (the analyst). This part of
his utterance does not serve a regular referential function. Rather, it refers
to words—not to any arbitrary words but to those words that the analyst
purportedly uttered at some other time. Through this reference, Darío also
collapses different time frames. By drawing on the analyst's words, Darío is
bringing in a reference about listening, making explicit that the analyst
is positioning her ear in reference to symbolic sounds. We can see the difference between Darío's first instance of indirect quotation (line 4)—where

he transforms the analyst's speech through subtle changes in deictic, tense, or pronoun change—and the second instance (line 6), in which he quotes the speech of the analyst directly. In the first quotation we have:

(a) "My analyst says that I am fifteen years old."

We could infer that the original statement (made by Andrea, the analyst) was:

(b) "Darío, you act/look/sound as if you are fifteen years old."

Yet, Darío did not exactly listen to option b. Instead, he quotes his analyst as saying there is a *sonic* relationship between his speech and that of the analyst's son, who is "around fifteen years old." He is making an inference derived from the proposition made by the analyst. We do not have enough context to understand what the analyst meant when she said, "It seems as if I am listening to my son Manu when I am listening to you." What we do know is that Darío heard "You are fifteen years old," presumably as an assessment of his level of emotional maturity. We can assume that this exchange happened inside the clinical setting, since one of the most important stipulations of psychoanalytic theory is that the analysand and the analyst should not have any social relation outside the clinic. Their relationship is purely therapeutic. This discrepancy—between what the analyst actually said and the interpretation that Darío is making of it—shows us that in psychoanalysis, what is quoted is far from being a direct or indirect attribution but a new reconfiguration of the words, a new grammatical form.

In line 7 we see a formulation of the *What you really mean is* form of quotation when Andrés says, "No, *what your analyst is telling you is* that she thinks of you as her child." This belongs to the same group of expressions as the one uttered by the taxi driver ("I think that you mean something else") and Palazzo's "in reality, what they are seeking is . . ." From one perspective, reported speech—which incorporates a past utterance into a new dialogical context—may be viewed as a reconstruction of that past utterance, one that revitalizes it with a present significance.

The *What you really mean is* form of reported speech—which can be described as intersubjective reported speech—affords a new "hearing/ listening" in a necessarily different context. It is essentially deprived of the words' original significance by the author's current interpretation. For example, in the exchange above, Andrés is telling Darío what the analyst really meant with her words. He is simultaneously presenting the third-person perspective of the reported speaker and the first-person perspective of the reporting speaker. He suggests that the analyst is bringing the figure of her son into the therapy to indicate to Darío that she sees him as a son, thus stating clearly that she is not available for any sexual encounter. While this statement is meant as a joke, Andrés is clearly reproducing, if artificially, how to listen psychoanalytically, disregarding the words of the direct quotation brought up by Darío and offering a different analysis. The one voice has been replaced by a series of new statements.

Bakhtin had envisioned some of these problems when he presented his concept of double-voiced discourse. In "Discourse in the Novel," Bakhtin (1981, 261) describes the novel as a complex set of "several heterogeneous stylistic unities." From this perspective, the novel is not a single unified form but a genre that subsumes several subgenres. Unlike monological lyric poetry, the novel is dialogical or heteroglot, expressive of a multiplicity of points of views that Bakhtin called *voices*. Such speech constitutes a special type of double-voiced discourse, serving two speakers at the same time and expressing two different intentions simultaneously: the direct intention of the character who is speaking and the refracted intention of the author. These voices are "dialogically interrelated, they—as it were—know about each other (just as two exchanges in a dialog) and are structured in this mutual knowledge of each other; it is as if they actually hold a conversation with each other" (324). Double-voiced discourse, Bakhtin tells us, is internally dialogized. So, one way in which the *What you really mean is* quotation can be interpreted is as representing a double-voiced discourse, which has a particular intentionality (a therapeutic one) and is open to different interpretations.

Alterity inside One's Own Self

In psychoanalysis there is a radical form of alterity: the unconscious. Derrida (2005) called it an "intruder," or the other in you that is internal but gets expressed externally through actions, among other behaviors. The recognition that there is something we cannot control that is nevertheless represented by our drives, our fears, and our repressions is a modern idea performed in many casual encounters in Buenos Aires. But unlike other forms of alterity, the idea of the unconscious does not necessarily need another person to recognize that it is there (although most of the time it happens inside an interchange). It can happen inside one's own dialogue.

Psychoanalytic listening is cumulative: it functions through aural residues that, little by little, give sense to an incoherent group of sounds or perhaps superimpose one set of ideologies and practices of listening over others. This is the main reason that temporality is a crucial element in psychoanalytic listening and one of the "justifications" for some therapies to last many years. Listening can happen at any time, as the following example demonstrates.

Adriana is a forty-three-year-old theater teacher who lives in Caballito, a middle-class neighborhood in the geographical center of Buenos Aires. She has been in and out of therapy for approximately thirty years. She classifies her therapies as "important" and "unimportant." The important ones lasted approximately seven to ten years, and Adriana has had three of these. There were some smaller therapies between the important ones that lasted just a few months. Adriana told me that her first therapy— which started when she was just ten years old—was not her decision but her mother's. Adriana did not have a good relationship with her mother, which influenced her decision to continue therapy once her first important one ended. Adriana suggested her problems were related to a house that her grandfather bought her when she was ten years old to provide her with financial stability in the future. But when Adriana became an adult, her mother, who had separated from her husband and needed money, did not want to leave the house. Adriana told me that this situation created a lot of friction between mother and daughter; at the age of twenty-one, Adriana felt forced to leave the house—*her* house—and to find odd jobs to support herself.

She was telling me about her last important analysis, which ended in 2007, when the following monologue ensued:

1 It was great because I was able to notice that everything that I had
2 come to look for, I was beginning to resolve. So, in one session I told [the
3 analyst] "I believe so and so ..." and it was just, contemporary to when
4 I bought my apartment. I bought my home, not the one that my grandfather,
5 where my mom lives. And that was a subject that, if in reality I have to tell you
6 about it ...

[Long pause of forty-eight seconds]

7   Oh my God, this is crazy! This is crazy!

[Another long pause of thirty-four seconds]

8   Cristina [the analyst] told me "that house is yours," and I fought for a long
9   time with my mom for that house, at one point I wanted to sell it and that
10 we share the money, but at the end we didn't sell it, my mother didn't have
11 a job. It was a big conflict, *and now I realize, talking with you,*
12 that in 2007 when I bought MY own house, something got resolved.
13 *What I am telling you is that just now, I am realizing something very important.*

[Pause of thirteen seconds]

14 Well, my mother also felt guilty and responsible, because she witnessed
15 that I worked a lot in order to pay the rent, and she felt that she was
16 living in my house. But she didn't have any money, and no job, and
17 the house is very small and in the suburbs, so even if we had sold
18 it you can't afford to buy two smaller ones. No way. So, a very
19 tense situation generated between me and my mom. I think that right now
20 our relationship is better, because that issue was resolved. And my mom, when I
21 bought the house, my mom could not believe it! She told me, "I could
22 imagine that you would win an Oscar, but never that you would buy
23 a house."

[Pause of twenty-four seconds]

24 And I realized now talking with you . . . this is crazy . . . talking
25 about that. It is as if I am listening to something, as if I am
26 closing an incomplete circle now just by telling you this.

[Long pause of thirty-eight seconds]

27 The truth is that I am just now realizing the meaning of what I told
    you:
28 that I started therapy at ten years old, right after they bought me
29 ours/the/my house, mine and my mom's. Mine. And then it ended
30 when I bought my house ... I have never made that connection.
31 Nevertheless, that affected me deeply and was circulating in my
32 unconscious. And it made my relation with my mother hard,
33 that I felt the instability, the lack of parameters, until
34 something finds a closure. And that affected me, it really, really af-
    fected me and it
35 affected our relationship. Like when ... do you understand?
36 And I say, I never brought it up to a conscious level,
37 until now *after I told you about it and hear myself telling you.*
38 But nevertheless, it determined the way I acted.

Adriana has been to therapy for almost thirty years. She has talked
for many years to different therapists, and she has talked to her friends
about her feelings; consequently, she has listened to herself for a long time.
Through all of this exposure, she is capable of uncovering many aspects of
her own utterances, ones that are not self-evident to the neophyte listener.
If we compare Adriana's listening with the taxi driver's example, the first
thing to notice is that he does not possess an aural accumulation about the
woman he is trying to interpret. He might have that accumulation with
other people he is closer to and with his own self, but the interpretations that he is bringing up may or may not resonate in the psyche of the
woman he is addressing. In Adriana's case, on the other hand, it was her
own aural accumulation that facilitates not an interpretation but a discovery. In her own words, she was able to listen to something that was
circulating inside her psyche but was never articulated before. An aural
accumulation of thirty years finally found a form by her listening to her
own words.

Adriana, through a variety of metalinguistic remarks (lines 11, 13, 24, 26,
27, 36), points to how she is listening. It is by listening to herself, she tells
us, that she has discovered something important: *I never brought it up to a
conscious level, until now after I told you about it and hear myself telling you*
(lines 36–37). Adriana is bringing to light an unconscious self.

This interesting discursive formation of the emergence of a new self resonates with Émile Benveniste's (1966) view that subjectivity depends on the ability of speakers to posit themselves as a subject in language. In his view, subjectivity emerges through dialogue and the performative and in-dexical properties of language: "consciousness of self is only possible if it is experienced by contrast. *I* use *I* only when I am speaking to someone who will be a *you* in my address. It is this condition of dialogue that is constitu-tive of *person*, for it implies that reciprocally *I* becomes *you* in the address of the one who in his turn designates himself as *I*" (224–25; emphasis in the orig-inal). Although focused only on pronominal usage, this dialogic perspective may be extended to narrative practices generally and to the manifold ways in which communicative acts create subject positions linking speakers (or authors), texts, and audiences (real or imagined). For psychoanalytic listening as a genre, the contrast that Benveniste is describing has the potential to emerge within a dialogue with one's self. The position between the pro-nominal *I* and *you* in Adriana's case remains inside her internal discourse. When in line 27 she says, "The truth is that *I* am just now realizing the meaning of what *I* told you," the *I* is coming from her unconscious self, as is the word *myself* in line 37. My presence serves the function of an external depositary—probably the same function that an analyst holds—but the dialogue is not between me and Adriana (you can see the long pauses); the dialogue is happening inside her own self(selves). The creation of an alter-ity in this example is not the equivalent of imagined voices of the school-girl talk that Japanese intellectuals are constructing, as in the case Inoue describes; it is a particular form of alterity that inhabits one's own self, and it comes to life only through words and through *listening* to those words.

As Adriana's example presents, not all dialogues are between physically embodied voices. Even when the "other" I address appears to be a physi-cal person standing in front of me, I may well be addressing and listening to a particular cultural voice. For example, if I am talking about my own research, and my interlocutor brings up concepts that I associate with a particular aspect of my research, I might find myself engaging with that particular concept rather than with my interlocutor as a concrete person. In this way, I am listening to a particular discourse, independently of who is uttering it. This is why listening in genres is of so much importance. The way we turn the ear into a particular genre reduces and creates particular cultural context.

* * *

When Theodor Reik (1948, 144) explained that psychoanalysis consists of "not so much a heart-to-heart talk as a drive-to-drive talk, an *inaudible* but highly expressive dialog" (emphasis added), he was pointing to the importance that listening holds in the psychoanalytic setting. Once defined as the talking cure, psychoanalysis emphasized the verbal utterances produced by the analysand. But focusing on the attention to listening practices prompts us to ask: How is the listener interpreting sounds symbolically? How do speakers who are undergoing therapy speak in ways that anticipate psychoanalytic forms of listening?

These questions help us to appreciate the enormous display of different contexts that emerge by positioning the ear inside a particular genre. By understanding how listeners listen, we are also able to witness the emergence of different ideological constructs that, just as utterances do, help to anchor a particular interaction inside a specific interpretive framework. In this chapter I have demonstrated how listening psychoanalytically has become a social practice in Buenos Aires by pointing to specific ideologies about how *porteños* are listening. By focusing on how social actors talk about themselves and psychoanalysis outside the clinical setting, we are able to see the performative aspect of this listening genre and how it points to the emergence of modern subjectivities by reproducing a radical form of alterity.

4 The Psychoanalytic Field in Buenos Aires

In Buenos Aires there is a lack of engineers and a surplus of psychoanalysts.

Popular saying

I always say that if you are in Argentina and you go to a gathering, let's say of educated middle class, but not necessarily, and you happen to question the very existence of the unconscious it would be like being at a synod surrounded by bishops and questioning Mary's virginity.

(Digo siempre que si uno está en la Argentina y va a una reunión, digamos de clase media ilustrada, pero no solamente, y se le ocurre cuestionar la existencia del inconsciente se debe sentir como estar en un sínodo de obispos y cuestionar la virginidad de María.)

Mariano Ben Plotkin

Psychoanalysis occupies an important position in Argentina, partially and symbolically structuring other fields and many discursive arenas. We can find psychoanalytic narratives and concepts outside the clinical setting: in newspapers, TV and radio shows, sports, theater, and advertisements, among many other forums. Psychoanalysis in Argentina, but especially in Buenos Aires, is not only an institutionalized form of a therapeutic practice but also a way of relating to the world. This means that psychoanalysis has become a framework that helps to explicate some experiences of everyday life, influencing ways of acting and thinking and nurturing social identities and lifestyles. There is a direct relationship between the clinical and pedagogical institution of psychoanalysis and everyday experience (see Plotkin 2001; Plotkin and Ruperthuz Honorato 2017; Visacovsky 2001).

A signature statement of psychoanalysis is that particular acts, verbal or not, will stand for something else (*When you say X, I hear Y*). There is a figurative meaning to actions, saying, and hearing. But it is not always verbal. For example, I was once sharing food with friends in Buenos Aries, and after cutting a tart, I accidentally handed someone a knife from the blade rather than from the handle. "Why are you doing this?" my friend responded. "Are you trying to tell me something?" I did not understand and gave no answer, but another friend replied to the interjection, "Stop projecting your own neurosis onto other people."

This kind of interaction, where something I said or did was interpreted as meaning something else, was a common experience throughout my fieldwork. At the beginning of my research, I concluded that in Buenos Aires, many individuals have a tendency to "overinterpret things." It was not until later that I started to realize it was a reflection of something else: the prevalence of psychoanalysis as an interpretive framework, clearly expressed through listening practices. In Buenos Aires, people have habituated their ears to listen to that which is not said. They look for meanings that are attached not to a particular referent but to a particular framework of interpretation: psychoanalysis.

Some of its followers and disseminators think of psychoanalysis as a clinical theory of universal properties, immune to the specificities of each national or regional adoption. According to Plotkin and Mariano Ruperthuz Honorato (2017), one of the peculiarities of writing a history of psychoanalysis is that in important sectors among diverse psychoanalytic movements, there is the belief that only those who have experienced psychoanalysis and, in some extreme cases, only analysts are able to understand the field. For these individuals, psychoanalysis cannot be thought of as a field: "Psychoanalysis would not be susceptible of being analyzed with the methodologies and analytical tools of the social sciences because its development would happen outside of the social practices. This view situates psychoanalysis almost in the place of an *a priori*, a unique and pre-determined object, that would emerge as 'situations' in the different cultural spaces where it became to a certain extent rooted" (13)."[1]

But, in pushing back against the idea that psychoanalysis is not a field, Plotkin and Ruperthuz Honorato have argued that precisely because it has evolved into different schools, each with claims of expertise, psychoanalysis is, in fact, a clear example of Pierre Bourdieu's definition of the field as hierarchical and shaped by fights for resources and legitimation. Being a field, as they show in their work, psychoanalysis developed unique features and specificities inside the different countries in which it grew.

The way psychoanalysis has manifested in the United States is a useful example of how it takes on the specificities of each community in which it lands. It has been argued that in the "optimistic" United States, psychoanalysts would rebel against Freudian ideas of irreversible determination of character, favoring instead a sort of individual reform through therapy (for examples of this trend, see Erikson 1993, 1994). In her classic book *Psychoanalytic Politics*, Sherry Turkle (1992, xxiii–xxiv) explains that "in America, where there is no strong intellectual tradition of the Left, optimistic versions of Freud focused on an adaptation to a reality where justice was rarely challenged." By contrast, in France, where there is a strong intellectual and political Left, psychoanalysis "became deeply involved in radical social criticism, and French social criticism became deeply involved in psychoanalytic thinking" (xxiv).

Argentina also developed its own interpretation of psychoanalysis. As in Paris, Buenos Aires embraced the abstract theories of Lacan, even becoming disseminators of his ideas to other countries.[2] Far from sharing an "optimistic" outlook with the United States, residents of Buenos Aires explain the pervasiveness of psychoanalysis in their city by pointing to what many, including scholars and analysts, describe as the "melancholic character of Argentines." For example, the constant repetition of writer Jorge Luis Borges—"Argentines are Europeans in exile"—suggests to many that immigration created a "motherless anxiety that prompts Argentines to seek some kind of reassurance, something that analysis provides," as one renowned senior analyst told me.

Studies about the diffusion of transnational commodities, lifestyles, and knowledge demonstrate the importance of the local conditions of reception (see Latour 1993, 2001; Plotkin 2001; Turkle 1992). In other words, the diffusion of ideas, concepts, and even goods does not remain unchanged but is provided with meaning according to prevailing local modes of cultural interpretation (Inda and Rosaldo 2002). Forms of knowledge defined as "expertise," such as psychoanalysis, do not escape the rule; although they have cognitive universal pretensions, they are primarily social practices rooted in cultural traditions and networks of signification, composed, performed, and appropriated in particular contexts.

This chapter looks into the specificities of this form of knowledge in Argentina: what does psychoanalysis mean in the Argentine context, what are the particularities of this practice, who are its disseminators, and how is this practice learned? The brief reconstruction of the historical context in which psychoanalysis has been conceptualized by scholars, mental health providers, analysts, and students in Buenos Aires will focus on the institutional training needed to become an analyst. This is an important element, since becoming an analyst is a long and sometimes difficult process that is frequently indexed as "learning how to listen," contributing to the creation of a genre of listening and ultimately its circulation in the country in a diversity of social contexts. This chapter also pays attention to the hegemony of psychoanalysis inside the Buenos Aires National University (UBA), which helps to explain how psychoanalysis has been institutionally favored to the detriment of other psychological specialties that historically have been relegated to secondary status.

A BRIEF HISTORY OF THE PSYCHOANALYTIC FIELD IN BUENOS AIRES

Using data from 2015 to 2017, depending on the country, the World Health Organization estimated that Argentina has 226 psychologists—including psychoanalysts—for every 100,000 inhabitants, the highest number per capita in the world. Costa Rica, which ranks second, has 142 psychologists per 100,000, followed by the Netherlands (123), Finland (109), and Australia (103)—rates that are around half or less than half that of Argentina (World Health Organization 2021). By contrast, the United States has only 30 psychologists for every 100,000 inhabitants.[3] A recent study on Argentina by Modesto Alonso, Paula Gago, and Doménica Klinar (2015) shows that the proportion grows in the capital city of Buenos Aires to an astonishing rate of 1,572 psychotherapists (or even by the most conservative estimate there are at least 750 psychotherapists) for every 100,000 inhabitants, more than three and perhaps up to seven times the national ratio.

What specialty do these psychotherapists actually practice? As stated by several historians and specialists, the numbers are tricky because psychoanalysis is often confused with other forms of mental health therapeutics (Dagfal 2009; Lakoff 2006; Plotkin 2001; Vezzetti 1983). When I interviewed the late Germán García, an internationally prominent figure within the school of Lacanian psychoanalysis and director and founder of the Descartes Center, a training institution for Lacanian psychoanalysis in Buenos Aires, he insisted that the majority of the people who call themselves psychoanalysts are, in fact, psychologists. "Every time I speak to French, Italian or Spanish people," he told me, "I got tired of explaining to them that there are not that many psychoanalysts in Argentina. [Argentina] is the only country where the psychologist is called psychoanalyst. In Spain, for example, there are sixty thousand, or eighty thousand psychologists, who knows? But they call themselves psychologists, and they say, 'I am a clinical psychologist,' 'I am a cognitive psychologist.'"[4]

Germán García and other scholars are pointing to the semantic intersection of different mental health disciplines. In Argentina, psychoanalysis has *somehow* overlapped with other disciplines that have in common the idea of a therapeutic as the means to heal some emotional distress and the idea of mental disorder. Accordingly, psychology and even psychiatry are part of the exchangeable semantic nuance when one refers to the practice of psychoanalysis, and vice versa. People use the word *psychologist* when they are going to analysis, the word *psychiatrist* when they are referring to a psychologist, or the colloquial *el loquero/la loquera* ("crazyologist," jokingly referring to experts in dealing with "crazy" people).[5] Psychoanalysis is thus inserted into a broader field of mental health that scholars of psychoanalysis in Argentina refer to as *el mundo psi* (the psy-world) (see Balán 1991; Dagfal 2009; Lakoff 2006; Plotkin 2001; Visacovsky 2002).

Yet sharing a semantic reference does not fully explain how or why psychology, psychoanalysis, and sometimes psychiatry are so often conflated in Argentina while, in most of the world, the fields remain separate.

This question has been the research focus of Alejandro Dagfal (2009), a psychologist and author of the erudite book *Entre París y Buenos Aires: La invención del psicólogo* (Between Paris and Buenos Aires: The invention of the psychologist). He explains what he calls the "cultural French exception," pointing to the connection and exchange between Paris and Buenos Aires to understand how, in Argentina, psychology followed an alternative path to the cognitive paradigm linked to the Anglo-Saxon scientific tradition. Through the French influence, Buenos Aires subtracted much of the biological component of psychology and inserted instead a subjective dimension that draws the field closer to the humanities. Another contributing factor is that there were few psychology professors when psychology entered the curriculum at public universities (1955 in Rosario and 1957 in Buenos Aires). Thus, many philosophers, self-taught amateurs, and psychiatrists with some psychoanalytic training taught psychology, bringing their conceptual framework to the emerging field. Dagfal (2009, 31) writes, "In our country there was a big anti-positivist reaction during the 1930's, after which the experimental or naturalist modern currents, from any direction, didn't have a strong resonance inside the universities." Psychoanalysis became a dominant force in this period and did not leave its hegemonic position, "unlike Brazil and even France, where psychoanalysis became threatened by more scientific approaches after the sixties, and had to fight to maintain its central place" (31). As a consequence, the "Argentine exceptionality"—the counterpart of the French exception—was born. As Dagfal notes, "Buenos Aires not only mirrors Paris, but creates its own image, its own hybrid idea of the reflected image" (47).

The close relationship between France and Argentina, extending beyond psychoanalysis, is complex and well documented (see Carpintero and Vainer 2004; Dagfal 2009; Plotkin 2001; Vezzetti 1983, 1996). This historical association allowed many psychologists in Buenos Aires to closely follow philosophical and political debates originating in France.[6] The "subjugation," as some authors have called it (see García 2005), of Buenos Aires to French culture has been one of the most recognized points of departure for understanding the idea of an Argentine exceptionality.[7] In the case of psychoanalysis, it made its way into learning institutions through the psychology curriculum. Also, because Argentina has one of Latin America's oldest and most extensive public welfare systems, the synergy between the university (also public) and the health system allowed psychoanalysts to extend their practice beyond the private clinic, reaching vast sectors of the population through free services at public hospitals (Balán 1991). Since the 1970s, the same political and economic crises that undermined those public systems strengthened the role of psychoanalysis as an interpretive and therapeutic tool (see Damousi and Plotkin 2009; García 2005).

Psychoanalysis also benefited from a growing client base at the right time. In the 1960s the social sector comprising the natural potential clientele for psychoanalysis—a relatively affluent and highly educated middle class—expanded quickly.[8] As a result, changes in traditional concepts about family and women's role in the home and in society opened another area for the reception of psychoanalysis (Plotkin 2001). Previously, the International Psychoanalytic Association (IPA) had accepted only medical doctors to practice and study psychoanalysis.[9] But as Jorge Balán (1991) points out in his book *Cuéntame tu vida* (a title that roughly translates as "Tell me about your life" and was inspired by the Spanish title of Alfred Hitchcock's 1945 film *Spellbound*, which revolves around psychiatry, love, and dreams and features sets designed by Salvador Dalí), in Argentina the wives of some of the main historical figures that brought psychoanalysis into the country began practicing as psychoanalysts without licenses. Hence, the estrangement of psychoanalysis from medical institutions made it an attractive career for women whose entrance into medicine was frustrated by the medical establishment.[10]

The IPA prohibition was lifted in 1967 when the association passed Resolution 2282, which stated that psychologists could be medical auxiliaries of doctors and, as such, could perform some peripheral clinical observations (always under the general supervision of a medical doctor). However, in 1985, and coinciding with the university's creation of a subject field of psychology separate from the school of humanities, where psychology was previously housed, that resolution was repealed, authorizing psychologists to perform psychotherapy (Carpintero and Vainer 2004). During the period when only medical doctors were admitted to the IPA and the Argentine Psychoanalytic Association (APA), the relationship between psychologists and psychoanalysts was problematic because psychoanalysts "embodied a kind of paternalistic elitism, where they would show in their private clinics to psychologists the secrets of a practice that supposedly they should not practice, and the benefits of a practice they could never have access to" (Dagfal 2008, 28–29). In this era, psychoanalysis created a sort of cultlike culture among intellectual elites. According to Alejandro Vainer, the estrangement of psychoanalysis from the medical realm turned the APA into a "big family," blurring the boundaries between a professional practice and a "way of living." This created a discourse that psychoanalysis, like a religion, should be a project that transforms the individual as well as society (Vainer 2014).

Throughout the modernization process and social restructuring that Argentina experienced after the 1960s, psychoanalysis became "simultaneously used as a therapeutic method, a means to channel and legitimize social anxieties, and an item of consumption that provided status to a sector of the population obsessed with the concept of modernity" (Plotkin 2001, 72).[11] Above all, it became an interpretive system. According to Plotkin, "if neurosis was *the* modern disease, then psychoanalysis was *the* modern therapy to deal with it, and it was touted as such by numerous magazines and other publications" (73). At the same time, the reaction of the middle classes against President Juan Perón, whom they perceived as authoritarian and antiliberal, employed psychoanalytic concepts: they judged his regime "schizophrenic" and "neurotic," beginning a long tradition of describing political and economic circumstances through a psychoanalytic frame.[12] To this day, the appropriation of psychoanalysis as an interpretive instrument by the intellectual Left—and to a lesser extent, the intellectual Right—is an important factor in the dissemination and legitimization of psychoanalysis in Argentina.[13]

To understand the relationship between Freudianism and the Left in Argentina, it is imperative first to recognize the difference in cultural consumption between what historian Hugo Vezzetti calls the "plebeian" culture and the elite cultural circles. In Vezzetti's (1996, 129) view, Freud entered Argentina's Left through an *izquierdismo plebeyo de masas* (a plebeian, mass-oriented leftism), thanks, in part, to the Left's political agenda of introducing the "great" authors to the masses. Affordable editions of Freud's texts began to circulate among the "plebeian" masses in the 1930s. Freud was well received by his new readership, Vezzetti speculates, because of the open character of his work and, as other critics have argued, the essayistic nature of his writings (131). The most acclaimed cultural journals of the early twentieth century, such as *Nosotros*, a literary magazine published from 1907 to 1943, and *Revista de Filosofía*, which catered to the cultural elites, were not immediately drawn to Freud's ideas and sometimes openly criticized them.[14] It was not until the late 1960s, especially with the introduction of Lacan's ideas, that the more "enlightened" Left began to embrace psychoanalysis.[15] The introduction of Lacan's theories—focusing deeply on listening and resonance—would contribute to the dissemination of psychoanalytic listening as a genre.

But the Left often kept its distance from psychoanalysis. On important occasions the Left considered the IPA and the APA as protecting the interests of the ruling class.[16] Also, as historian of psychology Luciano García (2016, 33) discusses, the theories of Ivan Petrovich Pavlov were "the only competitor that psychoanalysis had in Buenos Aires in the forties and fifties." In the 1950s and 1960s, the Pavlovian school, or reflexology, played an important role at the University of Buenos Aires. Psychiatrists that wanted a theoretical connection with the official Marxism of the Communist Party formed this school. Psychoanalysis had been rejected for being a "product of the bourgeoisie," and thus Pavlov and his followers offered the possibility of integrating ideology and psychiatry.[17] Psychoanalysis and reflexology fought to have a prominent space inside the public university. As Juan Carlos Volnovich, a psychiatrist in training during those years, recalled, "In that era there were roundtables with Marie Langer, with José Itzigsohn, and others. There were times where the fight between the reflexologists and the psychoanalysts was not resolved. It was like a Boca-River [the derby between the two most popular Argentine soccer teams] of mental health" (cited in Carpintero and Vainer 2004, 173).[18]

The decline of the Pavlovian approach was crucial to the consolidation of psychoanalysis. Through its links to the Communist Party, the Pavlovian school was strong in the public university from 1957, when the subject field in psychology was created, to 1966, the year of the anti-Communist and anti-Peronist military coup d'état. After 1966, psychoanalysis gained the upper hand in the psychology department. Historians credit three important issues that made room for psychoanalysis at the expense of Pavlovism (see Carpintero and Vainer 2004). First, reflexology's theories were clinically weak. Second, several reflexologists already had one foot in psychoanalytic theory and used psychoanalysis as a personal therapy. And finally, *la noche de los bastones largos* ("the night of the long batons") in 1966—a violent dislodging of students and teachers who had occupied the university to protest the political intervention by the military government, which wanted to revoke the academic freedoms established in 1918—made many reflexologists lose their institutional positions at UBA. Many renounced their jobs as an act of solidarity, and some never got these positions back.

In 1959, Enrique Butelman, the second director of the emerging department of psychology, invited José Bleger, one of the few psychoanalyst members of the Communist Party and one of the most influential figures in establishing psychoanalysis in Buenos Aires, to teach the introduction to psychology course. Bleger had just published a book titled *Psicoanálisis y dialéctica materialista* (Psychoanalysis and materialist dialectics), which led members of Argentina's Communist Party to ostracize him. According to Gervasio Paz, a member of the Pavlovian school, Bleger "was criticized starting from the title; first for putting psychoanalysis before Marxism and second for putting dialectics before materialism. In other words, Hegel before Marx" (cited in Carpintero and Vainer 2004, 174). Nonetheless, Bleger's classes "captivated from the beginning a student body as eager for a new psychology as for a meaningful social and political commitment. Thus, the first psychologists to graduate from the UBA had a unique training, which, among other authors, included Freud and Marx, [Alfred] Adler and [Carl] Jung, [Melanie] Klein and [Kurt] Lewin, [Georges] Politzer and [Daniel] Lagache" (Dagfal 2007).[19] From this point forward and continuing to the present day, psychoanalysis has been an extremely important subject at UBA.

The entry of Lacanian psychoanalysis into Argentina in the 1960s had a significant impact on the dissemination of psychoanalysis outside of the clinical setting. Unlike the psychoanalysts affiliated with the IPA-connected institutions, which required a medical degree to perform psychotherapy, most Lacanians did not come from the medical profession, and many were not psychologists either. Rather, their training and previous activities were linked to philosophy and literature. This circumstance, added to Lacan's focus on linguistics and structuralism, favored the emergence of a new kind of figure: the "intellectual psychoanalyst," less attached to the strictly therapeutic dimension of psychoanalysis and more to the intellectual currents of the time (Plotkin and Visacovsky 2008). Thus, psychologists with no medical degree found a welcoming space where they could develop their interests in psychoanalysis, which the APA, through the prohibition of the IPA, had previously denied them. According to Sergio Rodríguez (1998), a psychoanalyst who elaborated a list of the "good" and "bad" things that Lacanian psychoanalysis produced in Argentina, Lacanism "saved Freud and psychoanalysis from disappearing from our country." At a time of mounting discomfort toward the APA for being too centered in "Kleinian theories" and of struggles between different sectors within the APA—resulting in the renunciation by Plataforma and Documento of their affiliation with the association for being too conservative—Lacan came to offer a more "creative" and broader alternative. Lacan's formulation that "an analyst only authorizes himself"—with all the problems this created—allowed for a proliferation of students of psychology who focused on a more humanistic ideal and, above all, were able to become analysts without a medical degree. Thus, the "return to Freud" that Lacan proposed entered Argentina through a noninstitutionalized psychoanalysis.

Lacan was introduced to the Argentine intellectual milieu by Oscar Masotta, a charismatic, self-taught philosopher, aesthetician, and later psychoanalytic theorist. Although Masotta never ceased to define himself as a Marxist, his link with the leftist parties was tense, to the extent that his intellectual activity did not match the models of the "committed intellectual" (reflected in Jean-Paul Sartre's ideals) or "organic intellectual" (à la Antonio Gramsci) that prevailed at the time (Longoni 2017, 18). He was the first translator of the works of Lacan into Spanish, and in 1974 he founded the Escuela Freudiana de Buenos Aires (Freudian School of Buenos Aires), modeled on Lacan's École Freudienne de Paris (Shullenberger 2016, 417). In 1964 Masotta gave his first public talk on Lacan at Torcuato Di Tella University, with the title "Jacques Lacan o el inconsciente en los fundamentos de la filosofía" (Jacques Lacan or the unconscious in the fundamentals of philosophy). This historic talk is posited as the first incursion of Lacan into the country. By 1969 Masotta taught The Ideas of Jacques Lacan course at Di Tella, which would become his institutional home.

In Argentina, as in France, between 1962 and 1967 structuralist discourses began to replace Sartrean humanism, and Lacanian work played an important role. In Argentina, left-wing psychoanalysts considered Kleinian psychoanalysis conservative and ideologically reactionary. Through Louis Althusser, they found in Lacan the "return of Freud" that allowed them to question Kleinian ideas. If Masotta was Lacan's introducer, not only in Argentina but in the Spanish-speaking world, Lacan's ideas spread thanks to Althusserian structuralism. By the early 1970s, Masotta had become the point of reference for Lacan's ideas in Argentina, and interest in Lacan's work began to expand from the same kinds of projects that Masotta had been developing: philosophy study groups, conferences in nonpsychoanalytic or APA spaces, and several publications (Carpintero and Vainer 2005). Masotta left Argentina on December 7, 1974, and after a brief stay in England he settled in Spain, where he continued training people on Lacanian psychoanalysis. His abrupt departure has been explained as a combination of two factors: the repressive atmosphere of prosecutions and assassinations that would culminate in the 1976 military coup and his personal aspirations of learning German and doing his own readings of Freud (Carpintero and Vainer 2004; Izaguirre 2009; Vezzetti 1998).

The strong presence of Lacanian psychoanalysis in Buenos Aires prompted many detractors and critics. The main critique regarded Lacanians' supposed obstinacy in a difficult, baroque rhetoric and its "surrealist nuances" (S. Rodríguez 1998, 1), which enabled an elitist, cultlike following. The political critique can be exemplified by León Rozitchner, Masotta's friend and collaborator in the leftist journal *Contorno*, who expressed that Lacanism was "a group that excluded precisely analysis—in my view Lacan excluded it—from everything that had to do with the social problem" (cited in Carpintero and Vainer 2005, 124). A strong critique thus came from the Left for the so-called individualism of Lacanian psychoanalysis and his distance from social medicine. Also, Lacanians' emphasis on reading texts more than working in the clinic created friction among the more traditional analysts.

Another important aspect of the dissemination of psychoanalysis outside the clinic is the circulation in popular magazines, journals, and periodicals of psychoanalytic columns of varied degree of difficulty and specialization. In a country of virtually full literacy and a strong readership culture, women's magazines of the late 1950s and early 1960s developed weekly and monthly editorials directing women toward new ways of getting to know themselves through such techniques as psychotests and quizzes wherein women psychoanalysts became "experts" in women's issues (Plotkin 2001; Vezzetti 1983). The emergence of these printed materials coincided with developing discourses about the family as a vehicle for individual self-fulfillment rather than as a mere cell for the reproduction of the species.

One important editorial source for the circulation of psychoanalysis was the publishing house Paidós, founded in 1958. Initially devoted to child psychology, it was the creation of Enrique Butelman, the second director of the UBA department of psychology, and Gino Germani, a renowned sociologist of Italian origin who was at the forefront of reviving Argentine sociology and was one of the promoters of the psychology department at UBA. Thanks in part to the avid readership of the local public, and to the decline during Francisco Franco's rule of publishing activity in Spain, which had previously been a main source of print media in Argentina, Paidós prospered very quickly. Butelman and Germani created numerous collections whose common denominator was the desire to expand the intellectual and scientific arena with novel authors and create more subjects of research. A decade later, "these former students of philosophy and literature would not only manage one of the most important publishing houses in the field of the human sciences, modulating the tastes of the public with the choice of books they translated or published, but would also be in charge of the country's first two academic departments devoted to psychology and sociology" (Dagfal 2007).

Thus, the circulation in lay magazines of topics and discussions infused with psychoanalytic theories and the proliferation of books on psychology, psychiatry, psychoanalysis, philosophy, and sociology helped to circulate humanistic and social theories about the self outside the clinical setting. More recently, the proliferation of radio and TV programs that broadcast live sessions between analysands and analysts or that show psychoanalysts analyzing television celebrities and sports icons, as well as advertisements that use the figure of the analyst in its most iconic representation, contributes to the circulation of psychoanalytic language in Argentina. All of these factors were decisive in the evolution of psychoanalysis and its eventual manifestation as a genre of listening in the country today.

THE PEDAGOGY OF PSYCHOANALYTIC LISTENING

To recognize the circulation and expansion of psychoanalysis in Buenos Aires it is important to understand the steps necessary to become an analyst—particularly the crucial role that listening plays in this process.

In Argentina, psychoanalysis is part of a broader psy-world, and its boundaries are not always well defined. As a result, it often surpasses its own discursive ground. For example, the orthodox practice of psychoanalysis in Argentina—the highly ritualized private contract between a psychoanalyst and an analysand—takes many forms. Psychoanalysis is offered at public hospitals and at small public clinics where there is no couch but a desk that separates analyst and analysand. These exchanges last between twenty-five and thirty-five minutes instead of the fifty-minute average of Freudian psychoanalysis, and there is no payment, which in the practice of traditional psychoanalysis is a precondition to analysis.[20] Psychoanalysis also takes place in groups in the form of multifamily sessions inside a large auditorium with several psychoanalysts and as many as eighty analysands in the room. There are also TV shows where people are "analyzed" before the cameras, as well as comic books illustrating the vicissitudes of analysis, among many other representations.

By being part of the psy-world, psychoanalysis gets to share different positions within society, and sometimes these positions are not entirely within the doxa. For example, one psychoanalyst I spoke to who does not consider himself an "orthodox psychoanalyst" (he rarely uses the couch, does group analysis, and works at the hospital on twenty-four-hour shifts) admitted that he finds the "overuse" of the *psy* stem problematic.[21] "The prefix *psy* or *psycho* can be followed by anything," he said. "You can find 'psychotarot' and aberrances like that everywhere. . . . In this career we don't sign blueprints, you know; architects have to sign something."

This critical point of view expresses two different propositions. The first is the creation of cultural hybrids that continue to be part of the psy field, no matter how unorthodox they may be. The second involves the legitimization of a social arena that has surpassed its own limits. Until 2005, when a master's degree in psychoanalysis was created at UBA, there was no psychoanalytic degree recognized by the university system.[22] Instead, psychoanalytical institutions recognize the training they provide but do not certify the students.

The question of how (or by whom) a psychoanalyst becomes legitimized remains an open one. Currently, in order to practice in Argentina, an aspiring psychoanalyst must have a *licenciatura* (a five-year degree that is between a bachelor's degree and a master's) in either psychology or psychiatry. But the question of how to confer legitimacy is still part of a large, ongoing debate in Argentina and in other countries, including France and the United States, where psychoanalysis is still strong (see Lézé 2006). Nevertheless, the *licenciatura* in Argentina provides a powerful foundation in psychoanalytic theory and the listening practices associated with psychoanalysis and represents an important element in the broader presence and circulation of psychoanalytic listening in the country. Generally speaking, the lack of specific degree-granting institutions has not diminished the prestige or prevalence of psychoanalysis in the study of psychology, either at the university or in the most prominent training institutions for people hoping to practice clinical psychology professionally. On the contrary, psychoanalysis remains central to these institutions. Hence, these educational and postgraduate training contexts have also been important for the growth of the listening practices associated with it. What I refer to as the genre of psychoanalytic listening in Argentina is partly rooted in these clinical contexts. The rest of this chapter provides an overview of these educational and training experiences and highlights the importance of psychoanalytic listening in the analyst's development and, consequently, its eventual circulation outside the clinic.

Public University: University of Buenos Aires

People aspiring to work in the field of psychology and mental health will typically have their first formal exposure to the theories and practice of psychoanalysis during psychology training at the University of Buenos Aires (UBA), the largest and most prestigious university in the country, with more than three hundred thousand registered students. The curriculum for this path of study is overwhelmingly geared toward psychoanalysis, psychopathology (Lacan), and clinical psychoanalysis. As a result, from the very beginning, people interested in working in psychology will be strongly influenced toward key elements of psychoanalysis and its specific listening models.

Within the syllabus of psychology at UBA, the number of classes devoted to Freud, the so-called French and English schools of psychoanalysis, psychopathology (Lacan), and clinical psychoanalysis significantly outnumber other specialties, including behavioral, cognitive, and developmental psychology (Facultad de Psicología, n.d.). Indeed, there are eight elective psychoanalytic options compared to only one course in systemic theory, one in group therapy, one in legal psychology, and so on. And because the curriculum is also the dominant framework used in the entrance exams for key professional pathways after university study—exams that will affect where future psychologists can work, whether they can compete in the world of private health insurance, and what kind of private practice they will be able to develop—the overwhelming curricular focus on psychoanalysis is also built into larger economic and professional incentives, further solidifying its central influence for the psychological field.

The popularity of psychology as a degree in Argentina is considerable. In 2004, for example (the most recent year for which data are available), there were 24,052 psychology students registered at UBA (Universidad de Buenos Aires 2004, 82). If students registered in psychology at other universities and postgraduate institutions are added in, the total number of registered psychology students in the country is 62,243, of whom 37.6 percent are at UBA. The overwhelming majority of students are focused on developing careers where they work directly with patients in a clinical setting. During my research, I interviewed over a hundred psychology students at UBA and found that 84 percent wanted to pursue a clinical psychology career compared to the remaining 16 percent, who wanted a different career path, mostly in cognitive brain research or some kind of biological psychology. These numbers help illustrate what I witnessed during my own experiences attending psychology classes at UBA: the courses in psychopathology, psychoanalysis, and clinical psychology are so popular that there is not enough space for all the students who want to attend. Classrooms that can usually seat sixty students hosted one hundred or more. Students sit on the floor or stand during class. In comparison, there are approximately fifteen to eighteen students (sometimes even fewer) in behavioral psychology and neuroscience classes. The massive attendance starts to decrease after the third year, and not everyone registered finishes the degree. According to recent statistics (Alonso, Gago, and Kilnar 2015), 1,542 students come out every year with a psychology degree at UBA, most of whom become clinical psychologists.

Training the Psychoanalytic Ear: The Public Hospital

The heavy emphasis on psychoanalytic theory and psychoanalysis during the five years of study for the *licenciatura* is also a major emphasis of the entrance exams for the postgraduate program in clinical psychology in Argentina's public hospitals, which is considered the most prestigious path toward a career in psychology. This too has an important impact on the larger structuring of the field.

For aspiring psychoanalysts in Argentina who have obtained a *licenciatura*, there are several possible paths, with different levels of complexity. The three most common paths are to apply for a paid *residencia* (residency) or an unpaid *concurrencia* at a public hospital, which lasts four or five years, respectively; to enroll at one of the many psychoanalytic associations that offer training for clinical supervision for approximately two to three years; or to start a private clinical practice. No matter which path they take, aspiring psychoanalysts must themselves undergo analysis throughout their lives, an experience that plays an important role in the way they learn to listen to themselves, and to their analysands, psychoanalytically.

The most prestigious path is to obtain a paid residency at a public hospital. As part of the application process, applicants must take a competitive one-hundred-question, multiple-choice exam administered by the government health department in each city. Aspiring residents in Buenos Aires take a standardized test meant to assess their knowledge about general psychology. [23] Designed by a group of psychologists with different areas of expertise, the test changes each year and reflects the psychology curriculum at the University of Buenos Aires. Students with the highest exam scores and top undergraduate grade-point averages are offered the residencies. The whole process is meant to be a fair competition that will result in a meritocratic and democratic practice, and anyone with a degree in psychology can compete.

Although the residencies at public hospitals officially prepare graduates to work in clinical psychology rather than psychoanalysis, the entrance exam is heavily focused on the latter. In each of the last eleven years, for example, out of the one hundred questions on the Buenos Aires exam—which is developed specifically to test for a comprehensive knowledge of psychology—forty-seven to fifty-five were directly related to psychoanalysis. The questions are either about classical psychoanalysts (Freud, Lacan, Klein, and Donald Winnicott) or more recent psychoanalysts (Eric Laurent, Silvia Bleichmar, Henri Ey, and others). For example, in 2015 the first twelve questions were explicitly related to Freud's texts and the next seven about Lacan's theories, followed by questions about Laurent, Diana Rabinovich, Klein, Winnicott, and other psychoanalysts. In total, forty-seven questions were related to psychoanalysis that year. Meanwhile, other fields of psychology, such as cognitive, systemic, behavioral, and structural, were underrepresented on the exam. Psychoanalysis is by far the most important theoretical framework needed to get a position at a public hospital.

Because of the prestige and the funding, the competition for a paid residency at a public hospital is fierce. Each year eight hundred to one thousand new graduates apply for approximately twenty-eight to thirty open positions. There are many benefits of getting a residency—including the training, exposure to patients of different backgrounds, the slow acquisition of expertise, and the professional prestige and symbolic capital—and together they put residents in a strong position to compete for tenured positions at public hospitals and to be part of the *pre-paga* system (private medical insurance), which will increase the likelihood of financial security. Despite the entrance exam's heavy focus on psychoanalytic theory, neither the residencies nor the tenured positions are psychoanalytic jobs. Instead, they are open to clinical psychologists, and depending on the student's preference (and luck), the position can be at a children's hospital, a women's hospital, a mental health emergency service, a psychiatric institute, or a private clinic.

But because of the extensive studies necessary for the exam, which is devised to reflect the psychology curriculum at the University of Buenos Aires, and because the vast majority of advisers in public hospitals are psychoanalysts, central elements of psychoanalysis and psychoanalytic theory—and the broader focus on psychoanalytic listening—remain at the center of this professional path. Indeed, many of the psychoanalysts working at public hospitals that I spoke with use both *psychologist* and *psychoanalyst* to refer to their profession. However, they use mostly psychoanalytic terminology to talk about their patients—for example, the word *Other*, which they emphasize is spelled with a capital *O*, referring to the Lacanian idea of radical alterity; or the term *unconscious*, to define the purpose of analysis; or *desire*, as in the *desire of the analyst*, the libidinal force that makes possible the analytic experience.[24] This should not come as a surprise, since the curriculum that informs the field of psychology is so heavily influenced by psychoanalysis, socializing professionals to speak inside a particular psychoanalytic ethos.

The other way of obtaining a position in the public hospital system is through *concurrencias*, a less prestigious path than a paid residency but one that nevertheless immerses people in the professional vocation of psychology and inculcates in them key tenets of psychoanalysis, including psychoanalytic listening. A *concurrencia* is a five-year commitment to work four hours, three or four times a week, at a public hospital and perform similar duties to those of residents. Both *concurrentes* and residents are exposed to patients after approximately three weeks of working at the hospital, both receive clinical supervision from senior psychologists/analysts (at least 85 percent of the supervisors are psychoanalysts), and both are expected to spend 60 percent of their time in clinical training and 40 percent in patient care. Residents, however, work eight hours a day, five days a week, for four years, whereas *concurrentes* work part time for five years and do not handle emergencies. The rotation between external, internal, and primary consultation also varies. But the main difference between a resident and a concurrent is that *concurrente* positions are *ad honorem,* or unpaid.[25]

From a merely economic perspective, *concurrencias* represent free labor. Yet since there are so few paid residencies, many aspiring residents are forced to get a *concurrencia.* Each class of *concurrentes* provides 6,400 hours of free labor a week or 1,664,000 hours over the course of five years. But because training in a public hospital is considered the most prestigious, and because of the strong influence of psychoanalysis in this training—which remains central to the broader field in Argentina—*concurrentes* accumulate important professional capital during these years. By working at a public hospital, with its strong emphasis on psychoanalysis, they are inserted into the institutional framework of mental health, where they can compete for a tenured position (one must be a resident or a *concurrente* to apply for a permanent position in a public hospital). After the completion of the residency/*concurrencia* at a public hospital, the analysts in training has only six months to apply for an open position. This is a strict limit. And since there are so few openings, many *concurrentes* stay past their five-year commitment to keep their status and wait for an opening. This strategic move helps both the public institution—which receives free labor for an extended period of time—and the *concurrente,* who will have a better opportunity to get a tenured job at this institution when and if there is an opening. Another form of capital that *concurrentes* develop is that they become more appealing to private health insurance agencies, which value hospital training over any other kind.

While *concurrentes* gain symbolic capital during these years in a hospital, another important reason they pursue this path—through five long years of unpaid labor—is that "there is a strong ideological component of supporting public institutions in Argentina," as Diana Rabinovich, a prominent psychoanalyst who was a personal friend of Lacan, told me. And there is another factor—one that points to the importance of the knowledge sharing among the field's leading psychoanalysts. The *concurrentes* may be in a position of financial difficulty, but the opportunity to work with prominent supervisors in the field is highly valued. For example, as Alberto, a second-year *concurrente,* explained when I asked about working without a salary for five years: "The term *ad honorem* is a beautiful one. It is an honor to bring this service to the hospital, and what we charge, we charge with our formation. I mean, the people whom we work with and who supervise us, and what those people give us back to our professional formation—it gives us what an ATM [automated teller machine] could never give to us."[26]

Most supervisors at the public hospitals, even while working *ad honorem*, are well known and respected analysts and have successful private practices. They have accumulated enough symbolic capital to make a comfortable living. So why spend many hours supervising new residents and *concurrentes*? The answer can be summarized in the response of a well-known psychoanalyst who supervises new residents and *concurrentes* at the public children's mental health hospital, who told me, "It is absolutely imperative that we [renowned psychoanalysts] support public health systems to avoid the mercantilism structure of private health corporations. If we don't do it, who will?"

Working as a supervisor, with no economic remuneration, at a public hospital represents an act of support for a fair system that will provide quality services even to those who are unable to afford them. It also signals the analyst as a good person, and, more selfishly, it helps analysts to develop their own schools of thought. Unpaid positions not only invest subjects with experience and knowledge and the opportunity to be part of an institutional organization; they also mark individuals as occupying specific social positions that are immersed in a sea of ideological constructions, ethics, and power relations.

Residencies, *concurrencias*, and unpaid supervisions exemplify the strategic nature of the psychoanalytic field in Buenos Aires. Inside the mental health institution, being exposed to patients from different socioeconomic and cultural backgrounds is highly valued, and economic remuneration—although highly desirable—is not the key motivation for this social field (at least in the early stages). The exposure to different circumstances (i.e., internal patients, external patients, emergencies), the process of getting inside the public hospital structure by way of the entrance exam, and the opportunity to study and work alongside prominent psychoanalysts create specific symbolic capital that—considering the state's lack of institutional mechanisms for recognition—provides an alternative legitimization in the training of psychoanalysis. After being trained, or working at a hospital for four or five years, the capital accumulated during those years is there to stay, playing an important role in helping aspiring psychoanalysts secure careers in the field.

By developing key exams based on psychoanalytic theory, and with 85 percent of the supervisors in public mental health hospitals being psychoanalysts, Argentina's mental health field has developed an inherent strategy that has transformed psychoanalysis into the dominant professional capital, surpassing in prominence other psychology specialties. It shows that defining the boundaries of the field of psychology, and determining who is inside that field, is a matter of constant struggle (Bourdieu 1992). But it also shows that, in Argentina, psychoanalysis is clearly dominant in that struggle.

An additional aspect of the training received at public hospitals that directly informs the development of a practice strongly based in psychoanalytic theory is the exposure to patients and cosupervision, which also highlights the importance of psychoanalytic listening practices. Once defined as the "talking cure," psychoanalysis has always emphasized language. By being able to articulate into words the unconscious (repressed) drives that guide our behavior, one can liberate oneself of such disturbances as neurosis, anxiety, and hysteric episodes. But as Lacan suggests, another way of understanding psychoanalysis is by listening in a particular way. Psychologists in Argentina described to me how one can "become" an analyst by switching the ear and listening in a particular way. There is a performative act by switching the ear into psychoanalytic listening that provides the listener with social attributes; in this particular case, it transforms the subject into a psychoanalyst.

This idea—that listening is one of the key components to becoming an analyst—is commonly held among psychoanalysts in Argentina. The mastery of particular listening practices defines whether or not you have become an analyst.

For example, Celia, a fourth-year resident working at the children's mental health hospital Tobar García, recounted the following story:

Last year [2011] we were in the hospital emergency room when a woman of about fifty was admitted with some scratches and small wounds in her face. She seemed scared. You could tell she was from a low-income background and she didn't look right. But despite the fact that she was bleeding—she had a cut next to her right ear—she asked to talk to the psychologist. My supervisor, Dr. F., and I went to see her. She sat down and started talking almost without looking up, about the problems she had with her husband, and her fear that *la nena* [referring to her youngest daughter] was going out with the wrong crew. I was very moved when suddenly, Dr. F. interrupted her and told her, "Why don't you make an effort and *tell us what you really want to say.*" Immediately after that, the woman began to cry and said, "I have cancer, I am really scared, and I don't know how to tell my family." It was shocking! Evidently Dr. F. *was able to listen to something that I, despite all the work I have been doing in the hospital, couldn't hear.* That's the kind of training that we receive in the hospital. And I don't think that there is a better place to be exposed and understand what analysis is about.

Celia's comments about being exposed to psychoanalytic listening, and her admission that she did not master it, were common in interviews with residents and *concurrentes*. They frequently described their experience working inside the public hospital as if it were a world with its own modes of communication, and one day they would learn this language, as well as how to listen. As one third-year male *concurrente* described it: "It's all about paying attention to the signs. They can be verbal or not. You have to learn to read between the lines; *you have to listen*. Yeah, *it pretty much comes down to listening, something that can take a life to achieve*." He also noted, as he described his own problems trying to understand the "human psyche," that things are "not really what they look like on the surface."

As many residents and *concurrentes* at public hospitals regularly affirmed, listening is a pivotal element that analysts have to learn to become effective psychoanalysts. Aspiring analysts are exposed to psychoanalytic theories throughout their undergraduate education, but they regularly articulated the importance of training their ear. To be able to provide psychoanalysis inside the public clinic, many people pointed out, they need to *listen* as a psychoanalyst. For example, Alicia, a young psychologist/analyst who had been working in the drug and alcohol division of the mental health hospital Florentino Ameghino for the past five years and who had recently started to see individual clients at her private practice, described how her work required her to develop an ability to listen psychoanalytically. When I asked if she considered her work with clients at the hospital to be psychoanalysis, she pointed to listening in a particular way as being the determining factor:

> It depends how you define psychoanalysis. For me, I don't need to have a couch, a quiet space, and a picture of Freud on one of the walls to do psychoanalysis. When I am talking with my patients, *I'm listening as an analyst*, and that's how I think psychoanalysis is done inside public hospitals. It is far from being an "orthodox kind of psychoanalysis" [*she makes quotation marks with her fingers*], which would be closer to what I do at home, but what really defines psychoanalysis for me is the *psychoanalytic listening* (*la escucha psicoanalítica*).

Like Alicia and Celia, descriptions of a specific practice of listening were common among those training to become analysts in the public hospital in Buenos Aires. Nevertheless, it is interesting to note that it was not until recently (from 2004 on) that analysts—other than Lacanians—began to write about listening practices in psychoanalysis (see Akhtar 2013; Connor 2004b; Wilberg 2004). Freud never fully developed the listening component of his remarkable theory. It was Theodor Reik and Otto Isakower, two of his closest disciples, who would later develop a theory of listening in the psychoanalytic field. In Argentina today, however, the idea of learning how to listen *differently* is fundamental in the analyst's training, and while not always explicitly stated, it is always there.

Learning and Listening at the EOL and the APA

Large numbers of Argentine psychoanalysts develop the listening practices associated with psychoanalysis at one of the many postgraduate psychoanalytical training institutions that operate in the country. Enrolling at such an institution is the second-most common path to becoming an analyst in Argentina (though a small percentage of recent graduates do both—start a residency/concurrency and enroll at a psychoanalytical institution). Hundreds of institutions offer psychoanalytical training, some more popular than others, some more difficult to enter than others, and some affiliated with international and more prestigious institutions. Two of the most important and internationally recognized psychoanalytic institutions in Argentina are the Escuela de la Orientación Lacaniana (EOL) (School of the Lacanian Orientation) and the Asociación Psicoanalítica Argentina (APA) (Argentine Psychoanalytical Association). The EOL is part of the Instituto del Campo Freudiano in Paris (ICFP) (Institute of the Freudian Field in Paris), and the APA is part of the International Psychoanalytic Association (IPA). Both institutions have played an important role in the historical trajectory of psychoanalysis in the country, and each is in high demand among aspiring analysts. Both have high standards for admission (though they are sometimes flexible) and are recognized as being among the best institutions in Buenos Aires. In contrast with public hospitals, where 90 percent of the focus is on the patients, these institutions focus more on the theoretical aspect of analysis. While there are clinical modules where particular cases are analyzed, the majority of courses are geared toward developing an understanding of Freud, Lacan, and other renowned analysts' theories.[27] Although the pedagogical and training methods for aspiring analysts are different from those in the public hospitals, these institutions also contribute to the genre of psychoanalytic listening in Argentina.

School of the Lacanian Orientation

The EOL provides the equivalent of a master's degree in psychoanalysis through the ICdeBA (Clinical Institute of Buenos Aires), a postgraduate private institution founded in 1992, where Jacques-Alain Miller (who is married to Lacan's daughter and owns Lacan's copyright) is a member and constant visitor. Its mission is to "teach and disseminate the philosophy of Lacanian psychoanalytic orientation throughout different levels: teaching, research and clinical practice" (Escuela de la Orientación Lacaniana. n.d.). While Freud and many other authors are part of the curriculum of the institute, the core of the program is to understand and apply Lacan's teachings through his writings, as well as through texts of renowned analysts who have engaged with Lacan's theories. Consequently, all of Lacan's and Miller's books and essays are assigned. No matter what subject is being reviewed (e.g., transference, trauma, anxiety), it is always centered inside Lacan's framework.

The school follows a semester model. During my research, I attended two introductory classes for almost an entire semester that are mandatory for students: psychosis and neurosis. Most classes are restricted to registered students, and the director of the ICdeBA in 2012 made sure that I understood she was making a big exception by letting me attend (she later told me that she was curious to know what an anthropologist would say about the ICdeBA). The classes last two hours and are taught every other week. They are held inside a big room and enroll between 100 and 120 students. The classes on neurosis are always packed, whereas classes on psychosis have many empty chairs.

While students pursuing a *licenciatura* at the University of Buenos Aires and other universities include people from different socioeconomic backgrounds, those who go on to study at the ICdeBA are mostly middle and upper-middle class. Women make up the majority of the student body but by a smaller percentage than at UBA. Since the classes are graduate seminars, everyone already holds a psychology title, and many already have a private practice. An economic investment is necessary to have a private practice, so from a financial standpoint, the program is more elitist than that at UBA.

The most noticeable aspect of the classes, and of the institution as a whole, is the personality cult around Lacan. As a Freudian psychoanalyst told me when referring to Lacanians: "They are immersed inside a hierarchical structure, and they will always be, because no one knows what

Lacan said, not even Lacan! So the interlocutor, translator, or the person who 'thinks he knows' would always be in a position of power."[28]

The format of the two classes I was able to observe followed a lecture style. An expert in a particular topic would present a Lacanian concept or text, followed by a period of questions. The lectures were mostly theoretical and very dense, with many mathematical symbols that made it almost resemble a physics class. Every concept presented was transformed into a mathematical algorithm. For example, the presenter would explain that if a patient uttered a word that the analyst thought was a signifier, the analyst should annotate S_1. If the patient continued to utter that specific signifier in relation to another signifier, the algorithm would read something like this:

$$S_1 \rightarrow S_2 + 1$$

Where S_1 symbolizes the emergence of the first and *master* signifier, the arrow represents the connection to the second signifier, and S_2 characterizes the second signifier (also known as the field of knowledge) attached to +1, indicating that it was uttered twice. This basic formula will take many forms, and many other symbols will be added, depending on the concept.[29] Consequently, knowledge about the symbols was required to understand the lectures, which resulted in classes where almost no one participated. Instead, students were taking notes incessantly and quietly.

This formulation, $S_1 \rightarrow S_2 + 1$, is relevant to psychoanalytic listening because the chain of signifiers that roam the analysand's psyche is what creates the *resonance* that certain sounds (signifiers) produce and to which the analysand is unable to assign a concrete referent. During the classes I attended, there was direct allusion to this phenomenon. Listening psychoanalytically entails the suspension of attention to tune in with the resonance in the analysand's psyche.

Although there was no one particular class dedicated to developing a theory about listening in the psychoanalytic encounter, listening was an important element in class discussions, and it was mentioned in almost every class I attended—especially when the presenter discussed the analyst's role as an *escuchante* (listener) whose function is to make sure the analysis takes place by listening to the patient through a psychoanalytic framework. In other words, analysis will not begin until the analyst *listens* psychoanalytically. This idea is best exemplified through a conceptualization that is of special importance for Lacanian psychoanalysis: the "preliminary interview," a notion that, according to most Lacanian psychoanalysts, is key for the development of a successful therapeutic encounter (Lacan 1997). Lacan's expression "preliminary interview" is in some ways similar to Freud's ([1913] 1958) "preliminary treatment." The expression indicates that there is a threshold to be crossed to enter into the analysis—but not simply the threshold the analysand crossed when entering the analyst's office. It is a preliminary working period, prior to analysis proper, which begins only after a rupture of some kind occurs within the exchange—"a cut," as Jacques-Alain Miller describes it, "that qualifies a change and determines a before, a preliminary, and an after. This cut corresponds to the crossing of the threshold into a new social bond, which in our case would be the analytical discourse" (Lacan 1997, 41).

The success of this preliminary interview is directly related to the cultivation of the analyst's listening skills, and it is a point that has lasting import for understanding the centrality of listening to psychoanalysis and the expression of this form of listening as a genre. Indeed, as Ernesto Sinatra (2004, 17)—a friend of Miller, a full-time professor at the EOL, and one of the most influential interlocutors on Lacan's ideas in Buenos Aires— describes it in his book *Las entrevistas preliminares y la entrada en análisis* (Preliminary interviews and entry into analysis):

> The beginning of analysis is not an automatic procedure that will be secured just through a number of encounters between patients and analysts. It requires a particular device in order to develop the conditions for the possibility of analysis. The preliminary interviews fulfill this need, and it is essential to evaluate that that person, in that moment and no other, will begin a psychoanalytic treatment with that specific analyst. One session— and sometimes more—is needed to make an evaluation. And it is in this session that the analyst must *listen carefully* to see if the possibility of analysis opens.

Sinatra discussed this idea in more detail during a class I attended at the ICdeBA and told the following clinical vignette: A man called, saying he had a question that needed an answer, and asked if he could have one, and only one, clinical session. Sinatra explained that this was an unusual request, but he agreed to the meeting because it piqued his curiosity. The man's question was simple: his girlfriend did not want to have intimate relations with him, and he wished to know why. Throughout the session, the patient kept talking about the woman and how he felt humiliated by her lack of response toward him. Right when he uttered the word *humiliation*,

Sinatra recounted, the patient started talking about his father, describing him as an absent figure who had treated him badly throughout his life. At some point, when the patient was about to mention his girlfriend's name, he uttered the first syllable of his father's name instead. At that moment, the patient realized that his girlfriend was precisely the type of woman his father would like, possessing all the characteristics that his father would approve of. After this "discovery," the patient became quiet. Sinatra then stopped the session, and the patient asked to continue the treatment.

This preliminary interview, according to Sinatra, represented a success. In this particular case, he could detect a possibility for analysis because, as he explained to the class, he was listening through a psychoanalytic framework:

As analysts, you have to pay attention to the words, but not too much attention. The purloined letter (*la carta robada*) is always there, in your face, but you have to let intuition run first. If you look too much for it, you won't find it. I was annotating things while the patient was talking, and at one point I had written: *novia y padre* (girlfriend and father), as the two signifiers that began to organize the discourse in that moment. At some point, as I looked back to my notes, I read: *no vía padre: no había padre* (no father way: there was no father). *I did not listen to this homophony consciously*, but I was able to capture the essence of what the analysand was trying to express, by *listening not to the content of the words, but to the signifying chain*.[30]

The next session, Sinatra asked the students if they had questions, since he did not have time for inquiries during the previous class. The students seemed intrigued about the interpretation (or listening) of the binomial *novia-padre*. One student offered a different reading: "After looking at my notes, I realized that the interpretation presented was not accurate. It seems to me that the subject's discourse is not referring to *no había padre*, but to *no vi al padre* (I did not see the father) instead. The fact that he chose a woman who humiliates him, who replicates what the father does, and the fact that this is a woman that the father would like, or approve of. For me it represents that he wasn't able to *see* his father in this woman."

Sinatra warned about the temptation to overinterpret. "Following that reasoning," he explained, "we can even say that the binomial can be interpreted as *vía del padre* (via/through the father). Overinterpreting is risky— risky in that there is an aggregated plus on our behalf, that is coming from us, not from the patient." He then referred to a classic oxymoron that Lacan

(1997) adopted "learned ignorance" (*docta ignorantia*), a sort of "wise ignorance" that allows the subject to suspend all referential meaning and "let the analyst to be taken by the occasion." This, according to Sinatra, is what the analyst in training should do: suspend all judgment and will to interpret and let "ignorance" guide the session.

The pedagogical question crucial to Lacan's own teaching is: Where does a text (or a signifier in the patient's speech) make no sense? In other words, where does it resist interpretation? Where does what the analyst sees and reads resist understanding? Basically, where is the resistance to knowledge (what Lacan calls ignorance) located (Lacan 1998)? The problem that the student of psychoanalysis inside the Lacanian framework will face is "how to ignore what he knows" (Gorney 1978, 20). In Lacan's (1968, 242) own words: "There is no true teaching [psychoanalysis] other than the teaching which succeeds in provoking in those who *listen* an insistence—this desire to know which can only emerge when they themselves have taken the measure of ignorance as such—of ignorance inasmuch as it is, as such, fertile—in the one who teaches as well" (emphasis added).

When I asked Sinatra how an aspiring analyst is trained to become immersed in an analytical framework, he answered that the position of alterity is indispensable: "Knowledge is what is already there, but always in the Other. Knowledge is not a substance but a structural dynamic. It is not contained by an individual but comes about out of the mutual apprenticeship between two partially unconscious speeches that both say more than they know." Dialogue is thus the condition through which ignorance becomes structurally informative in analysis. It is the ignorance of referential meanings—through the Other in each partaker—that will allow some kind of communication that will surface as such only after the fact.

TABLE 4.1 Binomial Novia–Padre (Girlfriend–Father)

Novia–Padre	Girlfriend–Father
No *había* padre	There was no father
No *vi* al padre	I did not see the father
Vía del padre	Via/through the father

The students of psychoanalysis at the EOL are thus pushed to "learn by unlearning" in an environment that fosters the ignorance necessary to establish a dialogue between the analyst and the analysand's unconscious. When Lacan argued that the unconscious is structured like a language, what is at stake for the unconscious is precisely grammar, which has to do with repetition, a pattern. Here is where Lacan's ideas about resonance appear. The students need to find those signifiers that will give shape to a discourse that appears as a resonance of particular words uttered by the analysand. If the analyst is able to *listen* to these words unconsciously, analysis is possible. Hence, the preliminary interview, as the key moment for deciding whether there will be analysis, is a listening exercise where knowledge will become evident if the analyst is listening inside this particular genre. Analysts must develop trust in self and must "let go" of reference first.

The formulations I witnessed at the EOL circulate outside the clinical setting. I am not claiming that these interpretations are the same as those produced by a trained psychoanalyst or have equivalent value. But the idea that words have meaning beyond their pure denotation is present in Buenos Aires's culture, in the addressivity form *What you really mean is....* These classes allowed me to understand where this form of communication comes from.

Argentine Psychoanalytic Association

The APA is the oldest psychoanalytic institution in Buenos Aires and is more traditional than the EOL. While it differs in important ways from the EOL, the APA, through its extensive teaching programs in psychoanalysis and psychoanalytic theory, shares its emphasis on the role of listening in the psychoanalytic encounter.

The APA takes pride in being part of the IPA, which was founded by Freud in 1910. When reading about its history, APA members believe that the introduction (or "discovery," as it is framed) of Freud in Argentina is the result of a society "marked by immigration and a lost past trying to make sense of their loss and their new environment" (Melgar and Rascovsky de Salvarezza 2004, 23). The APA was founded by a group of young professionals, both immigrants and Argentines of European descent, who in 1942 decided to create a unified institution that would encompass medical, psychiatric, and psychoanalytic theories (Carpintero and Vainer 2004; Vezzetti 1996). Ángel Garma, a renowned Spanish psychoanalyst who was analyzed by Theodor Reik and later immigrated to Argentina, was one of the founders and the first president of the APA. In the 1950s, thanks to the active role of some APA members who worked at the University of Buenos Aires in different capacities (as professors, lecturers, and administrators), psychoanalysis was introduced to the public university.

The APA, through the Instituto de Psicoanálisis Ángel Garma, provides a four-year program to become an analyst that includes a range of classes relevant to psychoanalysis. Among the most important requisites to become an analyst are attending weekly analytical sessions with a current member of the APA throughout the duration of the program; engaging with Freud's work by taking at least twelve courses dedicated entirely to Freud's theories; selecting seminars that are pertinent for the student's chosen specialization; and completing at least two supervised clinical sessions. One example of a specialization that students can choose is sports and psychoanalysis, dedicated to understanding the transferential relationship between the athlete, the manager, and the public; the development of narcissistic personalities among participants; the representation of violence inside a game, and so on. Other specializations focus on new media technologies and the psyche, sociological approaches to the self, and eating disorders, to name just a few. There are also many introductory classes that are mandatory for all students, on topics such as the Oedipus complex, introduction to the clinic, and repression and the unconscious. Additionally, students of psychoanalysis at the APA are encouraged to attend meetings at the Multi-Family Structured Psychoanalytical Therapeutic Communities (MFSPT; see chapter 2), as they provide opportunities for students to witness clinical cases and learn about multisessions in psychoanalysis.

The APA is one of the most important psychoanalytic institutions in Buenos Aires; it has smaller branches in different provinces (e.g., Córdoba, Mendoza) that are interconnected, with a significant number of registered students among them. The APA provides what it calls "Freudian psychoanalysis," and unlike the EOL, where in some cases sessions can last only five minutes, it provides the traditional fifty-minute sessions and is less interested in finding the structure of signifiers than in paying attention to the historical account of the analysand. But there is an element in which both institutions coincide: the importance of listening in the clinical setting. As one of the clinical directors at Institute Garma told me:

> The institute's focus is on clinical practice. We provide the students with all the necessary tools to understand the works of Freud. But obviously, that's not enough. You can know in theory how to launch an aircraft, but it is not

until you try and experiment with the theory that you learned that you know what to do. Here, our emphasis is on the clinic, which means that students early on are exposed to patients. It is the transferential relationship in the clinic, where the student will learn *to listen to the unconscious of the patient.* There is no other way to learn how to be an analyst but to *sit down and listen to your patients.*

The APA has had many detractors (including the psychiatrists linked to the Communist Party and practitioners of positivist medicine), and yet it continues to be an important institution in Buenos Aires. Through *Revista de Psicoanálisis* (Psychoanalysis magazine), the first psychoanalytic publication in Spanish, founded in 1943 (and now with nearly eighty uninterrupted years of dissemination), the APA has become a constant presence and one of the disseminators of the most current ideas and developments in psychoanalysis in different academic and scientific circles in the Spanish-speaking world.

The APA's emphasis on the clinical formation of the aspiring analyst makes it an attractive option for psychologists who are more interested in clinical practice than in theoretical inquiries. That the APA's founder was analyzed by Theodor Reik could help explain why listening is such a strong component of psychoanalysis in Buenos Aires, rather than the focus on language that is common in Anglo-Saxon countries.[31]

* * *

The specificities of psychoanalysis in Argentina—that it entered public universities in the 1950s after being mainly introduced by European immigrants and rapidly developed into a local autonomous field; that aspiring analysts show a commitment to working for years inside public hospitals without any economic incentive; and, more importantly for our purposes, that there is an explicit metalistening in which talk about listening practices is present, demonstrating that listening is one of the most important aspects of analysis (i.e., when the analyst listens inside a psychoanalytic framework, analysis is realized)—mark the country, and especially the city of Buenos Aires, as a unique place where psychoanalysis became a social practice.

In Buenos Aires, this listening practice has traveled outside the clinic and has become a way to listen in everyday conversations. The history of the psychoanalytic field is not linear and has introduced many social actors and institutions that belong outside of the psychoanalytic doxa, even though they are also a quintessential part of it. It is by the performative aspect of listening (psychoanalytically) that new subjectivities and professions emerge—listening creates an analyst.

There are many potential explanations for why psychoanalysis has become so prevalent in Buenos Aires—some historical, some more based in folklore. I am less interested in *why* than in *how* it circulates and has become a social way of interacting in Buenos Aires. Listening becomes a key piece of the puzzle: it is one of the main traits that maintain the circulation of psychoanalysis outside of the clinic.

5   The Mass Mediation of Psychoanalytic Listening

There is no innocent drawing. All drawings always express something, even in spite of the cartoonist; and then in those drawings that apparently didn't make sense, sense appears, anger appeared—I don't know, all kind of things."

(No hay dibujo inocente. Todos los dibujos siempre expresan algo, incluso a pesar del dibujante; y entonces en esos dibujos que aparentemente no tienen sentido, aparece el sentido, aparece la ira—no sé, todo tipo de cosas.)

Graphic humorist Tute, "Tute en APA, con 'Humor al diván'" (July 12, 2018)

Today I am going to be a subject, not a person.

(Hoy voy a ser sujeto, no persona.)

Gabriel Rolón, celebrity psychoanalyst on the TV show _Animales sueltos_ (2012)

Anyone spending an extended period of time in Argentina would be hard pressed to miss that psychoanalytic discourses circulate in several media outlets. A number of television and radio shows engage directly with psychoanalytic theory or indirectly by using psychoanalytic ideas and frameworks to explain a diverse set of phenomena. Many shows feature analysts who discuss an assortment of topics, ranging from Twitter exchanges between politicians to personal questions about the anchor's private life to the behavior of celebrities. At times, they are called on to discuss big questions:

What is love? What is solitude? And the one that recurs most frequently: What is wrong with Argentines?

Television shows feature an array of formats. There are one-on-one interviews (*Animales sueltos, El ángel de la medianoche, Tiene la palabra,* to name just a few), where the anchor simply asks questions and the analyst responds. These interviews explicitly invoke psychoanalytic theory. Analysts demonstrate their expertise by speaking about Lacan's theory of desire or Freud's conceptualization of the superego, and they usually bring up examples from their private practice to illustrate their points. The tone of these interviews resonates with self-help materials that give advice on how to cope with personal emotional problems. They also tend to make broad generalizations about different demographics—as, for example, when claiming that women's habit of wearing makeup and stockings makes them fetishists, while men do not share this quality.[1] Other shows (*Cortá por Lozano, Pura química, Políticos al diván*) invite guest analysts, or hosts who are themselves analysts, to "psychoanalyze" celebrities. On live television, a celebrity sits or lies down on a couch while a psychoanalyst asks questions and interprets their answers using psychoanalytic theory. Alternately, these shows might present short excerpts of celebrities speaking on tape, followed by analysts making assessments and interpretations ("what they really mean is . . ."). These shows usually include more than one anchor/presenter, and the tenor tends to be less serious than in the one-on-one interviews.

Television is not the only medium where psychoanalytic discourses are mediated for relatively broad public consumption. Radio shows such as *Radio Lacan, Programa radial psi,* and *Freudiana radio: La voz psicoanalítica del mundo* (The psychoanalytic voice of the world), also feature one-on-one interviews, following more or less the format used on TV. They might revolve around a discussion of the difference between neurosis and psychosis or relate Lacan's mirror theory to compulsive behavior in adolescents. There are also programs that incorporate the participation of listeners who call the studio and ask the analysts to provide guidance and counseling. Being a quintessential listening experience, radio shows emphasize the importance of listening and direct their audience to pay attention to particular words or concepts. They also ask what those words "invoke" in listeners, once more displacing denotation in favor of a hermeneutical interpretation.

In Argentina, the figure of the analyst is so pervasive that it even functions as a promotional character to sell products. Commercials draw upon the stereotypical figure of the analyst—a well-dressed, bearded man in his fifties in a nice office. This figure is used to sell diverse products, from beer to potato chips, auto repairs, and aperitifs, to name just a few.

Psychoanalysis is also present in graphic humor, which has a long-standing presence in Argentine culture and the public sphere. In the three most widely circulated newspapers in Argentina, *Clarín*, *La Nación*, and *Página 12*, established cartoonists persistently depict humorous situations using the analytic encounter: an analysand on the couch and an analyst sitting with a notebook and a pen in hand. Some of these cartoons are allegorical representations of the analytic encounter. For example, a caricature by cartoonist Tute features an analysand—a man lying on a couch—with his speech represented in a huge bubble with a long text towering above him. The analyst, a woman, stands on her chair and seeks to read the "other side" of the text—that is, the "other meaning" of the analysand's uttered words (*When you say X, I hear Y*) (figure 5.1). In other cartoons, analysts and analysands address topics through discussion. For instance, cartoonist Fernando Sendra depicts a man telling an analyst, "Doctor, women scare me." The analyst responds, "Well . . . let's look at your childhood," and the man replies, "What if my mother finds out?" (figure 5.2).

Beyond graphic humor, most newspapers include one or more columns written by psychoanalysts and psychologists, either focused on psychoanalytic theory or using psychoanalytic frameworks to discuss political issues. For example, in August 15, 2019, the *Página 12* weekly psychology section included a note titled "Occupation Army: A psychoanalytic view on the saturation of uniformed agents in public space." Here Cristian Rodríguez (2019), a psychoanalyst living in Buenos Aires, describes the parallels between the recent proliferation of blue and yellow vests used by the city and transit police and the militarization of Buenos Aires during the dictatorship of the 1970s. Using concepts such as *transubjectivity* and *functional psychical repression*, Rodríguez embarks on a metaphorical psychoanalytic analysis of the vests, revealing how they trigger repressed memories of urban militarization. In 2019, another newspaper, the widely circulating *Clarín*, published in its psychology section the article "Apply the Marie Kondo method to order your life and your bonds. Psychologist Alejandro Schujman (2019) "and Laura Escobar, a disciple of the Japanese woman, give the keys to take it to the inner world." The word *bonds* (*vínculos*) make explicit reference to a psychoanalytic term that describes the way in which a person relates to others by establishing a relational structure. Thus, Kondo's book—globally popular for urging readers to declutter their houses in order

FIGURE 5.1 Cartoon by Tute (*Humor al diván*. 2017, 152).

FIGURE 5.2 Cartoon by Fernando Sendra (n.d.).

to achieve order in their lives—gets embedded in a conversation about psychoanalytic theory.

There are numerous other prominent examples of the presence of psychoanalytic discourse in media production in Argentina, across the political spectrum. *La Nación*, a conservative newspaper, has an online channel with a weekly show called *Terapia de Noticias* (News therapy), hosted by Diego Sehinkman, who is both a psychologist and a journalist. The show begins with a vignette on a particular political discussion in Argentina (e.g., a senator debating a government policy), followed by Sehinkman's monologue in which he gives "different readings" or "possible scenarios" regarding the meaning of the presented topic. The word *therapy* (terapia) in *Terapia de Noticias* conveys the idea that there are many possible interpretations of the things politicians say. The recurrent phrase *"¿Qué habrá querido decir?"* (What would he/she have meant?) resonates throughout the show. Since 2012 Sehinkman has hosted another show, *Políticos al diván* (Politicians on the couch), also on *La Nación*, where he interviews politicians in his role as analyst, replicating the analytic encounter. In his own words, the interviews seek to emulate "a first therapy session" and take "the best X-ray that can be taken of these characters" without judging or placing oneself "in a moral place." The metaphor of the X-rays once again conjures the notion that there is something hidden, ready to be discovered (*When you say x, I hear y*).

That a show like this is produced by one of Argentina's major newspapers is striking. Even more remarkable is the fact that many politicians are willing to participate. Sehinkman (2014) has conducted so many interviews with prominent politicians that he published a book based on these interviews, the subtitle of which translates as "the unconscious ones that govern us."

Psychoanalytic discourse also has a strong presence with other major elements of Argentine cultural production—such as tango, the quintessential Argentine music genre. An assemblage of psychologists and tango dancers called Tango-Psi have framed tango as having a direct connection to psychoanalysis. Mónica Peri, a psychologist and tango dancer who is affiliated with Tango-Psi, has written two books—*Tango: Un abrazo sanador* (Tango, a healing embrace) (2015) and *PsicoTango: Danza como terapia* (Psycho-Tango: Dance as therapy) (2010)—in which she describes finding a Freudian parallel between the embrace of tango dancing and "the first embrace we received from our mothers" (2010, 35). Peri (2009, 5) suggests that since tango has been "demonstrated to be an object of psychoanalysis, we can compare it to play, inasmuch as in playing, the dance of the tango allows us to put ourselves in contact with our unconscious. *Bodies that speak and are heard. Incarnate bodies, in which life is manifested*" (emphasis added).

Psychoanalytic discourse is also widely present in the theater. The famous opera *María de Buenos Aires*, written in 1968 with music by Ástor Piazzolla—one of the most celebrated Argentine tango composers—presents the story of María, a prostitute "born one day when God was drunk" who dies and is resurrected as a ghost. Her specter wanders the streets, finding a rare circus run by Los Analistas (the Analysts), in whose arena remorse, complexes, and nightmares are portrayed by reckless acrobats. When one of the acrobats, Analista Primero (First Analyst), tries but fails to interpret María's memory of a shadow, she believes she has fallen prey to a strange madness.

The proliferation of cultural representations of psychoanalysis outside of the clinic in Argentina extends to rock music lyrics, astrology, numerous social media groups, and TV series, among many others. Although, as historian Mariano Ben Plotkin and anthropologist Nicolás Viotti (2020) have argued, psychoanalysis may be declining as a clinical practice in Buenos Aires, these examples suggest that the dialectic between the clinical practice and its commoditized forms persists. All the TV and radio shows, newspaper columns, and comics I have described continue to be produced today, with no sign of flagging interest.

This chapter analyzes in detail examples of three cultural representations: graphic humor, psychoanalysts on television, and advertisements. These examples can help us understand how these discourses have permeated popular culture and how they circulate; the metacommunicative messages embedded in psychoanalytic discourses; and how listening psychoanalytically, as a genre, is present within these representations, helping to disseminate the listening ideology that there is a hidden meaning within the utterances available for interpretation (*When you say X, I hear Y*). In these analyses we can see the dialogic movement between the constitution and circulation of psychoanalytic listening and the cultural production of discourses based on psychoanalysis.

But to approach these examples we need to understand first how psychoanalysis became a *framework of interpretation* to be used for different purposes. In what follows I outline a brief history of how psychoanalytic ideas permeated other fields.

PSYCHOANALYSIS AS AN INTERPRETIVE FRAMEWORK

People in Buenos Aires often say, "In Argentina, psychoanalysis has expanded beyond the clinic; you can find it everywhere!" This statement is likely based on the amount and variety of the field's cultural representations. Yet psychoanalysis has left the clinic and acquired different forms almost since its inception. This has occurred most notably in academic settings, as scholars of the humanities and the social sciences began to analyze data and texts and create theories using the so-called psychoanalytic framework.

Thus, when analysts and lay people discuss the expansion of psychoanalysis beyond the clinic, it is important to answer some key questions: What part of psychoanalysis has migrated outside the clinic? Does this mean that information about psychoanalysis and psychoanalytic theories are available to everyone? Does it imply that psychoanalysis is accessible and provided almost everywhere? And what, then, does psychoanalysis mean in the context of this broad circulation?

In its early days, psychoanalysis borrowed terminology from medicine—not only in an effort to give psychoanalysis prestige but also because most of the early analysts were doctors (Balán 1991; Frosh 2010). The consulting room became the key site of psychoanalysis because it was where treatment took place. The professionalization of psychoanalysis followed the structure of medical settings (e.g., sessions were expected to have a certain duration, emotional involvement with the patient was restricted, and specific places were assigned to the patient/analysand and the analyst in the consulting room). Since psychoanalysts were already doctors who provided medical care, the figure of the psychoanalyst consolidated as that of a therapist (Dagfal 2009; Roudinesco 1990).

In a very concrete sense, the therapeutic clinic became the source of psychoanalysis, and its theories and practices were developed to be applied inside the clinic (Dagfal 2009; Frosh 2010; Roudinesco 1990, 2003). However, over time the "clinic" in psychoanalysis came to extend beyond its original physical space and became a metaphor.

From this perspective, psychoanalysis is not just a medical science but a practice. It involves the presence of an analyst and an analysand in which the analysand's aim is to uncover the hidden (repressed) source of a particular ailment and to learn to live a life where suffering may not necessarily disappear but is kept at bay. The analyst helps in this process by being both a *listener* and a witness to the presence of meaning in what, for the analysand, is unspeakable or meaningless (Edelson 1975). This process happens within a very specific framework that involves transference (the unconscious way in which patients relate to or "use" the analyst to advance their treatment), countertransference (the analyst's response to the transference of the patient), and, most importantly, the certainty that at some point unconscious impulses will emerge.

Under this definition, psychoanalysis is a *live encounter* that necessitates face-to-face interaction. As a senior analyst in the first-year introductory psychopathology class at the University of Buenos Aires (UBA) described it: "Without analyst and patient, both being together in their transferential relationship, interpretation in the psychoanalytic sense cannot take place." In order to have an analytical session, very specific steps and processes need to be present; otherwise, no psychoanalysis takes place, and the proceedings are no more than an intimate conversation with a friend or acquaintance.

Stephen Frosh (2010, 4), one of the most important historians of psychoanalysis, has discussed the same idea in detail: "When a literary author's work is interpreted in terms of childhood trauma, it is not psychoanalysis; or when a political commentator draws on ideas about unconscious national impulses, it is not psychoanalysis; or when a social psychologist philosopher uses the idea of intimacy and stability of selfhood to understand identity conflicts, it is not psychoanalysis." Frosh agrees with the UBA professor and many other psychoanalysts: that what defines psychoanalysis is the therapeutic encounter, which implies the co-presence of both analysand and analyst.[2] Thus, whatever social theorists are doing when they use psychoanalytic explanations, it is not psychoanalysis. Instead, they are using a particular framework to explain a collection of different social phenomena.

Frosh ascribes blame for this misuse of psychoanalytic ideas to Freud and early students such as Carl Jung. After all, Freud himself published studies of creative artists in which he used psychoanalysis to bring to light aspects of their psychology (see Freud [1910] 1964). In *Civilization and Its Discontents*, Freud ([1930] 1962) expanded his focus to encompass society as a whole in an effort to make sense of the bleak aftermath of the First World War. Consequently, psychoanalytic interpretation in its beginnings served as a framework to interpret social behavior partly because "its rich account of unconscious processes inserts an appreciation of the 'irrational' into theories that otherwise find the unexpected, self-destructive or fanatical eruptions of social disorder hard to fathom" (Frosh 2010, 67).

But this is not the sole reason for using psychoanalysis to perform social analysis. Psychoanalytic theory is able to eschew fixed meanings and instead posit interpretations of particular people in particular contexts. This flexibility opened the door to an array of different uses for the psychoanalytic framework, especially for the so-called postmodern theorists: feminist studies (Butler 1990; Mitchell 1974; Spivak 1987), critical theorists (Adorno [1938] 1978; Althusser and Balibar 1971; Marcuse 1955), art (Ogden 1999), literature (Kristeva 1984, 1987), and postcolonial studies (Bhabha 1991a, 1991b; Chakrabarty, Majumdar, and Sartori 2007), among many others. All of these studies use particular aspects of psychoanalytic theory, from different schools of psychoanalysis, to achieve varying aims.[3]

The use of psychoanalysis as an interpretive tool in academic circles for the study of an array of social phenomena has a long history. Through this relationship, some analysts have become public intellectuals, generating sufficient cultural capital representing "cultural authority" (Zelizer 1992) to endow them with the right to talk about almost any cultural phenomenon.

This has happened in several countries. In France, for example, Lacan began in 1951 to hold private weekly seminars in Paris in which he urged students to study what he called "a return to Freud" that would concentrate on the linguistic nature of psychological symptomatology (Marta 1987). Due to its popularity, this seminar became public two years later and lasted for twenty-seven years, ending only when Lacan's life was in its final stage. These seminars became highly influential, not only inside psychoanalytic circles but also in Parisian cultural life. Lacan was famous for his difficult prose and entangled propositions, but nonetheless, he appeared on televised shows to talk about many aspects of everyday life experience, sometimes being recognized more as a public intellectual than a practicing psychoanalyst (Roudinesco 2003).

When he emerged as a public figure in France, Lacan followed a trend that was already in place in other countries. In the United States in the 1940s and 1950s, for instance, this phenomenon took the form of books and magazines intended for lay audiences. In his book *The Fifty-Minute Hour: A Collection of True Psychoanalytic Tales*, Robert Lindner (1954, ix) quotes historian Max Lerner as saying that "one of the by-products of the post-Freudian age has been the emergence of a new genre of American writing—the work of the writing psychiatrist or psychoanalyst, who applies his insights to the problems of the day or tells of some of his adventures with his patients." It was this genre that prompted the circulation of psychoanalysis outside the clinic in the United States and elsewhere.

Such interpretations and circulation of psychoanalytic discourses are possible thanks to the plasticity of psychoanalytic theory. It was lifted from its interactional and institutional origins and transformed, among other practices, through the process of entextualization, or "the process of rendering discourse extractable, of making a stretch of linguistic production into a unit—a *text*—that can be lifted out of its interactional setting" (Bauman and Briggs 1990, 73), and also through the process of contextualization, the accommodation of those texts to new institutional surroundings (Silverstein and Urban 1996).

So, what does it mean that psychoanalysis in Argentina has moved beyond the clinical setting, having infiltrated contexts that do not necessarily comply with the clinical setting? What circulates outside of the clinic is an entextualized and mediatized (Agha 2011) form of psychoanalysis that takes different shapes, depending on the context in which it has been placed (e.g., the university, radio and television shows, or advertisements). Consequently, when we hear such declarations as that of Yamil—a neuropsychologist who states that psychoanalysis is everywhere in Argentina due to its "hegemonic presence" in the national universities—what has become ubiquitous is not necessarily the clinical practice of psychoanalysis (although the number of people who attend analysis is very high compared to other countries) but particular texts that are decentered from its interactional and institutional origin and recentered into different contexts (Bauman and Briggs 1990) through their mediatized forms, which link institutional practices to processes of communication and commoditization (Agha 2011).

Within the process of circulation and mediatization of psychoanalytic discourses, and more broadly over the course of these discourses' reproduction and dissemination, listening is key in that there is a common denominator that relates all the different modalities in which psychoanalysis is discussed outside of the clinical setting; it is the quality described elsewhere as *When you say* x, *I hear* y—that is, there are things we do that we are unconscious of but that have meaning beyond our understanding. Once the cumulative resonance of experiences, sounds, and words finally finds a referent, then we are able to perceive the "real" meaning of a particular experience.[4]

When one looks at Argentina, for example, it is clear that these processes develop in practice, meaning that it is through the actions and exchanges between social actors that the mediatization of psychoanalysis surfaces. Discourses of psychoanalysis in the country rely on sociohistorical models (i.e., the idea of unconscious practices, the Oedipus complex) through which cultural forms are produced and reproduced, and these are further circulated in an array of mediatized forms. The rest of this chapter illustrates this phenomenon by looking closely at three cultural representations of psychoanalysis in different media outlets while also underscoring the crucial role that listening plays in this dissemination.

PSYCHOANALYSIS AS A CULTURAL PRACTICE

When discourses of psychoanalysis are inserted into new contexts, the boundaries between expert knowledge, lay reception, and the later replication of this knowledge mix. The communication and listening models associated with psychoanalysis play a prominent role in this process.

The direct and indirect exposure to psychoanalytic discourses creates a lay audience with a tendency to freely provide psychoanalytic interpretations. This exposure may result from an individual having gone to analytic sessions for many years or through information shared by family members or close friends who are analysts. More recently, however, the significant presence of psychoanalysis in Argentina's media has also directly contributed to the creation of this audience, leading to a prolific circulation of psychoanalysis in Buenos Aires and to its interpretative framework becoming part of the cultural and social life of the city. In brief, psychoanalysis as an explanatory model has become socially significant in Buenos Aires. Exactly *how* the circulation of psychoanalysis became so socially significant is attributable to the *communicability* of its textual form (Briggs and Hallin 2007).

It's important to note that what is circulating is not "psychoanalysis" itself but a particular discourse based on the practice of psychoanalysis.

The concept of "communicability" helps us to understand certain discourses as effective, and therefore contagious, because they communicate successfully while others do not. Charles Briggs (2007, 556) explains, "Communicability suggests volubility, the ability to be readily communicated and understood, and microbes' capacity to spread," adding that "communicability is infectious—the way texts and the ideologies find audiences and locate them socially/politically" (see also Briggs 2005, 2011). Texts and discourses project a wholesome final product, failing to show all the ideologies that emerge when discourses circulate. Focusing on the concept of communicability helps disentangle the ideological dimensions that create "legitimate" producers of certain discourses (e.g., medical, legal), on the one hand, and supposedly passive receivers of information (texts), on the other. In the case of psychoanalysis in Buenos Aires, both consumers and producers of discourses based on psychoanalysis are responsible for its circulation and dissemination, so the boundaries between "authoritative" psychoanalytic discourse and the "lay" representation of psychoanalytic discourse are not as fixed as in other fields. By contrast, in biomedical discourses, science is the backup for any assertion, serving as a consistent and trustworthy technique for the development of our understanding of the natural world (Foucault 2010; Latour 1993, 2001, 2005). Scholarly works on medical discourses (J. Anderson 1998; Briggs and Hallin 2007; Capra 1982; Good 1994; Kleinman 1980) have demonstrated that these constructions never exist at a purely conceptual level; they are always applied through sets of material practices. The material understanding of human illness is thus reflected in the material practices of the medical profession, which has become a dominant discourse through the application of scientific knowledge. It is through such practices that the power of the biomedical discourse of health and illness has become socially embedded (Briggs 2011, 2005, 2004).

While psychoanalysis also has to do with health and illness, it does not invoke the same legitimation that science confers on biomedical discourses. Becoming an analyst entails a long and idiosyncratic process in which one must earn legitimacy after a long personal engagement with analysis. In France, though psychoanalysis enjoys high cultural prestige, it does not possess the social legitimation that is expected from a university profession (i.e., the title of psychoanalyst is not recognized by the university) (Lézé 2006). Since the boundaries of psychoanalysis are porous, and the legitimation of the analysts is not always supported by a learning institution, the overlap between analysts and lay audiences is common. Such a dilution of expertise is anathema in the biomedical realm, where institutional accreditation grants doctors the authority to diagnose and prescribe medication.

That these concepts are so far removed from biomedical discourses is, to an extent, part of their appeal. The communicability of psychoanalytic discourses does not project the authority that biomedical discourses do. And although Argentina has recently created university programs that confer "legitimate" degrees in psychoanalysis, the overuse of the prefix *psy-* (as in *psychotango* and *psytrance music*, among many others), the presence of psychoanalysis in so many different fields of cultural production, and the perceived antiempiricism of some disseminators of psychoanalysis suggest that psychoanalytic discourses are communicable because they appeal to a universal quality of humanity related to personal emotions and feelings mediated by unconscious practices.

Graphic Humor

The medium of graphic humor is useful for understanding how psychoanalytic discourses and depictions of listening psychoanalytically circulate in Argentina. Numerous graphic humorists, some of whom have large international followings, incorporate psychoanalytic frameworks into their works. In addition to a vast number of lay readers, psychoanalysts participate in this media ecology—as both artists and audiences—pointing to a broader ambiguity regarding the legitimate and authentic site for psychoanalytic discourses. Yet these ambiguities ultimately help to allow key aspects of psychoanalytic discourse and its listening practices to flourish well outside the clinical settings.

One fascinating example is the 2017 book *Humor al Diván* (Humor at the couch) by Juan Matías Loiseau, a famous Argentine graphic humorist who publishes under the name Tute. In the summer of 2018, Tute became the first cartoonist ever invited to present his work at the APA. Alicia Lagarrigue, the APA's communications director, explained that she decided to invite Tute because "for me, he is the representative of psychoanalysis in all of us" (Tute 2018).

On July 12, 2018, the auditorium of the APA in Buenos Aires was packed. A heterogeneous group composed of many psychoanalysts but also a good number of lay people had assembled to listen to Tute. The event was focused on *Humor al Diván*, a collection of cartoons depicting moments shared between analyst and analysands, short stories involving couples, and solitary dialogues with one's own psyche. This subject matter was familiar territory for

Tute, for he had produced other works concerning psychoanalysis. During the presentation, Tute was asked why he had become so interested in psychoanalysis. He paused and carefully selected his words before responding:

On the one hand I'm interested in psychoanalysis as a technique. I think it's a weird [*volada*] technique.... I mean, I think it's a very ingenious idea created by a madman [*laughs*].... I have been going to analysis for many years, so I began to learn things—only as an analysand, because I never studied it, nor I am invested in reading psychoanalysis. But I'm interested. From the humoristic point of view, as a graphic humorist, I also find it superinteresting; it is a space that is very prone to humor, right? The little couch which is a kind of a little bed with a guy sitting there, and another one lying, and they do not know each other. And yet, they recount themselves... or at least the analysand tells his deepest, most intimate, most miserable things to a stranger. And there is supposed to be a cure taking place with the few words that the other subject—who every now and then says "Hmmm" [*laughter*].... On the other hand, I consider the psychoanalyst an artist.... It makes me laugh when [people] try to bring psychoanalysis into the realm of a discipline, as if it was an exact science. For me it's so far away; it's much closer to the artistic field than it is [to] science. (Asociación Psicoanalítica Argentina 2018)

The event included a panel discussion with distinguished figures in the field: Dr. Andrés Rascovsky, one of the most famous analysts in Argentina, former president of the APA, and the son of APA cofounder Arnaldo Rascovsky, who was among the primary disseminators of psychoanalysis in Argentina; and Liliana Pedrón, an active member of both the APA and the International Psychoanalytic Association (IPA), an editorial coordinator of the IPA's *Journal of Psychoanalysis Today*, and the APA's coordinator of cultural events and symposia.[5] Their presence further demonstrated that the APA considered this an important event in the institution's broader engagement.

Far from being just a celebration of the author's artistic achievement, the discussion was instead a psychoanalytic analysis of numerous elements relating to the book and the author. For example, using a psychoanalytic framework, Rascovsky addressed the subject of the father in Tute's work, noting that both he himself and Tute had followed in the footsteps of successful parents (Tute's father, Caloi, was also a famous cartoonist). His comments explored the continuity of the subjective bonds between father and son.

Pedrón similarly drew from a psychoanalytic framework, looking for "that which is not said (or drawn)" in each cartoon. She speculated about the meaning of some of Tute's drawings, wondering whether the sketch of what seems like a "floating stone" (depicting the moon—a frequent image in Tute's cartoons) represents *la culpa* (guilt) (figure 5.3). She remarked on the fact that Tute strikes out words in some of the cartoons and replaces them with new words, making her wonder whether it is because he drew in haste or if there is another motive. She warned that for psychoanalysts, the stricken word threatens to override the effect of the new word.

Tute's book was widely popular among lay readers, and its extensive discussion at the APA among distinguished psychoanalysts underscores how psychoanalytic discourse can be pushed well beyond the clinic, mediatized, and connected to the cultural milieu of Buenos Aires. Tute himself admitted that he does not read psychoanalytic theory but that his own experience as an analysand has enabled him to appropriate psychoanalysis as an interpretive framework through its artistic representation.

Moreover, the engagement of two prominent analysts in discussing the book using psychoanalytic techniques and discourses further legitimizes the use of psychoanalysis outside the clinic. When Tute states that he sees analysis more as a form of art than as an "exact science," he amplifies the separation of psychoanalysis from the clinic, although he concedes that

FIGURE 5.3 "My mom would have loved to meet you." Cartoon by Tute (2013).

there is some kind of healing during the interaction between analysand and analyst. Psychoanalysis is thus presented as a creative technique rather than as a clinical practice with a rigid nosology, a proposition that is implicitly backed by two prominent analysts.

The mediatization (the amalgamation of linguistic practices and commodification) of psychoanalytic discourses also plays an important role in the circulation of these discourses at a remove from the clinical setting. Mediatization links processes of communication to processes of commoditization (Agha 2011). It thereby connects communicative roles to positions within a division of labor. For example, in the analytic encounter, discourse is transversed by an economic transaction: there will be a payment involved at the end of the session.

The orthodox practice of psychoanalysis—the highly ritualized and private contract between a psychoanalyst and an analysand—takes a number of mediatized forms in Argentina, many of which involve communicative-commoditized practices that differ substantially from the face-to-face clinical interaction. For example, advertisements, newspapers, tarot, and tango are practices that not only are generated outside of the clinic but imply an economic transaction that produces revenue. Tute's presentation offered another example, as it provided an opportunity to sell books, which he graciously signed at the end of the talk. Through this process of mediatization, psychoanalytic discourses transform into a commoditized form: a book that sells for twenty dollars.

But as mediatized practices proliferate, concerns about authenticity tend to emerge. That Tute is considered by a spokesperson for the APA to be "the representative of psychoanalysis in all of us," even though he clearly stated that he is not an expert in psychoanalysis and is not interested in becoming one, suggests an ambiguity regarding who is authorized to use psychoanalysis as an interpretive framework.

When I interviewed Tute in his studio in San Telmo, he admitted that he did not like the lay psychoanalytic interpretations in which *porteños* engage. He found this practice intrusive and often "*cualquier cosa*" (nonsensical). In his work, he said, he employs creatively a theory that is open to anyone. He is not doing psychoanalysis but using the main ideas and concepts "to create something new." By recycling psychoanalytic discourses, Tute is decentering them from the clinical setting, yielding an amorphous variety of outcomes. In an interview with *En el margen*, a psychoanalytic magazine, he noted that in his childhood home "there was a language spoken very naturally that was completely foreign to me.

When different episodes or behaviors were repeated, there were interpretations or second readings. I didn't find any sense or logic in it" (Avolio 2020). This *language*, unknown to Tute at a young age, is learned through listening, by hearing the resonances—the music—in the words. This *music* circulates through different media and cultural practices, becoming a genre of listening.

In 2012, the cartoonist published *Tuterapia*, a play on both his pen name and the phrase *tu terapia*, meaning "your therapy." The book includes a foreword by writer and psychoanalyst Gabriel Rolón—arguably the most famous disseminator of psychoanalytic ideas to lay audiences today—who states that the psychoanalyst is searching "for a truth that hides behind the barrier of repression" (Tute 2012).[6] Tute's books feature many representations of this idea of "searching for [the] truth." For example, one cartoon depicts a man lying on the couch, talking. His words construct a cavernous maze that his analyst is investigating with a lamp on his hand. After a good amount of searching, the analyst's head comes out from one of the holes in the cavern, and he asks the analysand to continue next time.

Tute is hardly the only one using psychoanalytic ideas through a mediatized chain. Quino, the most important and widely recognized graphic humorist of Argentina (he is the creator of *Mafalda*, an iconic comic strip about a little girl that has been translated into over twenty languages), also uses the figure of the relationship between analyst and analysand in his work.[7] Another graphic artist, Rep (Miguel Repiso), developed the character Gaspar, el Revolú (a play on the words *revolucionaro* [revolutionary] and *reboludo* [the dumbest one]), an anguished leftist father whom Rep mostly portrays lying on the psychoanalytic couch talking with his analyst (figure 5.4). Rudy (Marcelo Daniel Rudaeff) is a psychoanalyst who produces cartoons with a political edge that often discuss economics, current events, and the character of politicians (figure 5.5). Fernando Sendra, a longtime contributor to the newspaper *Clarín*, also focuses on the analytic experience in drawing some of his characters. Through the process of mediatization, these graphic humorists, who are among the most recognized and influential in their field, transform psychoanalytic discourses into commoditized forms that create particular divisions of labor (cartoonists, publishers, institutions), all of which contribute to the circulation of psychoanalytic discourses. Moreover, these mediatized forms play a crucial role in the mass circulation of psychoanalytic listening as a genre in Argentina, directly disseminating specific listening models (specifically the idea that there is

FIGURE 5.4 "I did Freudian therapy, Lacanian therapy, Jungian, Gestalt, behavioral, and I finally know who I am. I am a guinea pig. *Gaspar, el Revolú*, by Miguel Repiso (Rep), n.d. Courtesy of Miguel Repiso.

FIGURE 5.5 Woman: I want a hysterical hamburger.
Rudy: A hysterical one, ready!
Woman: No . . . today, better not . . .

Man: I want an obsessive hamburger.
Rudy: What do you want with it?
Man: You decide.

Woman: A sausage!
Rudy: A phallic one, ready! What do you want with it?
Woman: All of it.

Rudy: I am making a lot of money since I started the "Fast Freud."

El Licenciado Rudiez, by Marcelo Rudaeff (Rudy) and Pati (n.d.). Courtesy of Marcelo Rudaeff.

something hidden that can be discovered) to audiences in an array of social contexts well outside the clinical encounters of analysts and analysands.

Psychoanalysis on Television

As psychoanalytic discourse becomes increasingly part of media, art, and cultural production in Argentina, listening continues to play a central role in the process of its circulation, not only in the way it affects people's interactions and social ideologies but also as a commodity that can be exploited, further facilitating the spread of psychoanalytic discourses through Argentina's market forces. A good illustration of this can be seen in the depictions of psychoanalysis and psychoanalytic listening on Argentine television.

Psychoanalyst Gabriel Rolón has become perhaps the most famous interlocutor between psychoanalysis and lay audiences in Argentina. He works as a clinical psychoanalyst in his own practice and has written nine books about psychoanalysis. Free of esoteric jargon, these books consist of easy-to-read prose that makes them accessible to readers who have little to no training or exposure to psychoanalysis. All of his books have become best sellers.

Rolón used to give talks about psychoanalytical concepts on Saturday mornings at Clásica y Moderna, a traditional bookstore and coffee shop in Buenos Aires's fancy neighborhood Barrio Norte. These sessions were open to the general public at a cost of thirty-five dollars per session—reservations had to be made weeks in advance due to their popularity. I attended some of these sessions, each of which lasted two hours and focused on a general theme (e.g., perversion). Rolón would reflect on the concept's meaning, how it had been developed by different psychoanalytic schools, and the significance that Freud and Lacan proposed for it, as well as how it can be seen in interactions. Like Rolón's books, these talks were intended to be accessible to nonexperts, and even though there were some psychologists present, most of the people in attendance were just curious to learn more about psychoanalysis.

Rolón's fame has transcended books and bookstore presentations, circulating psychoanalytic ideas to a mass media audience. He has appeared on numerous television shows (*Va X Vos*), *Siempre listos, Todos al diván, ¿A vos quién te ama?,* and *Animales sueltos,* to mention just a few) and has produced and hosted three radio shows of his own. On his radio show *Noches de diván* (Couch nights), listeners call in to describe a particular problem or situation. Rolón then gently "analyzes" the situation in psychoanalytical terms, suggests some outcomes, and offers advice to the caller. On television shows, he will provide "analysis" in numerous formats—from informally "analyzing" a whole group of people working as hosts of a late-night show to a more formal act of one-on-one analysis, where a celebrity lies on a couch as Rolón performs a "conventional" clinical session. His media appearances range widely and have even included guest spots on a sports program, where he discussed the phobias of famous athletes. Throughout these appearances, the format draws its appeal, in part, from the inviting nature of Rolón's psychoanalytic methods and discourses. The fact that he is "analyzing" people in public gives the audience the sense that they have been admitted into one of the most ritualized and private spaces: the therapeutic session.

The tremendous success of these therapeutic performances—evident in the large audience avidly consuming these mediatized forms of psychoanalysis through television and radio shows, popular books, café concerts, and commercial theater—points to the variety of ways in which psychoanalytic knowledge has circulated outside of the clinical setting.

When specific knowledge travels, disseminators and consumers play differing roles in the process (Briggs and Hallin 2007). Disseminators, whom we might also call experts, are separated from consumers of the knowledge they are disseminating, but this is not a direct separation so much as a negotiation of shifting roles. At times, consumers can become experts in their own right. This process is not simply the result of forming asymmetrical relationships with others; rather, it comes from learning to communicate knowledge from an authoritative angle—in other words, through the performance of expertise.

Expertise is intensively citational. Expert actors use linguistic and metalinguistic resources, such as jargon and acronyms, to structure their interactions (Bauman and Briggs 2003; Carr 2010a). As a result, expertise requires a mastery of verbal performance, including the ability to use language to index and instantiate states of knowledge (Silverstein 2003). Rolón exhibits this expertise in his talks by harking back to Freud and Lacan, describing mental health diagnoses and their etiology and, in some ways, performing the role of a doctor. He also includes other philosophers, such as Plato, René Descartes, and Friedrich Nietzsche, through reported speech: "Nietzsche has a phrase that describes well the personality of the psychotic . . . "

But it is not only language that constructs tropes of expertise. As can be seen in the mediatized practice of psychoanalysis in Buenos Aires, experts must also draw upon a mastery of listening.

On April 28, 2017, during the show *Cortá por Lozano*, Gabriel Rolón appeared to promote the release of the movie *Los padecientes* (*The Sufferers*), based on a book he published in 2010.[8] A voice-over introduced Rolón, saying, "Rolón is not only a psychoanalyst and author of best sellers; he is also an actor, musician, teacher, radio host, and a well-known face of television. . . . His books made him the country's most famous analyst and a successful writer. . . . Gabriel Rolón is the exception to the proverb that says, 'Do not spread too thin' [*El que mucho abarca poco aprieta*], because he performs each of his activities with an incomparable passion. But his multiple roles have a common core that is what he does best: *to know how to listen* [saber escuchar]."

Immediately after this introduction, host Verónica Lozano (VL) began conversing with Rolón (GR):

> **VL:** Very good, to know how to listen.
>
> **GR:** Which is not going to be of any use to me right now, because *it's time to talk*, isn't it? You see I, sometimes, I appreciate the possibility of being able *to give talks*, to *have conversations*. Because, as the opening report said, we analysts are a little bit—I do not say condemned, because it is a choice—but we are destined to listen. To always listen to what happens to the other, what hurts the other. And then, to have some *moments to talk*, to *be able to talk* about what happens to us, I always thank you, so thank you for the invitation.

Listening frames the interaction of this encounter from the beginning: Rolón is an expert listener. Through a series of metalinguistic remarks (which are underlined in the transcript), Rolón expresses his relief that he will not be listening but instead will talk about the things that happen to him and to analysts in general. But his desires will be frustrated soon after the beginning of the interview.

Following an emotional recounting of an experience Rolón had with his deceased father, Lozano (who is also a psychologist) takes advantage of a short pause to task Rolón with a new act of listening:

> 1 **VL:** How beautiful [what you just told us is]. Now I'm going to put you to work because we have to analyze a few lapses—Freudian slips, let's say.
> 2 **GR:** Let's say.
> 3 **VL:** Let's go with the first one and see what we can say about this . . .

They cut to a video of a priest performing a ceremony:

> 4 **PRIEST:** Por Dios, por la **plat/por la patria** . . .
> [**PRIEST:** For God, for the money/ for the fatherland . . . (money = *plata*, which sounds similar to *patria* = fatherland)]
> 5 **VL:** Por Dios, por la plat/por la patria.

6 GR: Oh, wow! Well, first let's make a clarification. You are a colleague, Vero, so you know Freud once said that sometimes a cigar is just a cigar. Right? So sometimes a mistake is just a mistake.

7 VL: In this case it would not look like that [*loud laughter*]. I allow myself [to interpret that].

8 GR: I love it, because we are analyzing it together. Why are we two therapists, two psychologists? So, I mean, Freudian slip or lapse is important when it is said in front of the analyst—that is, when it is said in front of someone to listen to it.

9 VL: OK.

10 GR: Right? Well, I tend to think it's possible that in many of these cases it's a Freudian slip or a lapse because the people [*el pueblo*] are an other who are there to listen.

11 VL: Sure, it's a big ear; it listens.

12 GR: It's a big ear to listen. But not in all the cases, but many times it can be. And therefore, it is necessary to know how to listen well when we choose, when we vote, and also sometimes to have the generosity to understand that someone comes from making twenty-six campaigns and/

13 VL: You can make a mistake…

14 GR: He was talking two minutes earlier…

15 VL: Or maybe counting a lot of money…[*loud laughter*]

16 GR: Or thinking to what sector, whom I was going to give this money to? This money is for whom?

17 VL: Right, right.

18 GR: And you were left with the signifier of the word spinning [in your head], and you do this, which condemns you publicly…[*laughs*]

19 VL: We send him a little kiss, and we have another one. This one is of a different kind; let's analyze it together.

Rolón reveals himself to be a savvy communicator and is careful not to casually lodge malignant interpretations. He begins by including Lozano in his interpretation ("You are a colleague, Vero"), thus expanding the interactional framework and positioning both of them in the category of experts. He continues by citing Freud's idea that sometimes discourses do not have double meanings. Lozano, having given him authorization to interpret, affirms that this is not a case of confusion (line 7). Rolón legitimizes her interpretation (line 8) by once again emphasizing that she is also a psychologist. However, he then changes the register.

Shifting into more formal language, Rolón explains that lapses or Freudian slips make sense only in the context of a listener. So as not to directly contradict Lozano, Rolón explains that listening can also be a collective experience that can legitimize certain interpretations. He provides different scenarios that can explain the priest's confusion. He closes by expressing sympathy about how one mistake can insert a subject into a discredited discourse. These discursive strategies allow Rolón to assert control over the exchange without having to contradict Lozano. He enacts expertise but also includes Lozano—even when he disagrees.

Besides featuring a bravura psychoanalytic performance, this exchange is rich with ideas about listening. Rolón expresses three such ideas: first, the indication that lapses or Freudian slips happen only when there is someone to interpret them as such (line 8); second, the figurative conceptualization that *el pueblo* (society) is "a big ear," allowing the interlocutor in a one-on-one interaction to be replaced by society at large (lines 10–11); and third, that since anyone can listen, it is the responsibility of the subject to "learn" to listen before making any important decision—overinterpretation is risky (line 12), and listeners must be generous and not jump to conclusions. As Rolón reminds us, there is an ethics of listening: it is the responsibility of the listener to avoid confusion and especially to avoid inserting subjects into wrongful discourses. Lozano tries in two occasions (lines 7 and 15) to force a particular interpretation: the priest is thinking about money and probably not about God. But Rolón stays away from that interpretation and continues to provide alternative explanations. During this part of the exchange, there is overlap between Rolón and Lozano (lines 12–15) until Lozano gives up, admits that this could be a simple mistake, and closes her intervention by sending kisses to the priest (line 19).

This exchange reveals how psychoanalytic listening as a genre circulates and how it is represented in its mediated form. The focus is explicitly on listening, and when Rolón explains, in his role of expert, that "*el pueblo*" is a big ear, he democratizes listening; thus *anyone* is authorized to listen and can make interpretations. If anyone can listen psychoanalytically, the *What you really mean is...* addressivity form emerges as an index of how people are listening and is far from being an imposition; it becomes a form of sociability in which one can be interpreted by another. This televised exchange serves as a pedagogical tool contributing to, or reflective of, the broader presence of the genre of psychoanalytic listening in Argentina.

But Freudian slips represent just one form of listening psychoanalytically. Although as Rolón explains, the slip needs to be heard to be interpreted as such, the focus is on the verbal performance. In the next example, Rolón explains how "listening slips"—the act of listening per se—are at the core of psychoanalytic listening.

Lozano presented another clip, this one from a television show, featuring a woman saying *"Tengo aval"* (I have a guarantor). The woman to whom she is speaking becomes noticeably upset and responds, *"Y traelo a Bal, tanto lo querés a Bal traelo"* (Bring Bal, you love Bal so much, bring him). She is quickly corrected by the first woman, who repeats *"aval,"* and from off screen we can hear a man saying, *"Aval, aval, para que le sostenga lo que dice"* (Guarantor, guarantor, to back up what she is saying). The woman who is upset seems to have *heard* the first woman refer to an actor—a man named Federico Fernando Bal—rather than the word *aval*.

When asked to offer an interpretation, Rolón responds:

20 **GR:** Well, you know that many times the lapse is not in what it is said, but in what is heard/
21 **VL:** What one interprets, right.
22 **GR:** And that shows what one has in mind. In reality, what the lapse tells us is about an unconscious idea, that one has kept, perhaps/
23 **VL:** And that is very common in conversations, that the other understands something else because he heard something else.
24 **GR:** That always happens, almost always. There's nothing more difficult than communicating, look/
25 **VL:** "But I told you this thing, no, you told me that other thing."
26 **GR:** Well, a few minutes ago I had a conversation with two people who said to each other, "You told me this because I . . ." and the other said, "No, no I did not tell you that"/
27 **VL:** "Hey you, Juan Carlos, weren't you listening?" There is usually someone else listening. [She is using the name Juan Carlos as a figurative witness.]
28 **GR:** That place [Juan Carlos's place] is the worst in the world.

Rolón explains that lapses often emerge not from the producing site but from the receptive end (line 20), highlighting the idea that listening can be a productive and not just a passive act. Rolón once again explains that the signifiers that roam our psyche are responsible for the mishearing.[9] Lacan (1997) has emphasized the importance of language in finding the unconscious, something that Rolón brings to many discussions, situating the unconscious at the forefront of any interpretation. Lozano's interjection (line 23) that mishearings are a common practice prompts Rolón to say that "mishearings" are *always* happening (line 24). Immediately, he hastens to add *"almost* always," but the idea remains: most communication entails the mishearing of utterances.

For years, linguistic anthropologists and sociolinguists have researched the idea that communication is anything but linear, contradicting Ferdinand de Saussure's model of the talking heads, where utterances travel from Person A to the ear of Person B and vice versa in an unproblematic and direct way. But Rolón's statement is different; the inquiry is directed not to speech but to the *reception* of speech. This conceptualization is slightly different from the *What you really mean is...* phenomenon. In the latter, the listener does not "mishear" but instead listens to "that which is not said," then adds a surplus of interpretation.

Rolón seems to be referring here to the polysemic reception of language, where the signifiers that roam the mind of the listener influence the later reception of particular utterances. Rolón adjudicates this phenomenon to the unconscious (line 22). And he argues that the worst position one can be in is that of the overhearer (line 28) because one would have to decide which is the best interpretation and thus would have to side with one of the parties involved in the misunderstanding. Once more, the idea that a witness is needed for the unconscious to emerge is present in this exchange.

These conversations between Lozano and Rolón offer a clear picture of how mediatized discourses about psychoanalysis circulate in Argentina. Lozano tells Rolón directly that she will put him to work (line 1). A division of labor is already established, where his labor is to listen. These exchanges are notable both for their descriptions of the importance of listening in psychoanalytic discourse and for the remarkable pedagogical focus of the discussion. The exchanges are—as a segment on television for broad viewing audiences and couched in the form of entertainment—directly teaching how listening models associated with psychoanalysis (*When you say X, I hear Y*) are mediated for large public audiences. Although there is no way to concretely measure the specific impact of this mediatization of psychoanalytic discourse on the broader presence and circulation of the genre of psychoanalytic listening throughout Buenos Aires and Argentina, its prevalence in social areas well outside the clinic suggests that this mediatization and the development of the genre of listening among diverse social contexts are intertwined. In the context of Rolón's television shows, writings, and other works, it is worth highlighting that these projects are created and sold in the context of a market economy, a market that is able to expand the circulation of a listening model that is structured around specific modern ideologies, with clear theoretical roots, and which, based on the wide popularity of these television shows, books, radio programs, and so forth, is supported through its commodification. As Marcel Mauss would say, there is no free gift. Rolón appeared on the show to promote a movie based on his novel, both commoditized products spawned by discourses on psychoanalysis. The air and publicity time Lozano granted to the movie based on Rolón's novel is offered in exchange for Rolón's willingness to perform the labor of listening psychoanalytically.

The circulation on television of psychoanalytic listening as a genre can also be seen in Rolón's interview on the show *Animales sueltos* (Loose animals), hosted by Alejandro Fantino. Throughout the interview, which aired on June 9, 2018, Fantino seemed excited and eager to speak with his guest, even telling him that he had been carrying around a notebook to record any interesting event he witnessed, in the hopes of asking Rolón about it.

An interesting discussion between the two began with Fantino telling Rolón that he once asked a famous tattoo artist to identify the most commonly requested tattoo design. The artist encouraged Fantino to try guessing the answer and provided this hint: "It is one word that many women ask for." Fantino volunteered the words *peace* and *love*, but the artist responded, "No, we tattoo approximately five or six times a day the word *soltar* [to let go]." Then this exchange ensued between Alejandro Fantino (AF) and Gabriel Rolón (GR):

1   **AF:** I start from that word, the most tattooed, for many, "to let go." What is it to let go? How does psychology understand, or how do you understand, what it is to let go? What is the meaning of letting go?

2   **GR:** Look, I think it's interesting that they choose that word, because we basically have the idea that we can't be happy because we carry a lot of weight. Right? So when they tell you, "Well, you have to let go"—let go of what? Let go of the commands, let go of the story, let go of a love story, specifically. Let's say you didn't let go of it and they tell you, "Let go, go out again, meet someone, let go of your past, to say ..."/

3   **AF:** But are you supposed to go around the world with little weight?

4   **GR:** Look, I think it's impossible to go around the world with little weight. What you have to try is to carry only the weight that is indispensable or inevitable.

5 **AF:** What do you call *weight* in psychology? Because I could tell you what weight is in physics, but I don't know what weight means for psychology. What do you call *weight*?

6 **GR:** Look, more than anything it's like a metaphor for . . . I would say . . . those things that . . . I don't know if for psychology . . . I try to translate what people tell me . . .

7 **AF:** Yes, exactly.

8 **GR:** When [someone] says to me, "I carry a lot of weight" . . . hmm, imagine this, OK? It is as if we were all born with a backpack, a backpack in which, little by little as we live, many people put things. Some things are good and other things are bad. We get phrases, words; someone places a stone that says, "You'll never be happy"; another places something . . . /

9 **AF:** Can they put that on you? Are there people who get that in their backpack, "You're never going to be happy?"

10 **GR:** But of course. "You're not good at anything." There are ways to introduce [the stone]. Look, when a mom or dad asks a boy to work on something, and two minutes later he [the father] comes and says, "Leave it, leave it, leave it. Leave it, I'll do it for you." What is he telling him? "You're not good for anything." "Let me do it for you because you are useless, you cannot do it."

11 **AF:** In that small act you are placing a stone that has that [inscribed] in the boy's backpack.

Perhaps most striking in this exchange is the polysemic nature of the words Fantino and Rolón deploy. They are having a conversation about the meaning of words; people from different professions assign distinctive meanings to words depending on the context. Fantino begins by asking what it could possibly mean that women tattoo the word *soltar*. He implies that there is some hidden meaning unavailable to him. He asks first what meaning psychologists assign to this term but rapidly shifts the question to ask how Rolón would interpret it. Rolón explains that *soltar* is related to the idea of carrying weight by accumulating experience throughout one's life. This prompts Fantino to ask about the word *weight*. He asserts that he knows what the meaning conveys in physics, but he is curious about what *weight* could mean to psychologists (line 5). Rolón starts to respond but immediately acknowledges (in an act of self-repair) that he will talk not about psychology but about what he interprets in the words of his patients (line 6) ("what they really mean is . . .").

Rolón explains that the word *weight* is used as a metaphor. To illustrate this idea, he presents an allegory of someone carrying a backpack where people deposit words and phrases that begin to feel heavy. Some people introduce words that feel like stones with the legend "You'll never be happy" (line 8). Fantino is surprised that someone could add those words to the imaginary backpack, and Rolón, now invested in his role as an analyst, explains that the *real meaning* of a parent's words when telling a boy to stop doing something he had previously been asked to do involves a cruel metamessage: "You are not good for anything."

Across all of Rolón's conversations with television hosts, the idea that everything has a meaning beyond pure denotation occurs again and again. As Rolón explains to Fantino (line 6), what he does is translate the words that people tell him. This translation depends on listening to "that which is not said," bringing to the fore unconscious practices, the real motives that drive one's behavior.

In this conversation between Rolón and Fantino, several key elements of the model of psychoanalytic listening are being mediated and performed for a broad television audience. The context of this performance and the remuneration that both Rolón and Fantino receive underscore how naturally and thoroughly the genre of psychoanalytic listening can be packaged and circulated through the media for public consumption.

For example, one of the four main elements that help define the genre of psychoanalytic listening is the fact that the way words communicate is dependent on how listeners receive them (see chapter 2). Rolón's comment on the word *weight* directly points this out to the show's viewers. Similarly, Rolón consistently affirms that everything has a meaning beyond pure denotation. In his response to Fantino's comment that *soltar* is the most tattooed word for women, Rolón links it to the idea of carrying weight by accumulating experience throughout one's life. This is a very effective illustration of this element of psychoanalytic listening.

It's not essential that viewers of shows like Fantino's consciously grasp the listening model that Rolón is describing. But Rolón and, to some extent, Fantino are both part of a larger media ecosystem wherein psychoanalytic discourse is part of their everyday lives and listening is key to understanding different aspects of their worldviews.

As we shall see in the next section, sometimes words are attached to complex stories, myths, and worldviews. In Buenos Aires psychoanalysis has become a cultural practice that depicts the world through particular ideologies of the self but also of gender, where the figure of the mother occupies an important role.

Advertisements

Mediatized discourses on psychoanalysis are communicable in part because the consumers created by these discourses' ubiquitous circulation continue to disseminate and recycle them. When the media deploy psychoanalytical discourses, they use a language that is attached to ideas and concepts that date back to Freud but that are nevertheless recognized among a big part of the population in Buenos Aires.

This language is impregnated with semiotic meaning capable of communicating many ideologies and beliefs. It is so powerful and recognizable that Argentine advertisers have come to use it to promote products and sell things. In this way, psychoanalysis is not just about a relationship between an analyst and analysand or about saying x and meaning y—it is also sometimes used to craft a relationship between discourses and commodities.

In his celebrated book *Wisdom Sits in Places* (1996), Keith Basso developed a fascinating analysis of how the Western Apache of Cibecue assign significance to places in their culture. There is a close relationship between landscape and language, where the invocation of the name of a place serves to educate and transmit the culture of Cibecue ancestors. More than being descriptive, place-names in the Cibecue community are accompanied by a story that usually conveys a moral lesson. In the chapter titled "Speaking with Names," Basso describes Louise, a woman who is worried about the reckless behavior of her brother. Several months previously, her brother stepped on a snakeskin and did not complete the necessary ritual to protect himself from this mishap. Now the brother is sick, and the sister is complaining to three friends, Lola, Emily, and Robert. While she is talking about the situation, Lola interrupts by saying, "It happened at Line of White Rocks Extend Up and Out, at this very place!" No one responds for thirty to forty seconds until Emily says, "Yes. It happened at Whiteness Spread Out Descending to Water, at this very place!" After another long pause, Lola utters another place-name. Louise starts to laugh softly, and Robert states, "Pleasantness and goodness will be forthcoming." After this exchange, Louise tells her dog that her brother acted foolishly, but she is visibly in better spirits than before.

Upon witnessing the interaction, Basso initially had no idea what had happened. For anyone not familiar with this form of communication, the exchange would seem incoherent. Through his ethnographic work, however, he later came to understand that speaking with names implies a very sophisticated metacommunication process in which each place-name is connected to a specific story. The long pauses between each exchange are necessary to visualize the place and thus remember the story connected to it. The stories behind the place-names that Louise's friends uttered conveyed a tale of a person who behaved badly, suffered the consequences of that behavior, but nevertheless had a happy ending. As Lola told Basso, the "pictures" that were sent with the names had a perlocutionary effect that calmed Louise's distress.

Perlocutionary acts are speech acts that "extend" the illocution of an utterance by having a direct impact or consequence on the listener (for example, persuading, inspiring, or promising). The illocution of the *What you really mean is* addressivity form is also a perlocutionary act because the listener usually accepts the interpellation. As the interpellation is accepted, doubts, worries, and uncertainties appear, generating a particular state of mind for the listener. In the example of the Cibecue people, the names attached to a story are performative and have a perlocutionary effect because, by being connected to a story, they produce different dispositions, feelings, and outlooks.

The Cibecue example shows how metacommunication plays a part in everyday interactions. The most ordinary words can carry meanings that go beyond their denotational capacity. Names specifically convey a particular form of cultural knowledge that circulates, and social actors associate differently with each name. Similarly, through the mediatized nature of psychoanalytic discourses, certain words and names in Buenos Aires are attached to a semiotic chain (e.g., myths and stories) that convey a particular cultural meaning of their own.

In the summer of 2018, I was watching television in Buenos Aires when an advertisement caught my attention. It was a commercial for Fernet, an Italian aperitif that is very popular in Argentina ("Nuevo Fernet 1882 RTD–Psicólogo" 2017). Fernet is a liquor that is usually mixed with Coca-Cola, and the commercial was introducing Fernet 1882, a new product that is already mixed with Coca-Cola and is ready to be served. The motto of the new packaging is "extremely practical," pointing to the advantages of not having to open and mix the content of two bottles. The ad begins with an analyst sitting in his modern office while a young man who has just arrived is starting to lie down on an empty couch. But before he lies down completely, the following exchange ensues between the psychoanalyst (P) and Julián, the analysand (J):

1   **P:** How are you, Julián?

2   **J:** I don't know.

3   **P:** It's your mother's fault.

4   **J:** Of course.

5   **P:** See you next week.

6   **J:** OK.

Just as Julián says, "OK," he starts to leave the couch. After the dialogue, a black background with the words *extremely practical* appears, followed by video footage showing a can of the new Fernet being opened. Then there is a cut to another black background with the name *1882 Sabor Fernet & Cola*, followed by the words *ready to drink*.

The commercial lasts fifteen seconds, and the exchange between Julián and the analyst is only five seconds long. But in this very short period an array of ideologies, stereotypes, and competing discourses are communicated.

In the Fernet advertisement we can *hear* a word that communicates a very idiosyncratic meaning: *mother*. In Buenos Aires, the word *mother*—meaning a female parent—conveys two stories that appear to be omnipresent, since they are found throughout so many discourses and in so many forms: the story of the mother as the source of psychological abnormalities and the story of Oedipus.

The first story, illustrated by Sendra's cartoon earlier in this chapter (figure 5.3), is linked to the ideology that the relationship with one's mother will shape most aspects of one's life. This relationship is usually associated with negative outcomes. Feminist scholars have argued that this belief is so prevalent that is almost axiomatic: both parents produce our selves, but our mothers are especially essential to this process.[10] There is an emphasis on self-scrutiny, looking for signs that point to "normality," "abnormality," and "pathology" that are the direct outcome of the relationship with our mothers (see Lawler 2000). As Valerie Walkerdine and Helen Lucey (1989, 15) put it, the mother has become "the guarantor of the liberal [democratic] order." Thus, it is the mother's task to produce the good, healthy, and well-managed self, which will in turn uphold democracy.

In the ad for Fernet, the word *mother* replicates this ideology. Whatever problem Julián experiences, it is his mother's fault. In his reply to the analyst's question about how he is doing, he expresses neither a lack of composure nor bad feelings; his response is neutral: "I don't know" (line 2). The analyst's reaction to Julián's statement is to implicate Julián's mother. Julián legitimizes the analyst's interpretation by quickly responding "Of course" (line 4), underlying the self-evident nature of this discourse. If we apply the commercial's motto, *extremely practical*—that is, you don't have to do anything but serve the contents of a can—to the interaction between Julián and the analyst, we find the following message: "as practical as knowing instinctively that mothers are responsible for all our problems." There is also a subtext that serves to mock the analytic encounter, suggesting that "you go to therapy for years just to realize that everything comes down to your relationship with your mother."

The negative association wherein "mother equals problems" is not unique to Argentina. Motherhood has long been conceptualized through discourses of extreme benevolence and sacrifice or as pathological and damaging (see Rose 1991). The hegemonic ideology that only some people count as "healthy," "good mothers," and "good children," while others are pathologized, is prevalent across many cultures. What is exceptional in Buenos Aires is the link between this negative association and psychoanalysis itself.

In the Fernet ad, we can witness how psychoanalysis frames motherhood and how these discourses are simultaneously being recycled by the media as they disseminate ideologies and create social identities. During my research in Buenos Aires, I lost count of how many times friends and acquaintances expressed a direct link between their problems and their relationship with their mothers. Only very seldom did they talk about their fathers. The word *mother* follows a particular semiotic chain through a story that links mothers with problems, and this story is very much present in psychoanalytic theory.

The successful communicability of this discourse lies in how internalized this story is in Argentina. Consequently, as with the Cibecue place-names, the word *mother* in Argentina triggers a particular story, albeit a negative one. Indeed, this idea has become so widespread in Buenos Aires that diverse companies are able to capitalize from it and use it to sell commodities.

The second story attached to the word *mother* is the Oedipus complex myth. (We saw an example in chapter 3, when Carlos alludes to the Oedipus complex to raise the possibility of sexual tension between Darío and his analyst.)

The word *mother* triggers a particular story: the complex emotions awakened in a child by the unconscious desire for the parent of the opposite sex.[11] This story is clearly illustrated in an Argentine commercial for Hellman's mayonnaise, first aired in 2004 to celebrate Mother's Day (Hellman's 2004). The ad—which many would consider cringe-provoking—lasts fifty seconds, as a love song called "*Algo contigo*" (Something with you), sung by famous Argentine singer Vicentico, serves as background music. The lyrics are about a desperate man who is madly in love with a woman and pleading to have a relationship with her:

> Do I really need to tell you that I'm dying to have something with you?
> Don't you realize how hard it is for me to be your friend?
> I can't get near your mouth without wanting it in a crazy way.
> I need to control your life, to know who kisses you and who embraces you.[12]

The ad presents the interactions of five boys, from approximately two to about eleven years old, with their respective mothers. As the mothers add Hellman's mayonnaise to different dishes, the boys look at their mothers in what can be interpreted as a lustful way. The first kid tells his mother, "Mommy, you are the love of my life"; the second stares at his mother in awe; the third says, "You are an incredible woman"; the fourth grabs his mother's arms, saying, "Did I ever tell you that I love you?," to which she responds with a surprised, tender look. The last kid, virtually a baby, tells his mother, "*Me encantás*" (which can be translated as "I really like you" but which is directed only to a romantic partner, not to a parent). The astonished mother asks him to repeat what he just said, and the boy replies by babbling. The commercial ends with the slogan "Hellman's is to give one's best."

The combined effect of the song, the lascivious expressions of the children, and the declarations of love give the impression that the boys are, in fact, infatuated with their mothers. Some of the comments on YouTube discussing the commercial corroborate this interpretation: "Oedipus Complex XD," "Emotional incest," "Ahh the Oedipus," "The Oedipus complex in a commercial with sexual connotation? Or am I just a pervert? :S."[13]

The Oedipus complex is one of the most widely circulated ideas spawned by twentieth-century psychoanalysis. It is a multifaceted concept that Freud developed throughout his career. It took Freud over twenty years after his first extended discussion of Oedipus in *The Interpretation of Dreams* to reassess his belief that the Oedipus complex was equally valid for girls and for boys (Leonard 2013). It is well known that Freud rejected Carl Jung's efforts to provide a comparable mythic narrative for girls in what he called the "Electra Complex" (Jung 1913). In his struggle to understand female sexuality, Freud also discussed the idea of a pre-Oedipus stage. But despite his recognition of female desire, Freud ([1926] 1959, 212) continued to declare his inability to understand female sexuality by notoriously asserting that "the sexual life of adult women is a 'dark continent' for psychology."

The Oedipus complex is a great example of how communicability disseminates an array of ideological tropes. The further recycling by lay audiences of the concept has taken many forms, sometimes completely unrelated to the original history. This later consumption and recycling by lay audiences establish hierarchies by situating ideologically the producers, disseminators, and consumers of certain discourses.

During casual interactions in Buenos Aires, the invocation of the Oedipus complex indexes a variety of social situations: for example, it can be a joke describing the close relationship that a male *porteño* has with his mother; it can take the form of a mother's complaint that her young son does not want to go to kindergarten because "he is still in the Oedipus phase"; or it might serve to justify the sexual attraction that a young man has for older women.

In the Hellman's ad we can see the lamination of a commoditized product—mayonnaise—and the semiotic chains that connect it all the way back to Freud. When lay subjects invoke the complex, we can still trace back its inception, but it is not mediatized since it is not commoditized and does not assign a division of labor. But it shows the internalization of particular stories attached to the concept of mother.

The two commercials—one for a liqueur, the other for mayonnaise—present stories linked to the word *mother*. One is attached to a strong ideology that links motherhood with identity, the other with a supposed passage that all male infants go through. Both stories emerge from psychoanalytic theories interpellating subjects as occupying very concrete social roles. There is a possible link between both stories: male subjectivity appears by having an unhealthy relationship (or attachment) with their mothers. When psychoanalysis is invoked, there are many ideologies attached to it, and they also appear. An important one is a gendered ideology represented through the figure of the mother that transmits messages depicting motherhood in a ruthless way. The perlocutionary force of summoning motherhood produces the same effect as the *What you really mean is . . .* form in that, although the denotation is clear, the concepts attached to it are idiosyncratic and differ significantly from the referent. We all speak in names one way or another; in Argentina, it is the concept of mother that awakens stories and concepts connected to psychoanalysis. And listening is key.

Consequently, as these discourses and their ideologies are depicted in the media, they also enter into the listening genres and listening ideologies of people throughout the country who may see the advertisements or simply be exposed to them later due to the circulation of these discourses, a circulation that is strongly determined by the specific genre of listening associated with psychoanalysis.

∗   ∗   ∗

Advertisements, television, radio, books, and other media provide a powerful vehicle for the mediatization and dissemination of key elements of psychoanalytic discourse outside the clinical setting in Argentina. The circulation of psychoanalysis in Buenos Aires takes a great many forms, and the dissemination and transmission of these forms are due to their communicability and their mediatization. Mediatization is always a communicative form—focusing on specific instances of communication like those in this chapter helps reveal how particular symbols emerge and become relevant. In the extreme case, the communicative form is a single syllable, the prefix *psy*. In other cases, as in that of Rolón, larger interpersonal routines are recycled in fragmentary ways.

In all cases, attention to what is recycled enables the identification of larger chains of communication (similar to Bakhtin's spheres of communication). Consequently, when one tries to capture how a particular social relation created inside a clinical setting—the relationship between analysand and analyst—gets replicated outside that setting, the concept of mediatization helps to shine a light on how this relationship gets reproduced and to trace the semiotic chain(s) that preceded and follow it. Communicability, on the other hand, is a crucial lens for grasping how, in Argentina's media ecosystem, the roles of producer, disseminator, and consumer of psychoanalytic discourses interact and how these relationships project a wholesome product to broad public audiences, indexing social actors as occupying specific roles. The success of the circulation of psychoanalytic discourses is due to its capacity to project ideologies as commonsensical and natural.

Listening is key to these processes. In all these examples, either listening is explicitly invoked and transformed into labor or the words summon in the listener particular stories that generate cultural models indexing stereotypical characteristics of interactional roles. The abundant examples of psychoanalysis in the media help to circulate the ideology that there is more to denotation in every statement uttered. In some cases, advertisements, television shows, and graphic humor replicate listening practices based on psychoanalysis by performing *What you really mean is* ideologies. In other cases, the perlocutionary reception of words triggers stories that are connected to mythical figures and ideologies of motherhood.

These representations underscore how the psychoanalytic discourses that permeate Buenos Aires and Argentina more broadly are founded on psychoanalysis as a genre of listening. Even in its textual form, psychoanalysis entails a huge component of listening. When Gabriel Rolón and Verónica Lozano discuss the behavior of people, or when Tute explains how his creative process resembles psychoanalysis, or when Sehinkman "analyzes" the evening news, psychoanalytic listening is strongly present. As a "social fact" in Buenos Aires, psychoanalytic listening as a genre is reproduced in numerous forms and places and with semiotic chains that can be traced all the way back to Freud—even though, in many cases, this listening genre has become so accepted and pervasive that the chains have become blurred.

Conclusion
Final Resonances

As I write these closing remarks, the COVID-19 pandemic has taken over the world. The first months, when lockdown policies were enforced, people began to notice changes in their everyday soundscapes. Some of the sounds they were accustomed to hearing, such as those coming from planes or honking cars, suddenly disappeared. New sounds surfaced instead: the singing of birds, the crushing of leaves, our own steps. Things appeared to be different. Sounds are part of our everyday life, and in their absence, our sense of normalcy was called into question.

The first difference I noticed in my usual soundscape came through the mundane experience of watching a *fútbol* game. When the Fédération Internationale de Football Association (FIFA) allowed tournaments to resume, it decided that no members of the public would be present in the stadiums. The first game after lockdown was on Saturday, May 16, 2020, between Borussia Dortmund and FC Schalke 04 for the German Bundesliga. During the televised game, instead of listening to the usual roar of fans, the spectator was left to hear lone sounds: coaches yelling instructions and players cursing and shrieking in pain when they were fouled. It was disorienting but also boring. Without the usual and expected sounds, the experience changed completely because the whistles, chants, and murmurs produced by the fans are intrinsic to the experience of watching a game. The attention shifted from the plays to individualized sounds. After the first few games, some clubs decided to artificially add to the broadcast recorded ambient sounds, such as celebrations and booing, that one would expect on the soc-cer field—with varying degrees of intensity, depending on the development of the match. With the added sounds, the games felt "normal" again, and, in fact, the attention went back to the plays. And yet there is something eerie in experiencing a game with a standardized, false ambient sound.

It was evident that without the expected soundscape the games would be experienced differently, and this accentuates how listening affects our apprehension of the world, without our even knowing it, by helping us to direct our attention. Listening to sounds has this capacity, and when the practice of listening becomes regular, genres of listening emerge, helping to anchor different social interactions. The pandemic has shown us in a direct way that listening structures social relations—in some cases, more than language does. Whether through the mastery of a particular listening genre, like the one described in this book, or by just following the systematic and habituating trail of diverse sounds, the act of listening serves as a cohesive force basting together a diversity of social situations. Absent this basting, the uncanny emerges because we forget the extraordinary structuring ca-pacity that listening generates.

In Buenos Aires, lockdown was incredibly strict for about four months after the first cases of the virus were detected in Argentina.[1] The govern-ment implemented Aislamiento Social Preventivo y Obligatorio (Preven-tive and Compulsory Social Isolation or ASPO in its Spanish acronym), and *porteños* needed a permit to go anywhere except to buy food. If caught roaming without a permit, the transgressor would be fined and also risk the embarrassment of being called a *boludo* (asshole) by passersby, as early videos showed.[2] The lockdown was effective in keeping the number of infections very low, compared to neighboring countries. And during this time, dozens of articles appeared in newspapers, magazines, and academic journals analyz-ing and explaining the problems generated by social isolation, many of them focused particularly on the psyche. Written in the heat of the social and in-dividual symptoms of the pandemic, some augured the end of an era—a para-digm shift—projecting either pessimistic or optimistic versions of the society to come. The former involved evaluation of the authoritarian trends that the containment of the pandemic would generate (see, for example, Orozco 2020; Salvatto 2020) or discussed how the sanitary distances that were im-posed between bodies influenced affects and the psyche (Canet-Juric et al. 2020; Chire-Saire and Mahmood 2020; Verztman and Romão-Dias 2020).

According to different sources (Antón 2020; Frittaoni 2020), the search for online psychotherapy in the whole country has increased at least

20 percent during the pandemic. This number does not include regular analysands who have continued their sessions using this "debated" new format.[3] Loneliness appears as the main problem of the confinement, presented as *más mortal que el virus* (deadlier than the virus). But another perspective comes from my friend Marcelo, who lives alone in Buenos Aires and who joked that he doesn't feel isolated because lockdown has made him listen to himself: "At all times I find myself listening to my inner dialogue. So, I don't feel that lonely because it feels as if I have company [*laughter*]." I asked if he could expand on this process, and he replied, in a serious tone, "It's like reviewing different moments of my life and understanding in a better way why I behave in a certain way." After a pause, he continued, "I think I finally hear what my analyst has been hearing all these years."

In this book, I describe a particular form of listening that emerges through dialogical encounters between speakers. I explain that what *porteños* are listening to is "that which is not said" but which is implied as they resonate with the speaker's statement. This is an embodied form of listening expressed by the reported speech formula *When you say x, I hear y* (*What you really mean is . . .*). Marcelo has been to psychoanalysis off and on for the past ten years, so he has been exposed to psychoanalytic listening for a long period of time and therefore is capable of finding this resonance in a dialogic relationship within his inner speech. In other words, he has habituated his listening practice to pay attention not only to external sounds but also to internal dialogue, a practice that he says has been nurtured by the pandemic. I asked how that differs from thinking and having an inner dialogue with oneself—a common practice among many people. He answered, "Every time we think or read, we listen to ourselves, so in that way it is similar. But I go beyond the meaning of the words and try to experience rather than reasoning—that's the difference." With the lack of "live" interlocutors, one has to ask whether experiences such as Marcelo's (or Adriana's, in chapter 3), in which listening habits within a psychoanalytic framework promote internal resonances, are common among *porteños* in lockdown. In a *culture of listeners*, such as the one that exists in Buenos Aires, the lines between the expert listener, the analyst, and the common listener became blurred. There is no passive reception of professional knowledge but a constant reproduction of it (Briggs and Hallin 2016; Carr 2010a).

The pandemic seems to have fostered the doxic idea that psychoanalysis and psychotherapy are "everywhere" in Argentina. Rafael, an established analyst, told me that "the pandemic created and accentuated many mental disorders; but in comparison with Spain, where the psychological help rose 200 percent in the past months, here [in Argentina] we don't see that number because we have been taking care of our mental health for a long time. We are a culture of listeners, and we have continued to do so with new means [online platforms]."[4] Centro DITEM, where multifamily sessions are conducted, has a similar outlook; in a long letter posted on their Facebook page on May 5, 2020, the center explained that they would remain open through virtual sessions, and in-person visits would be available only for crises. Corroborating Rafael's stance, they stated, "The average attendance for our virtual groups is 65 people per day. This number is higher than those who attend in person. The explanation for this is simple: there was a notable increase in the number of family members participating in our meetings. The same happens with the classes that are given weekly [at the center] for the professionals doing specialization internships."[5]

Centro DITEM began conducting online MFSPT sessions through the Google Meet platform during the summer months of 2020 and has continued to do so. Many patients and analysands commented via a Facebook thread on the importance of mental health services during lockdown. These ideas echoed the plea to the government by mental health providers to be considered "essential workers." An article titled "COVID-19: Los psicólogos piden ser declarados personal esencial de salud" (COVID-19: Psychologists ask to be declared essential health workers), published on June 25, 2020, in the newspaper *La Nación*, quotes Jorge A. Biglieri, dean of psychology at UBA, as complaining that the government was focused only on stopping the spread of the virus without taking into account "a conception of health in bio-psycho-social terms." Biglieri warns that "this biological reductionism produces a dangerous underestimation of the psychological and social effects of the Preventive and Compulsory Social Isolation (ASPO)" (Polack 2020).

The cultural milieu in Buenos Aires continued disseminating psychoanalytic ideas in spite of the pandemic. On August 16, 2020, psychoanalyst, actor, and theater producer Pablo Zunino, who for eight consecutive years produced and directed the successful play *El Dr. Lacan*, released an online representation of his new play, *Herr Professor Freud*. Inspired by Freud's daughter, who died during the 1918–19 influenza outbreak, Zunino tried to imagine Freud living through a different pandemic. In the play, Freud (played by Zunino) is represented as a modern figure who tries to make sense of new technologies (e.g., Zoom) and new epistemes. The streaming of dramaturgy became an important way to keep people entertained while at the same time keeping actors, producers, and directors employed. On July 18, Gabriel Rolón began streaming *Entrevista abierta* (Open interview), a "play" that he has been performing off and on for the past six years in different theaters around Argentina and neighboring countries. In these presentations, Rolón opens with a monologue about Freud, Lacan, and "philosophical" questions about love, fear, rancor, and the like. After the monologue the public asks questions, and Rolón answers them in the order received. In the streaming version, his wife, Cynthia Wila—a writer and actress—helped compile the online questions and find the common thread. (Access to the streaming cost five hundred pesos, the equivalent of six US dollars.) Although they belong to different domains, it is hard not to draw comparisons between Rolón's *Entrevista abierta* and the MFSPT, where the resonances of the participants' comments and questions trigger particular interventions and where a common theme is expected to emerge from the resonances. Another similarity is Rolón's emphasis that participants should "*escucharnos los unos a los otros*" (listen to one another) to mobilize affective entanglements.[6] The mediatization and circulation of psychoanalytic discourses have continued to flourish during the pandemic. The mediatized nature of communication has expanded the propinquity and frequency of psychoanalytic encounters and discourses. And listening continues to be invoked as the most important tool to help navigate lockdown.

Rolón thinks that Argentina is unique in the way its people are prompted to listen to one another. In a June 2020 interview with Alejandro Fantino, Rolón (2020) told the story of being at a party in Spain and seeing a woman sitting by herself. Rolón approached the woman and asked if she was OK. The woman was perplexed and responded that she was surrounded by friends but that no one at the party, except Rolón—a stranger—had asked if she was OK. Then she said, "No, I'm not OK. How did you notice?" Rolón answered, "I just saw you." Rolón then tells Fantino, "Because corporal language is also there to be listened to. And she said, 'Well, here nobody asked,' and I told her, 'If you lived in my country, we would have asked you ten times.'" He continued:

GR: Because we Argentines are more attentive to this. Our history has forced us to be attentive to this, Ale. Because when your grandfather came here, you know who he had next to him? A stranger, a stranger who at best spoke in Turkish, spoke in Arabic.

AF: This is great, that is to say, do you believe that the history of Argentinean migration forced us to be more attentive to the person next to us?

GR: Of course!

Rolón is reproducing folk theories about why psychoanalysis is so prevalent in Buenos Aires, which include the belief that because Argentines "come from ships" and "don't have a motherland," they have developed a collective trauma that needs resolution, which psychoanalysis can help provide. Rolón adds another reason why his country has a culture of listeners: the first migrants to what is now Argentina lacked linguistic competency. Therefore, attention to what the other was saying became an intrinsic trait of Argentines, who can listen to the body even before it speaks, as Rolón himself demonstrated when he saw the Spanish woman sitting by herself.

The pandemic has thus reinforced discourses about Argentine exceptionality in regard to being rightful consumers of mental health services. As psychologist Iafi Shpirer told Maya Siminovich in an interview for *Fuente Latina*, "People have to fight to maintain this unnatural sense of communicating online, of talking on the phone, of listening." Yet Shpirer believes talking and listening will be easy for Argentines because they like to share "personal stories" and do not hesitate to "talk about themselves" (Siminovich 2020). The commonsensical idea that Argentines like to share intimate aspects of their lives in conjunction with going to analysis on a regular basis is portrayed in a comic strip by graphic humorist Esteban Podetti (figure C.1). The strip, published on his Facebook page, depicts a woman lying on the analytic couch and expressing concern about the new terms and conditions allowing WhatsApp to share information with Facebook. The woman then explains that she alone possesses information about herself and, referring to the conspiracy theories and fake news that circulate on social media, says that she does not understand why "The New Order" wants her data. She is interrupted by the analyst, who verbally abuses her, calls her stupid, explains that she is a nobody and that Facebook wants to steal information only from important people, and then sends her home. In the final vignette, the analyst hands Facebook CEO Mark Zuckerberg an envelope and tells him, "Here is the data of Mrs. Paola, even her erotic dreams, Mark! All the dirt. Very good distracting maneuver on the part of *Guasap* [phonetic Spanish pronunciation of WhatsApp]! Nobody suspects where you get the info!"[7]

The idea that social media giants can get information about their customers through their psychoanalytic encounters is something that, as my good friend Daniel said, "can only happen in Argentina." But Daniel is not the only *porteño* who thinks that people in Buenos Aires have a tendency to "overshare" personal information, whether with their analysts, friends,

FIGURE C.1 *La Embarazada Mala*, by Esteban Podetti (2021). Courtesy of Esteban Podetti.

or even strangers. In the article "Why Argentinians May Be Finding Social Distancing Harder than the Rest of Us," published on April 23, 2020, in the national British newspaper the *Daily Telegraph*, reporter Clare Wiley explains that a longitudinal study of forty-two countries conducted in 2017 revealed Argentina as the country where people require the least amount of personal space to feel comfortable: two and a half feet away from strangers, much less than any other country.[8] Wiley quotes tango dancer Alejandro Gée, who explains that the embrace of physical contact by Argentines is a deeply ingrained part of the culture that also expresses itself in emotional openness: "You go to the market and there's someone you don't know, they start telling you about how they broke up with their boyfriend or girlfriend and they're crying. That's completely accepted, it's normal, nobody freaks out. Someone cries, someone is laughing—then they invite you to dinner and you don't even know them." I experienced firsthand the sociability Gée describes, where Argentines communicate aspects of their intimate lives with strangers. *Porteños* were interested in what I had to say, and in many cases they went beyond the denotation of my words to listen to "that which is not said" but which was implied in my words, regardless of how close we were. Argentina is a country of listeners, and the dialogic relationships that emerge through the attention placed on words, silences, and resonances are an undisputable fact in how *porteños* communicate.

The pandemic has given a boost and visibility to the importance of mental health to counterattack some of the psychosocial scarring that lockdown practices generate, and the importance of listening to each other reverberates throughout media outlets, casual conversations, and official news. Only time will tell whether psychoanalysis/psychotherapy will continue to have the important presence it currently has; but what is certain is that fundamental discourses based on psychoanalysis—the idea that unconscious practices guide structural aspects of our behavior, that talking about your personal ailments helps ease some of their immediate effects, and that listening to one another is the key to counteracting the psychic hurdles brought on by the pandemic—continue to circulate with a strong force in Buenos Aires today.

The city of Buenos Aires serves as a great case study to understand several aspects of listening because of the permeability of psychoanalytic listening as a genre. Through the close examination of the circulation of this genre of listening, this book presents different properties of listening that can be analyzed beyond the Argentinean context. First, listening is highly structured: no matter the setting, there is always a pattern in any listening act. Second, listening is not always automatic: many listening practices are learned and take time to master. Third, listening is multimodal: it can be deployed differently, generating an array of outcomes depending on how it is contextualized. Fourth, it is performative: it creates social roles, as when expert listeners, such as the psychoanalysts examined in this book, or anthropologists perform their social positionality by listening within a particular genre of listening. Fifth, listening provides directionality, helping the hearer to focus on particular actions and not on others—as I observed while watching a soccer game during the pandemic—or when "earslips" and mondegreens emerge, helping us to give sense to nonsensical sounds and thus to establish a meaning about indiscernible sounds. Last, listening has a perlocutionary force (as language does). Sounds sometimes linger and will find a referent at a later time after other sounds or words are heard; this aspect is crucial to psychoanalytic listening, since its goal is to disentangle the aural residues that accumulate throughout one's lifetime.

In this book I maintain that listening is one of the main channels from which psychoanalysis circulates in Buenos Aires. Psychoanalytic listening's prevalence is due to its exposure through the media, through the household, when family members discuss their own therapy sessions or are themselves analysts, and through going to analysis. This exposure has resulted in a culture of listeners interested in and willing to participate in the well-being of others. I purposely resisted analyzing the *What you really mean is* . . . reported speech as a form of power, as an imposition. Following philosopher Enrique Dussel (1973, 54), who discusses what he calls an "ontological generosity" when intersubjective encounters occur, I understand the *When you say X, I hear Y* dialogical exchange as based, most of the time, on a genuine effort to help subjects listen to themselves. Rather than just meddle in someone else's business, the lay listener challenges liberal ideas of atomized, self-sufficient individuals who master their own words and make them transparently reference their inner intentions, which can also be distinguished from their social and material being (Carr 2010a; Keane 2001). I understand this dialogical relationship as a way in which the psyche is connected to others, and I view the intervention on the part of the lay listener as a form of symbolic exchange.

The question of why some aspects of Argentina's sociability rely on psychoanalytic premises still puzzles many people. United States psychologist Martin Seligman, best known for his "positive psychology" approach—a methodology aimed at creating a science that investigates human qualities such as strength, virtue, and happiness—contends that psychoanalysis is, in fact, a negative methodology.[9] In a 2021 interview in *La Nación* newspaper, Seligman asked the interviewer—who had not even mentioned the subject—whether Argentina is finally leaving behind its "obsession" with psychoanalysis. The interviewer, in turn, inquired why he asked that question, and Seligman responded: "It would be good to know why Argentina is so psychoanalytic. Somehow, psychoanalytic thinking focuses on itself, paralyzing individuals, while modern cognitive-behavioral psychology deals with skills that help overcome problems in the external world. Perhaps it is that the psychoanalytic gaze aims at deep change. And there is something in the Argentine soul that appeals to a deeply underlying and self-paralyzing vision. I have wondered that about Argentina for almost 30 years now" (Mon 2021).[10]

Here Seligman contradicts the idea discussed in this book about the psyche as connected to others and qualifies going "deep" into one's consciousness as a paralyzing endeavor. There are in this view resonances of a liberal idea by which, in order to overcome problems, sufferers must adhere to an active methodology of optimism that, little by little, will liberate them from negative ideas. The paradigm of self-sufficiency is evident in Seligman's critique of psychoanalysis. Moreover, he inadvertently replicates common folk theories that depict Argentines as somber, sad, and melancholic, which are reflected in what he sees as the self-absorbed, paralyzing attitude that psychoanalysis fosters. The myth of Argentines as melancholic typically centers on their penchant for tango music, depicted as a gloomy genre, or the longing for a motherland. Others grieve a country that supposedly was, once upon a time, an economic powerhouse before its current decline. Now Seligman adds psychoanalysis as a possible trait to the mournful depiction of Argentines. That this was written in early 2021 underscores how psychoanalysis continues to be a referent in discussions of Argentina. Psychoanalysis is thus still attached to the idea of Argentina and continues to generate speculation about the "true" nature of the Argentine character, a favorite theme that has filled the country's literary and scholarly world for ages.[11]

Rather than pursue the ultimate cause that explains *why* psychoanalysis is so prevalent in Argentina, this book asks *how* it circulates and continues to reproduce itself in many different contexts by focusing on Buenos Aires as a culture of listeners. By analyzing listening as a genre, I hope to open the possibilities of expanding the examination of the different structures that listening generates and how these structures, which can be conceptualized as having boundaries—even if artificially delimited—create and sustain social relations. By studying how listeners resonate with the words of others, this book is a window into the crucial role that listening practices produce in creating identities and signifying the world.

NOTES

Introduction. A City of Listeners

1. Martin Heidegger (1962) would call this "being-in-the-world," grounded in a body in a world ready to occupy it in different ways.

2. A rich scholarship has focused, at least since the 1960s, on listening as a site of inquiry to understand social relationships. This interest began with artists/musicians such as Pierre Schaeffer and John Cage experimenting with the phenomenology of listening. Some recent representatives of this tradition are Becker 2004; Bull 2015; Horowitz 2012; Ihde 2007; Lacey 2013; Mikutta et al. 2014.

3. Another example of listening as an embodied practice can be found in Patrick Eisenlohr's *Sounding Islam* (2018). Through his analysis of "sounding atmosphere," Eisenlohr focuses on the phenomenological experience of "energetic flows and movement in sonic events" during the appreciation of mediated Islamic sermons (4).

4. Original: "A vos te faltó afecto. Bueno, eso es lo que *a mí me sonó* lo que dijiste. Te faltó el abrazo, y yo me siento identificada con eso también."

5. Julia Kristeva (1984) refers to these two realms—what I call denotation and resonance—as the level of the geno-text or the semiotic, and the pheno-text or the symbolic. The latter refers to the language as syntax, while the semiotic refers to the bodily and affective realm of prelinguistic and drive-based primary processes. Thus, for Kristeva, Lacan's resonance belongs to the geno-text, as did my friend's embodied experience of how my words sounded.

6. Linguistic anthropologists and pragmaticians have discussed in detail the problems with the unmediated nature of language; most famously, Mikhail Bakhtin's (1981) conceptualizations of dialogism and heteroglossia point to the polyphony of voices and plurality of consciousness that each individual brings to every interaction. From a different epistemological perspective, Martin Heidegger (1962, 165–67) explains "they-qualities" where "everyone is the other, and no one is himself. The 'they,' which supplies the answer to the question of the 'who' of everyday Dasein, is the 'nobody' to whom every Dasein has already surrendered itself in Being."

7. An exploratory study in 2008 by Candelaria Escalante, then a student of psychology, and medical psychiatrist Eduardo Leiderman interviewed 1,510 people randomly on the streets of Buenos Aires's twenty-two neighborhoods and found that 15.6 percent were attending psychotherapy at the time of the interview, while 21 percent of the interviewees had attended psychotherapy in the previous year and 41.6 percent had attended psythotherapy in the previous two years (Escalante and Leiderman 2008).

8. Original: "Cuando te encontrás con un paciente que camina como araña, que gime en vez de hablar, y que tiene una enfermedad en la piel, lo primero que hay que hacer es medicar. Una vez que el paciente está estabilizado, ahí hablar empieza a ser importante. Y ahí es cuando volvés a conceptos como desplazamiento, infancia, trauma, etc. Yo creo que como médico tenés que trabajar con la historia del paciente. Nosotros también curamos con la palabra."

9. In their book *The Transnational Unconscious: Essays in the History of Psychoanalysis and Transnationalism* (2009), Joy Damousi and Mariano Plotkin explain in detail how Buenos Aires became the epicenter of the diffusion of Lacanian psychoanalysis and how representatives of European institutions journeyed to Buenos Aires to be trained by Argentine analysts.

Chapter 1. For a Theory of Genres of Listening

1. Previous to Akhtar's work, Richard D. Chessick (1982) describes the importance of listening within the clinical setting.

2. Phenomenological approaches to listening do not consider a separation between listening and hearing. Listening is considered part of the intersubjective experience (see Duranti 2015) and thus is already mediated by the intentionality of the listener.

3. According to Chion (2012), this mode of listening has been the object of linguistic research. One crucial finding is that it is purely differential. A phoneme is listened to not strictly for its acoustical properties but as a part of an entire system of oppositions and differences.

4. For a comprehensive, historical, and critical analysis of the stethoscope, see Foucault 1977, 1986; Sterne 2001. For sounds inside hospitals and clinics, see Rice 2013. In the specific case of the medical realm, auscultation situates the body as "eloquent irrespective of its owner's capacity to speak" (Rice 2013, 64). The subjective experience of the patient is relegated second to the language of the body itself. Sounds are isolated and then treated as objective diagnostic signs. Consequently, when Foucault ([1973] 2008) discusses the emergence of the "medical gaze," he recognizes the importance of listening and touching as particular technologies of power that create subjugation, hierarchies, and social identities. There is a performative transformation inside the clinic through auscultation, which is multimodal in nature, involving language, touching, listening, and external signs that range from patients' robes to machinery.

5. Pragmatics is the branch of linguistics dealing with language in use and the contexts in which it is used, including such matters as deixis, the taking of turns in conversation, text organization, presupposition, and implicature.

6. I am referring to intentionality as proposed by Edmund Husserl (1982), who emphasizes the role of the agent in giving meaning to objects, people, events, etc., through what he calls "intentional acts," which in turn modify the agent's perception of the world (i.e., seeing, hearing, smelling, etc.). See Sokolowski 1964, 57.

7. Consciousness is not the defining element of psychoanalytic listening; on the contrary, listening through a psychoanalytic framework entails a sort of suspension of a conscious response. The consciousness of deciphering a sound through its semiotic imprint comes from the fact that sounds will always be attached to a referent when first heard.

8. An example of the contextual nature of listening can be seen when conscious judgment stops being involved in the act of listening and hallucinatory voices or sounds have the potential to emerge. If these are codified as pathological, this situation might be described as a schizophrenic auditory delusion. But if the sounds that surpass the conscious realm are heard in the context of a religious ceremony—where listening to the voice of God is the ultimate goal—far from being pathological, these sounds are regarded as a successful fulfillment of the ceremony (Schmidt 2000; see also Jaynes 1982; Freud [1923] 1995).

9. The idea that listening is able to produce a transformative force inside the social world has been explored by various scholars who began to inquire into other sensorial forms as a way of approaching culture, intending to limit the famous "textual paradigm" posed by James Clifford and George Marcus (1986) in the book *Writing Culture*. In *Hearing Cultures*—a play on the title of Clifford and Marcus's text—Veit Erlmann (2004) and other scholars call for the cultural and historical contextualization of auditory perception, paying attention to interaction through the sense of hearing in all its different capacities (see Bull and Back 2003; Feld 1982, 2017; Rice 2013).

10. Listening to sermons has yet another capacity, the gift of relaxation, peacefulness, and the enhancing of the listener's competence for discernment in the face of moral danger (Hirschkind 2006, 73). This particularity of listening relates to studies about how music is capable of transporting listeners into a different emotional estate (Juslin and Sloboda 2010; D. Schwarz 1997). Listening thus poses the capacity to constitute social roles, to direct action, and to transform the senses in ways that no other phenomena could perform.

11. I understand that "setting boundaries" to listening practices might be conceived of as naive, since many scholars have explained in detail why extracting and objectivizing a portion of ongoing social action and turning it into "blocks or atoms of shared culture" (Silverstein and Urban 1996, 1), and thus creating shareable and transmittable culture, decontextualize meaning, inserting it in a new context carrying meaning that is independent of the previous situation (see Silverstein and Urban 1996). All the studies in intertextual-

ity also point to the impossibility of isolating a particular text from other discursive/ textual formations (Barthes 1975; Bauman and Briggs 1990; Kristeva, Rey-Debove, and Umike-Sebeok 1971). I am aware that setting a boundary to listening practices is an artificial and problematic conceptualization. Yet, in order to begin to explore how listening transforms and creates social situations, I find it important to analyze listening practices as genres, and differentiate among them, as a useful tool to begin to understand how listening is a dynamic and transformative activity providing directionality.

12. For poetic structure, see Banti and Giannattasio 2004; Bauman 1986; Bauman and Briggs 1990; Bauman and Sherzer 1975; Briggs 1993; Jakobson 1960. For literary theory, see Bakhtin 1981, 1986; Barthes 1975; Jauss 1974, 1982; Todorov 1980. For music genres, see Kivy 2001; Rentfrow and McDonald 2010. For practice theory, see Hanks 1987.

13. According to Susan Ervin-Tripp (1972, 233), there are two dimensions of language structural co-occurrence: the horizontal and the vertical. Horizontal co-occurrence rules specify "relations between items sequentially in the discourse." This refers to the same level of language structure and follows a diachronic course. Vertical co-occurrence refers to predictability across the structural levels of language (selection of syntax, phonemic rules). The idea is that when the vertical axis is combined with the horizontal rules, the selection of the vertical (lexical terms, phonetics) would also affect future (horizontal) choices. Co-occurrence pertains to grammatical rules, but for it to "work," it has to be inserted into the social world.

14. An example is the emergence of the "fantastic genre" presented by Tzvetan Todorov (1980). In this form, the reader must be suspended between a "naturalistic and a super-natural" explanation in order for the genre to become visible. This idea is interesting because it hinges on a moment of hesitancy where the reader is confronted with not knowing what to make of a particular reading: "The fantastic occupies the duration of this uncertainty.... The fantastic *is that hesitation* experienced by a person who knows only the laws of nature, confronting an apparently supernatural event" (25; emphasis added). To exist within the text, then, the fantastic requires the fulfillment of three conditions in which the reader takes an active role.

15. Co-occurrence creates what Asif Agha and Frog (2015, 35) call "cultural models of 'kinds of persons' that shape the speech varieties felt to be appropriate in interact- ing with them." Listeners have definite expectations of just which forms of utterances may follow and which may not; they are capable of recognizing a style (or code) shift through recognizing language forms as patterns and through associating those patterns with social contexts of speaking.

16. For example, for Hans Jauss (1982, 94), genres are to be understood not as genera (classes) but rather as groups of historical families: "If one follows the fundamental rule of the historicization of the concept of form, and sees the history of literary genres as a temporal process of the continual founding and altering of horizons, then the metaphorics of the courses of development function, and decay can be replaced by the nonteleological concept of the playing out of a limited number of possibilities." Through his conceptualization of what he described as a "pre-constituted horizon of

expectations" available to a person experiencing a work of art (rezeptionsästhetik) (Jauss 1974, 285), a basic situation model emerges, helping to delineate the process of reception.

17. See Marsilli-Vargas 2014.

18. The process of inference is coconstituted between the analyst and the analysand. The analysand brings to the encounter a particular frame, the product of individual experience, and the analyst makes sense of it through a dialectic process between what it says and what is inferred.

19. *Cathetic energy* is a phrase generally used to describe various psychic impulses in terms of energy.

20. Isakower was a famous Viennese psychoanalyst (and later nationalized American) who is mostly famous for his contribution to the hypnagogic states while falling asleep, which later became known as the "Isakower phenomena" (see Townsend 1992).

21. Receptors for two sensory modalities (hearing and equilibrium) are housed in the ear. The external ear, the middle ear, and the cochlea of the inner ear are involved with hearing. The semicircular canals, the utricle, and the saccule of the inner ear are involved with equilibrium. Both hearing and equilibrium rely on a very specialized type of receptor called a hair cell (Barrett et al. 2015, chap. 10).

22. Moreover, a purely optical sense impression would not be able to account for the formation of logical or ethical judgment, as the auditory sphere does. According to Anne Karpf in her book *The Human Voice* (2006), the audio responsiveness of unborn infants to some sounds can be detected as early as fourteen weeks, at which point they can distinguish between male and female voices and, from within a group of people, can recognize their mother speaking and so be soothed or excited by her voice. Karpf explains that until the child is four years old, listening/hearing is the most important sense until another—vision—takes its place.

23. One of the techniques that Freud postulated as key for the recollection of relevant information is to develop a particular kind of attention: *gleichschwebend*, or mobile attention (commonly translated as "free-floating attention"). The idea is to avoid the dangers of focusing the attention toward one particular point because doing so (Freud warns us) would provide a mirror of the analyst's own expectations or inclinations. Instead, the analyst should pay attention to every detail equally.

24. This idea is closer to Steven Feld's (2017) concept of acoustemology, where being and sounding are one and the same.

25. Pierre Schaeffer (1952), the famous French composer, musicologist, and acoustician, also dissected the processes of listening and hearing to understand when exactly attention emerges. The dichotomy of listening versus hearing entails different levels of engagement that he divided into four categories: (1) *Ouïr*, which refers to the pure physiological process of apprehending sound. This is a category of pure hearing, as vibrations enter the receiver's ear canal without being selected for interpretation. (2)

Écouter, which focuses on the objective qualities of sound and is therefore intentional: "Je écoute ce qui m'interesse" (I listen to that which interests me) (13). This category places attention at the center of the listening activity. (3) *Entendre* describes the process of attending to particular aspects of sound: "J'entends, comme une fonction de ce qui m'intéresse, de ce que je sais déjà et que je cherche à comprendre" (I hear, as a function of what interests me, from what I already know and what I seek to understand) (13). It entails identifying the different characteristics and specific properties of a particular sound. (4) *Comprendre,* which constitutes an engagement with sound and its external references: interpretation. *Comprendre* is the equivalent of reasoning, which Plato envisioned as one of the main characteristics of listening (Demers 2010; Schaeffer 1952).

26. Feld's (2017) work among the Kaluli of Papua New Guinea exemplifies the interdependence of being and sounding, "a knowing-with and knowing-through the audible" (84), where there is an inseparable relationship between the sounding of songs and the environmental consciousness they produce. Acoustemology helps us understand that listening is not a passive enterprise but rather a complex web of interrelated fields of perception in which there is no separation between listening, creating sounds, and nature itself.

Chapter 2. The Music in the Words

1. Original: "Esas voces que escucho señalan cada problema o mala decisión que he tomado, son ensordecedoras."

2. Original: "Creo Hugo, que estas voces que ahora empiezas a oír estuvieron ahí todo el tiempo. No estabas escuchando, pero condicionaron tu vida. Ahora que estás solo, te ves obligado a escuchar y a enfrentarte a ti mismo. Pero no te sientas mal, se te está dando la oportunidad de escuchar e intentar hacer las paces contigo mismo. Escucharte me hace darme cuenta de la importancia de prestar atención, de detenerme y escuchar. Si agudizamos nuestros oídos, seremos capaces de escucharnos a nosotros mismos y, con un poco de suerte, cambiar."

3. Original: "No sé, que no hago las cosas bien, que no logré muchos objetivos que me propuse ... pero a veces es más un sentimiento que una voz. ..."

4. Original: "Esto es lo que llamo memoria experiencial, sonidos violentos sin representación o palabras."

5. For many years the MFSPT sessions were held at APA and Centro DITEM. In 2016 they moved permanently to Centro DITEM. I attended sessions at both locations.

6. The concept of *doppelgänger* here is informed by its literary conceptualization, which poses the paradox of encountering oneself as another. Hence, it is a metaphor that symbolizes the repressed material that the analysand brings to the analytic session.

7. For a medical perspective on different debates about the efficacy of psychoanalysis, see Launer 2005.

8. Transference does have strong affects of love and hate, which operate on the imaginary, but Lacan stresses the structural or intersubjective relation that transference consists of. This is the level of the subject, the symbolic; and though the affects are strong, the transference does not consist of emotions. Later Lacan stresses transference love. This operates as resistance to the analytic work and is usually a love for knowledge. The analyst is taken as the subject of the signifier or the subject who is supposed to know. This too is transference that opposes the work, and that is why the analyst has to vacate such a position in the countertransference relation. See Lacan 2015.

9. Original: "Basta por favor. Siento como que me estás acuchillando en el estómago. No puedo tolerar más tu maltrato" (Mitre 2016, 43).

10. Original: "De alguna manera, yo había logrado decirle a Andrés desde mi *verdadero self*, ya desidentificada de las presencias que me habían tenido atrapada a lo largo de muchos años, lo que no había podido decirle a mis padres. También tuve la oportunidad de descubrir que, de niña en mi casa, nunca supe defenderme ante situaciones de maltrato. Creo que esa escena vivencial, de la que los dos fuimos protagonistas, produjo un cambio psíquico en ambos" (Mitre 2016, 43).

11. Original: "Tenemos que escuchar desde lo vivencial. Si no uno solo llega a la realización intelectual del síntoma. Pero eso no te va a ayudar con el sufrimiento. Uno tiene que escuchar desde adentro, desde la experiencia vivida. Y eso es lo que experimentamos Andrés y yo. Andrés y yo escuchamos más allá de las palabras, aunque las palabras importan."

12. Henri Ey (1900–77) was an important French psychiatrist, psychoanalyst, and philosopher. In 1934 he developed the theory of "organo-dynamism," a materialistic approach to the psyche that combines organic elements with psychic energy. French psychiatrist Paul Guiraud (1882–1974) worked closely with Ey. His writings on delirium and his handbooks of general psychiatry were some of the most influential books of the time. See, among many, Guiraud 1922, 1925; Guiraud and Ey 1926.

13. My own research experience working with other psychoanalysts who participate in the MSPT also attests to the absolute faith that these therapists have in the groups. According to some, their belief in its therapeutic value is backed up by numbers. I could not find specific figures on how many schizophrenic cases have ameliorated through MFSPT therapy sessions. Most of the analysts who attend the APA sessions work at hospitals, clinics, and their own practice. It is mostly through the recounting of success stories that one can speculate that the treatment is, in fact, effective.

14. There are approximately thirty-two registered psychoanalytic associations throughout Argentina.

15. Ángel Garma Institute is the APA's main training organism, where aspiring analysts receive their education through a tripartite model: analysis, supervision, and seminars. The institute is named for Ángel Garma Zubizarreta (1904–93), a Spanish psychiatrist and psychoanalyst, and later a nationalized Argentine, who founded the Psychoanalytic

Institute of Buenos Aires in 1945 and created the psychology BA at the National University in 1957.

16. The sessions are always recorded through the microphone into a stereo, but I used my own digital recorder.

17. Rigid designators (in particular proper names) play a crucial role inside these encounters by establishing a relationship between the speakers and the listeners.

18. Jorge García Badaracco died September 11, 2010. In part because his death was so recent, and in part because he attended every MFSPT session until his health no longer allowed him to continue, those attending the meetings spoke of him often.

19. This idea is very similar to Lacan's chain of signifiers, in which one signifier will lead to another and so on. García Badaracco studied with Lacan, and thus there are many references to him in his work.

20. The names of the participants have been changed to protect their identities.

21. Original: "Mi nombre es Juan y he estado viniendo a las reuniones hace un año más o menos, y nunca he hablado antes. Es muy triste escuchar la historia de la señora. Evidentemente ella quiere decirnos algo, *si tan solo pudiéramos escuchar lo que quiere decir, lo que significa.* Pero la señora repite la misma historia sin producir ningún efecto."

22. Original: "Juan, lo primero es que estoy sorprendido por el 'Adela siempre repite la misma cosa, y no produce ningún efecto.' ¡Hoy te hizo hablar [risas] por primera vez! ¡Genial! Algo pasó en el que su insistente discurso finalmente encontró una respuesta. Porque vos pensaste 'tengo que decir algo.' Así que ella no está tan *equivocada al insistir en ser escuchada, porque al final, alguien la va a escuchar.*)"

23. Original: "*Hubo un momento en el que pude escuchar*, y pude ver que estaba equivocado, y que he estado equivocado por mucho tiempo. Estaba equivocado porque la verdad es que *no podía escuchar.* Y aquí [en la MFSPT], *me enseñaron cómo* [escuchar]. Porque cuando uno se deja llevar por un sentimiento, uno no puede pensar bien o escuchar. Y esa es la frase que uno debe llevarse a casa."

24. But the situated aspect that Lave and Wenger (1991) suggest carries some confusion. As they write, "On some occasions 'situated' means merely that some of people's thoughts and actions were located in space and time. On other occasions, it means that thought and action were social only in the narrow sense that they involve other people, or that they were immediately dependent for meaning on the social setting that occasioned them" (32).

25. Original: "La verdad es que ya no sé qué decir. Cada vez que voy a la casa de mi madre, lo único que oigo son quejas. No le gusta mi ropa, se molesta porque no la llamé a cierta hora. . . . El otro día incluso me dijo que estoy engordando. En fin, en sus ojos ¡yo no hago nada bien! Pero yo lo único que hago es laburar y laburar, me mantengo, pago mis cuentas con mi propia guita. Pero no sé, a veces pienso que no hago nada bien. El otro día en el laburo—como no puedo dejar de pensar en mis problemas—entregué

el presupuesto de la remodelación de un hotel en el Microcentro con un montón de errores. ¡No se pueden imaginar la vergüenza! ¿Qué va a pensar el cliente? ¡Que si no sé contar, no hay manera de que pueda participar en el proyecto remodelando! No he oído nada. ¡Obvio! Lo más seguro es que no quieren saber nada de mí, nunca jamás."

26. Original: "Lucía... yo, yo siento la necesidad de interrumpirte porque, porque... necesito que regresés. *La persona que está hablando no sos vos; es tu madre hablando, y necesito escucharte a vos, no a ella.* Te das cuenta ¿no? Vos desaparecés de la historia y solo escuchamos a tu madre hablando."

27. Original: "¿Sabés Lucía? Yo creo que la doctora está percibiendo algo correcto. Yo tampoco puedo reconocerte en lo que estás diciendo. Y ojo que esto no siempre es así, muchas veces cuando participás, está clarísimo que sos vos la que hablás. Pero hoy, no sé, *no me parece que la persona que estoy escuchando seas vos.*"

28. Original: "Sí, sí, a todos nos gusta echarle la culpa a cualquier otra cosa por nuestras desgracias en vez de verse a uno mismo. Eso es lo que tratamos de hacer aquí, mirar hacia dentro y parar el equipo de música."

29. Original: "Cuando hablamos con nuestros pacientes lo que es más importante para nosotros no es lo que dicen, sino cómo lo dicen. Nos enfocamos en la música en las palabras."

30. Original: "Ya estoy harto de los gobiernos que no hacen nada por nosotros. Uno que labura todo el día y que intenta como puede darle lo mejor a la familia. Los precios cambian todos los días, y yo ya no se cómo voy a hacer para sostener el negocio, mi familia, el tratamiento de Carlos. En la noche no duermo pensando en todas las responsabilidades que tengo y que no sé si voy a poder seguir sosteniendo. Todas las noches pensando en todo lo que se viene y yo haciéndome viejo."

31. Original: "Gonzalo, Gonzalo, esa música ya la escuchamos muchas veces. ¿Porque no nos decís cómo te sentís realmente? Dejá esa melodía que no te permite decir lo que realmente te pasa."

32. Original: "Y la verdad es que tengo mucho miedo. Yo no sé hacer otra cosa que no sea laburar. Me angustia pensar qué va a ser de mí cuando me jubile. No sé si me voy a poder reconocer en ese nuevo personaje. Me veo como un desvalido."

33. Original: "Escuchar a Gonzalo me recuerda de la necesidad de aprender a escuchar, de aprender a parar la música. La melodía de la que Diana hablaba estaba ocultando el verdadero miedo que está sintiendo. No es sobre el dinero; es sobre tener una nueva identidad y yo me identifico con ese sentimiento muy bien. Me retiré hace siete años y sigo la misma rutina de cuando trabajaba. Es difícil convertirse en alguien nuevo."

34. Lacan draws upon Freud's ([1900] 1953, 604) famous statement in *The Interpretation of Dreams*: "Dreams are the royal road to the unconscious." Lacan (1977, 45) substitutes *language* for *dreams*.

35. "¿Otra vez con esa canción, Marina?" "Rocío, ese discurso ya lo conocemos todos. ¿Podés hablar de lo que realmente te pasa?" "A mí me parece Rubén, que el ruido

que genera esa historia que te contás todos los días, no deja que el verdadero Rubén aflore." "Rosa, animáte a contarnos cómo te sentís. Queremos escuchar a la verdadera Rosa."

36. Lacan's theory of the Real, the Symbolic, and the Imaginary is too vast and has too many different interpretations to discuss in this section. The important thing to note is that for Lacan, the Real is impossible because it is impossible to imagine, to integrate into the symbolic order. This character of impossibility and resistance to symbolization lends the Real its traumatic quality.

Chapter 3. "What You Really Mean Is . . . "

1. Original: "No crean que buscan encarcelar a dirigentes políticos o dirigentes sindicales o sociales, como al compañero Juan Grabois hace poco. No buscan encarcelar dirigentes, ese será quizás un objeto de deseo lacaniano, como decimos nosotros acá. En realidad, lo que buscan es encarcelar las políticas de inclusión de participación y de inclusión que han desarrollado los gobiernos populares."

2. Original: "¿Quién otro, sino él, puede indagar qué es lo que implica que un dirigente gremial, concretamente Sergio Palazzo, bancario, haya citado, como citó, tan luego a Jacques Lacan, en pleno acto en Plaza de Mayo? Citó a Lacan, en efecto. Invocó su concepción del objeto de deseo, la planteó a la masa obrera que lo escuchaba al pie del palco."

3. The University of Buenos Aires is the oldest and most prestigious public institution in Argentina, providing free education to more than three hundred thousand students. Most of its budget comes from the federal government.

4. Original: "Un gesto claro dirigido desde el ámbito de los trabajadores hacia el ámbito del saber, para que, en el ámbito del saber, se reconozcan a su vez como trabajadores."

5. Original: "Quizás (y esto va en serio y con todo respeto) él percibió, o intuyó, que frente a la certeza delirante (otra expresión lacaniana con la que el narcisismo mauritocrático nos quiere marcar), frente a la negación de la realidad consuetudinaria con la que afirman que la inflación baja cada vez que los precios suben, o que es bueno perder el trabajo . . . el psicoanálisis sea, por qué no, una herramienta de resistencia, uno más de los caminos que nos permitan salir de esta extraña tormenta sedicente neoliberal."

Mauritocrático: an ironic play of words, combining the "meritocracy" praised by Macri and his first name, "Mauricio," when in fact he is the scion of one of the wealthiest families in Argentina.

6. I did not record this exchange, but I transcribed it right after it occurred to the best of my memory.

7. An important exception is Antoine Hennion (2001, 2010), whose analysis shows that amateurs' attachments and ways of apprehending music can both engage and form sub-

jectivities, rather than merely record social labels, and that their history is irreducible to the taste for works.

8. From a different epistemological perspective, philosopher Enrique Dussel (1973, 53) states, "To hear the voice of the Other, as another, provides an ethical openness." He continues, "In this manner the ethical conscience or metaphysical" is the "heart that knows to listen to the voice of the Other" (54). Dussel's ethical listening is neither an imposition nor an epistemic injustice; rather, it reflects an act of openness, something that Derrida (2005)—when analyzing the concept of *touching* in the work of philosopher Jean-Luc Nancy—conceptualized as an "ontological generosity." Listening to the voice of the Other implies advocating for the Other. Listening thus implies a form of care.

9. There are different epistemologies that may seem to frontally dismantle this idea. For example, Bakhtin's concept of "voice" and Goffman's "Face-Work" argue that there is no unified self. In the case of Goffman, rather than having a "unique" self, social actors perform rituals that help maintain our "interactional face" and thus perform many different social roles in every interaction. In Bakhtin's case, we as speakers are spoken through different social voices that inform our ideologies and worldviews. But psychoanalysis is not arguing against the idea that we are spoken through or that we perform many social roles unconsciously. The main proposition is that the experience of each individual is unique and helps to create an individual self.

10. Scholars interested in media studies have grappled with questions that connect the emergence of new technologies with particular epistemes. For example, in *Gramophone, Film, Typewriter*, Friedrich Kittler (1999) connects each media technology with Lacan's Real, Imaginary, and Symbolic. His main idea is that technologies are ontological and thus inseparable from being human. Walter Benjamin's famous "Work of Art in the Age of Mechanical Reproduction" ([1935] 1969) and Harold Innis's *Empire and Communications* ([1950] 2007) are other examples of scholars connecting modern subjectivities and new technologies.

11. Voloshinov (1973) showed how attitudes and social values shape the ways in which speakers report on someone else's speech. His classification system included direct (*oratio recta*), which evokes the original speech situation and conveys, or claims to convey, the exact words of the original speaker; indirect (*oratio obliqua*), which adapts the reported utterance to the speech situation of the report in indirect discourse (in this form, reporters relate the event from their point of view); and quasi-direct. The last one is difficult to define, and there have been different attempts to create terminology for it (see Coulmas 2011). Quasi-direct speech is phrased from the point of view of the narrator, but in terms of content, it belongs to the character's speech, thought, or perception.

Chapter 4. The Psychoanalytic Field in Buenos Aires

1. Original: "El psicoanálisis por lo tanto, no sería susceptible de ser analizado con las metodologías y herramientas analíticas propias de las ciencias sociales. Esta mirada ubica al psicoanálisis casi en lugar de un *a priori*, ya que se trataría de un objeto único y predeterminado, que solo admitiría distintas 'situaciones' en los distintos espacios culturales donde logró algún tipo de implantación."

2. It has been reported that after a strong immigration of Argentines to Spain during Argentina's military dictatorship, Lacanian psychoanalysis started to become prominent in Barcelona and Madrid (see G. García 2005; Izaguirre 2009).

3. A few years before the World Health Organization study, the American Psychological Association estimated an even smaller number for the United States: 27 per 100,000 inhabitants (Romero 2012).

4. Original: "Cada vez que hablo con gente de Francia, Italia, o España, me canso de explicarles que no hay tantos psicoanalistas en la Argentina. Es el único país en donde un psicólogo es llamado psicoanalista. En España, por ejemplo, hay sesenta mil, u ochenta mil psicólogos, ¿quién sabe? Pero ellos se llaman así mismo psicólogos, dicen 'soy un psicólogo clinico,' 'soy un psicologo conductista.'"

5. I am not trying to imply that people do not know the difference between these three fields, nor I am suggesting that there are no institutional differences. I am pointing to a linguistically interesting phenomenon where people use the same words to refer to dissimilar therapeutic situations. For a detailed analysis of the overlap of psychiatric, psychoanalytic, and psychology practices in public hospitals, see Vezzetti 1996; Visacovsky 2008.

6. For example, when the 2001 economic crisis erupted, psychoanalysts were asked to comment on possible reasons for the downturn. Their analyses used such terms as *narcissism* and *obsessive compulsive* to describe the causes of the economic collapse (see Bleichmar 2002; Plotkin and Visacovsky 2007). Diego Sehinkman (2014, 78), a psychologist, journalist, and the host of *Terapia de Noticias*, a program on the online channel of *La Nación* newspaper, likens Argentina to a patient with "borderline personality disorder. That is, someone who is emotionally unstable and, in this case, often seduced by strong but also abusive partners, or leaders." Izaguirre (2009) points to other examples when psychoanalysis intervened in politics, including a case in Brazil where a psychoanalyst was a torturer during the dictatorship and the role of psychoanalysis during Nazi Germany.

7. This term does not refer only to psychoanalysis. Many historians have used it to talk about aspects of Argentina that are considered different from other parts of Latin America.

8. From 1950 to 1960, Argentina ranked third in the world in the number of university students per one hundred thousand inhabitants (Germani and Sautu 1965).

9. The IPA is the world's primary accrediting and regulatory body for psychoanalysis. Its mission is to assure the continued vigor and development of psychoanalysis for the

benefit of patients. It was founded in 1910 by Sigmund Freud. Its first president was Carl Jung, and its first secretary was Otto Rank.

10. Women are still the dominant force behind psychology. An estimated 87 percent of registered psychology students are women (Alonso 2010). But institutional positions and successful private practices are equally distributed between men and women.

11. The idea of an inner self has been depicted by many scholars as the quintessential index of the modern subject (see Chakrabarty 2000; Deleuze and Guattari 1988; Gupta 2005; Inoue 2006).

12. See, for example, "Saber y autoridad: Intervenciones de psicoanalistas en torno a la crisis en la Argentina" (Plotkin and Visacovsky 2007), an examination of how psychoanalysis was used as a theoretical frame to explain the devastating economic crisis in Argentina in 2001.

13. For example, the late Silvia Bleichmar, famous psychoanalyst and author of the best-selling book *Dolor país* (which roughly translates as "country pain," in reference to the financial indicator "country risk," which was looming over Argentina in the economic crash of 2001), describes different economic crises in Argentina through a psychological lens.

14. *Revista de Filosofía* was a journal edited from 1915 to 1929 by José Ingenieros and his disciple Aníbal Ponce. It was a late product of biological positivism in Argentina that identified with the new climate of positivistic ideas that emerged in the early 1880s.

15. It should be noted that the IPA is considered by many historians and psychoanalysts to be a conservative institution.

16. Many psychoanalysts of the time participated in the Argentine Federation of Psychiatrists and in the groups Plataforma and Documento. These two groups resigned from the APA at the end of 1971, producing the first ideological rupture with the international psychoanalytic community, because they considered it to be at the service of the ruling classes. Plataforma led the separation and issued a statement addressing "mental health workers" and claiming resignation as the culmination of their line of work. Their intent was to organize a movement that included teaching, research, and assistance within the broad field of mental health from a perspective that analyzed unconscious determinants and the economic-political, and they urged psychoanalysts to take another place within the social, economic, and political process (Vainer 2014).

17. For an extensive analysis of Pavlovism, the Communist Party, and Argentina, see L. García 2016.

18. Marie Langer (1910–87) was an Austria-born Latin American psychoanalyst and human rights activist. She was a cofounder of the Argentine Psychoanalytic Association and one of the most important players in the dissemination of psychoanalysis in Argentina. José Itzigsohn was a psychiatrist and reflexologist who would later succeed José Bleger (one of the few psychoanalysts of the Communist Party) in teaching introduction to psychology at UBA (see Dagfal 2000).

19. Original: "Las clases de Bleger cautivaron desde el comienzo a un estudiantado tan ávido de una nueva psicología como de un compromiso social y político significativo. De este modo, los primeros psicólogos egresados de la UBA tuvieron una formación singular, que, entre otros autores, incluía a Freud y Marx, Adler y Jung, Klein y Lewin, Politzer y Lagache."

20. In "Psychoanalytic Technique," Freud ([1918] 2008) introduced the necessity of payment as a precondition to analysis. According to Freud, the absence of payment as a corrective force has serious consequences, since it would imply that analysis is beyond the real world.

21. Many psychoanalysts do not agree with the idea of using psychoanalysis outside of the clinical setting. In *The Four Fundamental Concepts*, Jacques Lacan (1998, 77) explicitly states, "Psychoanalysis is neither a Weltanschauung, nor a philosophy that claims to provide the key to the universe. It is governed by a particular aim, which is historically defined by the elaboration of the notion of the subject. It poses this notion in a new way, by leading the subject back to his signifying dependence." In Argentina, in spite of the opposition of many analysts, this definition does not apply.

22. Many students and professors explained that the master's degree is still in the process of getting the academic certification that other humanities degrees have.

23. The standardized test was implemented in 1988.

24. For Lacan, radical alterity, an otherness, transcends the illusion of otherness for the imaginary because it cannot be assimilated through identification. Lacan ([1966] 2006) equates this radical alterity with language and the law, and thus the big Other is inscribed in the order of the symbolic.

25. The expression *ad honorem* is actually used when talking about *concurrencias* at public hospitals and has a strong ideological semiotic value. It implies that the *concurrente* is invested in an honorific structure where material capital is relegated and where learning and care are prioritized.

26. It is important to note that I did not use the expression *ad honorem*. I specifically asked how he feels about working for five years at a hospital without a salary.

27. Both institutions have clinical sessions, but since they are closed to everyone except students and instructors, I did not have access to them.

28. Original: "[Los lacanianos] están inmersos dentro de una estructura jerárquica, y siempre lo van a estar, porque nadie sabe lo que dijo Lacan, ¡ni siquiera Lacan! Por lo tanto, el interlocutor, el traductor o la persona que 'cree saber' siempre estará en una posición de poder."

29. For examples of the many symbols and complexities of Lacan's mathematical semiology, see Florence 2011.

30. This anecdote is also found in Sinatra's book *Las entrevistas preliminares y la entrada en análisis* (2004).

31. To this day, the APA continues to provide strong clinical training, especially to women, who make up 85 percent of its students.

Chapter 5. The Mass Mediation of Psychoanalytic Listening

1. This is what Gabriel Rolón told Alejandro Fantino on the show *Animales sueltos*, aired on September 6, 2018.

2. Most recently, with the proliferation of new media technologies, analysts are using platforms such as Skype and WhatsApp to have analytic sessions with patients outside of their country of residence, thereby redefining what copresence means in the analytic encounter.

3. This is an important point, since the theories of Freud, Lacan, Klein, Miller, Jean Laplanche, and others vary greatly among them (see Frosh 1999; Gay 1988; Stolorow 2006).

4. The consumption of psychoanalysis in its clinical setting and its commoditized form (through mediatization) are bound up together in a dialectical relationship. They feed on each other, creating what Asif Agha (2011) calls "semiotic particles," the trail that forms a semiotic chain where one can trace how discourses are recycled and that travels through distinct mediums and different participation frameworks and cultural practices.

5. Arnaldo Rascovsky and Ángel Garma organized the Congress on Psychosomatic Medicine, and in 1960 Rascovsky was a founding member of the Latin American Psychoanalytic Federation (FEPAL).

6. "Una verdad que se esconde tras la barrera de la represión," Rolón, a self-proclaimed Lacanian analyst, uses the word *barrier* as a metaphor of Lacan's famous *barred subject*, the internal conflict that emerges in infants when the process of individuation begins.

7. In the book *Mafalda: Historia social y política*, historian Isabella Cosse (2015, 17) puts Mafalda in the same category as Ernesto "Che" Guevara (revolutionary icon), Carlos Gardel (the biggest tango star in Argentina), and Evita Péron (political and pop icon), saying that "without a doubt Mafalda is an Argentine icon. It is a figure and a strip with social, political and subjective meaning that cannot be ignored when it comes to understanding Argentines."

8. *Cortá por Lozano* is broadcast on Telefé, one of the main TV channels in Argentina. Covering a variety of subjects, the show is in the "magazine genre" and includes news, interviews, and humor. It premiered on January 23, 2017, and airs at five o'clock every afternoon. It is hosted by Verónica Lozano, a trained psychologist, who invites celebrities to be "analyzed" on air by sitting on a couch while she asks them questions. The show's title is a play on words, referring not only to the name of the host but to the phrase *cortar por lo sano*, which means to radically end a bothersome situation.

9. Here, Rolón diverges from the analysis proposed by literary critic Steve Connor (2009) (see chapter 1). In Connor's analysis, the mondegreen—the mishearing or misinterpretation of a nearly homophonic phrase—is the opposite of the Freudian slip because it serves to transform sound into meaning, while the Freudian slip does the opposite: transform meaning into nonsense. By contrast, Rolón is concerned not with sense but with the secret meaning that mishearings hide. Connor does not conceive of mondegreens as necessarily revealing a concealed meaning; rather, he is interested in how subjects always assign meaning to sound, whether or not they understand it. Rolón is interested in the possible "double" meaning of the mondegreen.

10. Freud developed psychoanalysis between 1895 and 1900 on the basis of his clinical experience with hysterical patients, most of them women. Hysteria as a female problem was a prominent subject of discourse during Freud's time. And, as the Fernet ad shows, the extension of these semiotic connections is still relevant today. For a feminist interpretation of hysteria in Freud, see Pierce 1989.

11. The positive Oedipus complex refers to a child's unconscious sexual desire for the opposite-sex parent and hatred for the same-sex parent. The negative Oedipus complex refers to a child's unconscious sexual desire for the same-sex parent and hatred for the opposite-sex parent. Freud considered that the child's identification with the same-sex parent is the successful outcome of the complex and that an unsuccessful outcome might lead to neurosis, pedophilia, and homosexuality.

12. Original: "¿Hace falta que te diga que me muero por tener algo contigo? ¿Es que no te has dado cuenta de lo mucho que me cuesta ser tu amigo? Ya no puedo acercarme a tu boca, sin deseártela de una manera loca. Necesito controlar tu vida, ver quién te besa y quién te abriga."

13. Original: "Complejo de Edipo XD," "Incesto Emocional," "Ayy el edipo," "¿El complejo de Edipo en un comercial con connotación sexual? ¿O yo ya estoy muy pervertido? :S."

Conclusion. Final Resonances

1. Unfortunately, after a few months of lockdown, the terrible economic legacy of former president Macri's government—combined with pressure from the opposition to the brand-new government of Alberto Fernández and irresponsible media coverage that misinformed the public and played down health policies—led Argentina to loosen lockdown enforcement, and by early 2021 the country had a very high infection rate.

2. In a highly publicized example of "bad behavior" during the pandemic, the TV channel *Crónica*—known for its sensationalist reporting—used the phrase "*habló el boludo*" (the asshole spoke) in covering the story of a "surfer" who broke quarantine rules (AN-Digital 2020).

3. Psychoanalysts have been debating for many years the use of media platforms to conduct remote psychoanalytic sessions. The younger generations of analysts tend to favor

these technologies, which allow them to reach people that do not have the means to travel or have obstacles that prevent them from going to a physical space for analysis. More conservative analysts argue that physical copresence is required for the *vínculo* (bond) to emerge between analyst and analysand and that these new technologies do not allow it to emerge.

4. Rafael is referring to news articles claiming that psychological services in Spain have grown 200 percent because of the pandemic (see Europa Press 2020).

5. Original: "La asistencia promedio a nuestros grupos virtuales es de 65 personas por día. Este número es superior a los que concurrían en modo presencial. La explicación de esto es sencilla: se produjo un incremento notable de familiares que participan en nuestros encuentros. Lo mismo pasa con las clases que semanalmente se dictan para los profesionales que están realizando pasantías de especialización en nuestro Centro."

6. In an interview with the newspaper *Página 12*, Rolón alludes to the therapeutic character of *Entrevista abierta* (Ranzani 2020).

7. Original: "¡Acá está la data de la señora Paola, incluso sus sueños eróticos Mark! Toda la mugre. ¡Muy buena maniobra distractoria de Guasap! ¡Nadie sospecha de donde recibís la info!"

8. The article refers to Sorokowska et al. 2017.

9. To understand the detrimental effects of the liberal ideology of positive psychology, see Cabanas and Illouz 2019.

10. Original: "Porque la Argentina es uno de los países más atrasados en el campo de la psicología positiva y el más 'casado' con el psicoanálisis, mientras que prácticamente todos los demás países importantes han abandonado el psicoanálisis. Sería bueno saber por qué la Argentina es tan psicoanalítica. De alguna manera, el pensamiento psico-analítico se centra en sí mismo, paralizando a los individuos, mientras que la psicología cognitivo-conductual moderna trata sobre habilidades que ayudan a superar problemas en el mundo externo. Acaso sea que la mirada psicoanalítica apunta al cambio profundo, y hay algo en el alma argentina que apela a una visión profundamente subyacente y auto-paralizante . . . Me he preguntado eso sobre la Argentina desde hace casi 30 años."

11. The dramatic inquiry into the very nature of Argentina and its people structured intellectual and political debates through interpretive texts, from *Civilización y Barbarie: Vida de Juan Facundo Quiroga* by Domingo Faustino Sarmiento ([1845] 2005) to *Radiografía de la Pampa* by Ezequiel Martínez Estrada ([1933] 2007), among others.

REFERENCES

Adams, Vincanne. 2016. *Metrics: What Counts in Global Health.* Durham, NC: Duke University Press.

Adorno, Theodor W. (1938) 1978. "On the Fetish-Character in Music and the Regression of Listening." In *The Essential Frankfurt School Reader,* edited by Andrew Arato and Eike Gebhardt, 270–99. New York: Urizen.

Agha, Asif. 2007. *Language and Social Relations.* Cambridge, UK: Cambridge University Press.

Agha, Asif. 2011. "Meet Mediatization." *Language and Communication,* no. 31: 163–70.

Agha, A., and Frog. 2015. *Registers of Communication.* Helsinki: Finnish Literature Society.

Akhtar, Salman. 2013. *Psychoanalytic Listening: Methods, Limits, and Innovations.* London: Karnac.

Alfandary, Isabelle. 2017. "The Function and Field of Scansion in Jacques Lacan's Poetics of Speech." *Paragraph* 40, no. 3: 368–82.

Alim, H. Samy, John R. Rickford, and Arnetha F. Ball. 2016. *Raciolinguistics: How Language Shapes Our Ideas about Race.* New York: Oxford University Press.

Alim, H. Samy, and Geneva Smitherman. 2012. *Articulate while Black: Barack Obama, Language, and Race in the U.S.* Oxford: Oxford University Press.

Alonso, Modesto. 2010. "Profesionales de la psicología en la República Argentina: Síntesis cuantitativa." *Anuario de investigaciones,* no. 17: 375–82.

Alonso, Modesto M., Paula Gago, and Doménica Klinar. 2015. "Los psicólogos en Argentina: Relevamiento cuantitativo." Poster presented at the VIII Congreso Internacional de Investigación y Práctica Profesional en Psicología, University of Buenos Aires, Buenos Aires, November 2015. https://www.researchgate.net /profile/Modesto-Alonso/publication/311703215_LOS_PSICOLOGOS_EN _ARGENTINA_Relevamiento_Cuantitativo_2015_Resultados_preliminares /links/58555c1808ae8f6955561605/LOS-PSICOLOGOS-EN-ARGENTINA -Relevamiento-Cuantitativo-2015-Resultados-preliminares.pdf.

Alonso, Modesto M., Paula Gago, and Doménica Klinar. 2018. "Distribución ocupacional de los psicólogos en Argentina." Poster presented at the IX Congreso Internacional de Investigación y Práctica Profesional en Psicología, University of Buenos Aires, Buenos Aires, December 2018. https://psicologossalta.com.ar /encuesta-nacional-de-distribucion-ocupacional-de-psicologos/.

Althusser, Louis. 1996. *Writings on Psychoanalysis: Freud and Lacan.* Edited by Olivier Corpet and Francois Matheron. Translated by Jeffrey Mehlman. New York: Columbia University Press.

Althusser, Louis, and Étienne Balabar. 1971. *Reading Capital.* London: New Left.

Anders, G. 2008. "The Normativity of Numbers: World Bank and IMF Conditionality." *PoLAR: Political and Legal Anthropology Review* 31, no. 2: 187–202.

Anderson, Benedict R. (1983) 2006. *Imagined Communities: Reflections on the Origin and Spread of Nationalism.* New York: Verso.

Anderson, Joan M. 1998. "Speaking of Illness: Issues of First Generation Canadian Women—Implications for Patient Education and Counseling." *Patient Education and Counseling* 33, no. 3: 197–207.

ANDigital. 2020. "Encuentran al surfer evasivo en Ostende: Está custodiado por 20 policías." *ANDigital,* March 25, 2020. https://www.andigital.com.ar/policiales-y -judiciales/item/84018-encuentran-al-surfer-evasivo-en-ostende-esta-custodiado -por-20-policias.

Antón, Marysol. 2020. "Terapias virtuales, psicólogos online: Cómo resuelven ahora los argentinos sus depresiones, miedos y ansiedades." *iProUP,* September 7. https://www.iproup.com/innovacion/16479-depresion-ansiedad-consultas-con -psicologos-y-psicoanalistas.

Asociación Psicoanalítica Argentina. 2018. "Tute en APA, con 'Humor al diván.'" You-Tube, September 14. https://www.youtube.com/watch?v=77-Qgh9914I.

Attali, Jacques. 1985. *Noise: The Political Economy of Music.* Minneapolis: University of Minnesota Press.

Austin, J. L. 1962. *How to Do Things with Words.* Cambridge, MA: Harvard University Press.

Avolio, Gisela. 2020. "Dos preguntas a Tute." *En el Margen,* July 1. https:// psicoanalisisalmargen.wordpress.com/2020/07/01/dos-preguntas-a-tute/.

Bakhtin, M. M. 1981. *The Dialogic Imagination: Four Essays.* Edited by Michael Holquist. Translated by Caryl Emerson and Michael Holquist. Austin: University of Texas Press.

Bakhtin, M. M. 1986. *Speech Genres and Other Late Essays.* Edited by Caryl Emerson and Michael Holquist. Translated by Vern McGee. Austin: University of Texas Press.

Balán, Jorge. 1991. *Cuéntame tu vida: Una biografía colectiva del psicoanálisis argentino.* Buenos Aires: Planeta.

Banti, Giorgio, and Francesco Giannattasio. 2004. "Poetry." In *A Companion to Linguistic Anthropology,* edited by Alessandro Duranti, 290–320. Oxford: Blackwell.

Bär, E. 1974. "Understanding Lacan." In *Psychoanalysis and Contemporary Science,* vol. 3, edited by Leo Goldberg, 437–544. New York: International University Press.

Barrett, Kim, Susan M. Barman, Scott Boitano, and Heddwen L. Brooks. 2015. *Ganong's Review of Medical Physiology,* 25th ed. New York: McGraw Hill.

Barthes, Roland. 1975. *The Pleasure of the Text.* Translated by Richard Miller. New York: Hill and Wang.

Basso, Keith H. 1996. *Wisdom Sits in Places: Landscape and Language among the Western Apache.* Albuquerque: University of New Mexico Press.

Basso, Keith H., and Henry A. Selby, eds. 1976. *Meaning in Anthropology.* Albuquerque: University of New Mexico Press.

Bauman, Richard. 1986. *Story, Performance, and Event: Contextual Studies of Oral Narrative.* Cambridge, UK: Cambridge University Press.

Bauman, Richard. 1992. *Folklore, Cultural Performances, and Popular Entertainments: A Communications-Centered Handbook.* New York: Oxford University Press.

Bauman, Richard. 2006. "Speech Genres in Cultural Practice." In *Encyclopedia of Language and Linguistics,* 2nd ed., edited by Keith Brown, 745–58. Amsterdam: Elsevier.

Bauman, Richard. 2012. "Performance." In *A Companion to Folklore,* edited by Regina F. Bendix and Galit Hasan-Rokem, 94–118. New York: Wiley-Blackwell.

Bauman, Richard, and Charles L. Briggs. 1990. "Poetics and Performance as Critical Perspectives on Language and Social Life." *Annual Review of Anthropology,* no. 19: 59–88.

Bauman, Richard, and Charles L. Briggs. 2003. *Voices of Modernity: Language Ideologies and the Politics of Inequality.* Cambridge, UK: Cambridge University Press.

Bauman, Richard, and Joel Sherzer. 1975. *Explorations in the Ethnography of Speaking.* London: Cambridge University Press.

Becker, Judith. 1986. "Is Western Art Music Superior?" *Musical Quarterly* 72, no. 3: 341–59.

Becker, Judith. 2004. *Deep Listeners: Music, Emotion, and Trancing.* Bloomington: Indiana University Press.

Becker, Judith. 2010. "Exploring the Habitus of Listening: Anthropological Perspectives." In *Handbook of Music and Emotion: Theory, Research, Applications,* edited by Patrik N. Juslin and John Sloboda, 128–57. New York: Oxford University Press.

Benjamin, Walter. (1935) 1969. "The Work of Art in the Age of Mechanical Reproduction." In *Illuminations,* edited by Hannah Arendt, 1–26. New York: Schocken.

Benveniste, Émile. 1966. *Problèmes de linguistique générale.* Paris: Gallimard.

Bhabha, Homi. 1991a. "Caliban Speaks to Prospero: Cultural Identity and the Crisis of Representation." In *Critical Fictions: The Politics of Imaginative Writing,* edited by Philomena Marini, 62–65. Seattle: Bay Press.

Bhabha, Homi. 1991b. *Nation and Narration.* London: Routledge.

Bijsterveld, Kerin. 2001. "The Diabolical Symphony of the Mechanical Age: Technology and Symbolism of Sound in European and North American Noise Abatement Campaigns, 1900–40." *Social Studies of Science* 31, no. 1: 37–70.

Bleger, José. 1958. *Psicoanálisis y dialéctica materialista: Estudios sobre la estructura del psicoanálisis.* Buenos Aires: Editorial Paidós.

Bleichmar, Silvia. 2002. *Dolor país.* Buenos Aires: Libros del Zorzal.

Boas, Franz. (1911) 1938. *The Mind of Primitive Man.* New York: Macmillan.

Borch-Jacobsen, Mikkel. 1988. *The Freudian Subject*. Stanford, CA: Stanford University Press.

Bourdieu, Pierre. 1977. *Outline of a Theory of Practice*. Translated by Richard Nice. Cambridge, UK: Cambridge University Press.

Bourdieu, Pierre. 1986. *Distinction*. Translated by Richard Nice. London: Routledge.

Bourdieu, Pierre. 1992. *The Logic of Practice*. Translated by Richard Nice. Stanford, CA: Stanford University Press.

Bourdieu, Pierre. 1993. *The Field of Cultural Production*. Edited by Randal Johnson. New York: Columbia University Press.

Briggs, Charles L. 1986. *Learning How to Ask: A Sociolinguistic Appraisal of the Role of the Interview in Social Science Research*. Studies in the Social and Cultural Foundations of Language, no. 1. Cambridge, UK: Cambridge University Press.

Briggs, Charles L. 1988. *Competence in performance: The creativity of tradition in Mexicano verbal art*. Philadelphia: University of Pennsylvania Press.

Briggs, Charles L. 1993. "Personal Sentiments and Polyphonic Voices in Warao Women's Ritual Wailing: Music and Poetics in a Critical and Collective Discourse." *American Anthropologist* 95, no. 4: 929–57.

Briggs, Charles L. 2004. "Theorizing Modernity Conspiratorially: Science, Scale, and the Political Economy of Public Discourse in Explanations of a Cholera Epidemic." *American Ethnologist* 31, no. 2: 164–87.

Briggs, Charles L. 2005. "Communicability, Racial Discourse, and Disease." *Annual Review of Anthropology* 34, no. 1: 269–91.

Briggs, Charles L. 2007. Anthropology, Interviewing, and Communicability in Contemporary Society. *Current Anthropology* 48, no. 4: 551–80.

Briggs, Charles L. 2011. "'All Cubans Are Doctors!': News Coverage of Health and Bioexceptionalism in Cuba." *Social Science and Medicine* 73, no. 7: 1037–44.

Briggs, Charles L., and Richard Bauman. 1992. "Genre, Intertextuality, and Social Power." *Linguistic Anthropology* 2, no. 2: 131–72.

Briggs, Charles L., and Daniel C. Hallin. 2007. "Biocommunicability: The Neoliberal Subject and Its Contradictions in News Coverage of Health Issues." *Social Text* 25, no. 4: 43–66.

Briggs, Charles L., and Daniel C. Hallin. 2016. *Making Health Public: How News Coverage Is Remaking Media, Medicine, and Contemporary Life*. London: Routledge.

Bryson, B. 1997. "What about the Univores? Musical Dislikes and Group-Based Identity Construction among Americans with Low Levels of Education." *Poetics* 25, nos. 2–3: 141–56.

Bull, Michael. 2015. *Sound Moves: iPod Culture and Urban Experience*. London: Routledge.

Bull, Michael, and Les Back. 2003. *The Auditory Culture Reader*. Oxford, UK: Berg.

Butler, Judith. 1990. *Gender Trouble: Feminism and the Subversion of Identity*. New York: Routledge.

Butler, Judith. 1993. *Bodies That Matter: On the Discursive Limits of "Sex."* New York: Routledge.

Butler, Judith. 1997. *Excitable Speech: A Politics of the Performative*. New York: Routledge.

Butler, Judith, John Guillory, and Kendall Thomas. 2000. *What's Left of Theory? New Work on the Politics of Literary Theory*. New York: Routledge.

Cabanas, Edgar, and Eva Illouz. 2019. *Manufacturing Happy Citizens: How the Science and Industry of Happiness Control Our Lives*. Cambridge, UK: Polity.

Canet-Juric, Lorena, Andrés María Laura, Del Valle Macarena, López-Morales Hernán, Poó Fernando, Galli Juan Ignacio, Yero Matías, and Urquijo Sebastián. 2020. "A Longitudinal Study on the Emotional Impact Cause by the COVID-19 Pandemic Quarantine on General Population." *Frontiers in Psychology* 11. https://doi.org/10.3389/fpsyg.2020.565688.

Capra, Fritjof. 1982. *The Turning Point: Science, Society, and the Rising Culture*. Toronto: Bantam.

Carpintero, Enrique, and Alejandro Vainer. 2004. *Las huellas de la memoria: Psicoanálisis y salud mental en la Argentina de los '60 y '70*, vol. 1 (1957–1969). Buenos Aires: Topia.

Carpintero, Enrique, and Alejandro Vainer. 2005. *Las huellas de la memoria: Psicoanálisis y salud mental en la Argentina de los '60 y '70*, vol. 2 (1970–1983). Buenos Aires: Topia.

Carr, E. Summerson. 2010a. "Enactments of Expertise." *Annual Review of Anthropology* 39, no. 1: 17–32.

Carr, E. Summerson. 2010b. *Scripting Addiction: The Politics of Therapeutic Talk and American Sobriety*. Princeton, NJ: Princeton University Press.

Carr, E. Summerson, and Yvonne Smith. 2014. "The Poetics of Therapeutic Practice: Motivational Interviewing and the Powers of Pause." *Culture, Medicine, and Psychiatry* 38: 83–114.

Carter, Paul. 2004. "Ambiguous Traces, Mishearing, and Auditory Space." In *Hearing Cultures: Essays on Sound, Listening and Modernity*, edited by Veit Erlmann, 43–63. New York: Berg.

Certeau, Michel de. 1984. *The Practice of Everyday Life*. Translated by Steve Rendall. Berkeley: University of California Press.

Certeau, Michel de. 1988. *The Writing of History*. Translated by Tom Conley. New York: Columbia University Press.

Certeau, Michel de. 2000. *The Possession at Loudun*. Translated by Michael B. Smith. Chicago: University of Chicago Press.

Chakrabarty, Dipesh. 2000. *Provincializing Europe: Postcolonial Thought and Historical Difference*. Princeton, NJ: Princeton University Press.

Chakrabarty, Dipesh, Rochona Majumdar, and Andrew Sartori, eds. 2007. *From the Colonial to the Postcolonial: India and Pakistan in Transition*. New York: Oxford University Press.

Chessick, Richard D. 1982. "Psychoanalytic Listening: With Special Reference to the Views of Langs." *Contemporary Psychoanalysis* 18, no. 4: 613–34.

Chion, Michel. 2012. "The Three Listening Modes." In *The Sound Studies Reader,* edited by Jonathan Sterne, 48–53. London: Routledge.

Chire-Saire, Josimar, and Khalid Mahmood. 2020. "Hope Amid of a Pandemic: Is Psychological Distress Alleviating in South America while Coronavirus Is Still on Surge?" arXIV.org, August 27, 2020. https://arxiv.org/pdf/2008.12289.pdf.

Cicourel, Aaron V. 1992. Review of *The Give and Take of Everyday Life: Language Socialization of Kaluli Children,* by Bambi B. Schieffelin. *American Anthropologist* 94, no. 1: 209–10.

Clifford, James, and George Marcus, eds. 1986. *Writing Culture: The Poetics and Politics of Ethnography.* Berkeley: University of California Press.

Collu, Samuele. 2019. "Refracting Affects: Affect, Psychotherapy, and Spirit Dis-Possession." *Culture, Medicine, and Psychiatry* 43, no. 2: 290–314.

Connor, Steven. 1997. *Postmodernist Culture: An Introduction to Theories of the Contemporary.* New York: Wiley.

Connor, Steven. 2004a. *The Cambridge Companion to Postmodernism.* New York: Cambridge University Press.

Connor, Steven. 2004b. "Edison's Teeth: Touching Hearing." In *Hearing Cultures: Essays on Sound, Listening, and Modernity,* edited by Veit Erlmann, 153–72. Oxford, UK: Berg.

Connor, Steven. 2009. "Earslips: Of Mishearings and Mondegreens." Presentation at the Listening In, Feeding Back conference, Columbia University, New York, February 14.

Cook, Nicholas. 1992. *Music, Imagination and Culture.* New York: Clarendon.

Corbin, Alain. 1998. *Village Bells: Sound and Meaning in the 19th-Century French Countryside.* New York: Columbia University Press.

Cosse, Isabella. 2015. *Mafalda: Historia social y política.* Buenos Aires: Fondo de Cultura Económica.

Coulmas, Florian. 2011. *Direct and Indirect Speech.* New York: De Gruyter Mouton.

Dagfal, Alejandro. 2000. "José Bleger y los inicios de una 'psicología psicoanalítica' en la Argentina de los años 60." *Revista Universitaria de Psicoanálisis* 2: 139–69.

Dagfal, Alejandro. 2007. "Psicobodas de oro." *Página 12,* March 15. https://www.pagina12.com.ar/diario/psicologia/9-81750-2007-03-15.html.

Dagfal, Alejandro. 2008. "Orientacion profesional y psicotecnia en la Argentina peronista (1943–1955)." *Revista de psicología general y aplicada* 61, no. 3: 313.

Dagfal, Alejandro. 2009. *Entre París y Buenos Aires: La invención del psicólogo (1942–1966).* Buenos Aires: Editorial Paidós.

Damousi, Joy, and Mariano Ben Plotkin, eds. 2009. *The Transnational Unconscious: Essays in the History of Psychoanalysis and Transnationalism.* New York: Palgrave Macmillan.

Darwin, Christopher John. 2008. "Listening to Speech in the Presence of Other Sounds." *Philosophical Transactions of the Royal Society B: Biological Sciences* 363, no. 1493: 1011–21.

Deleuze, Gilles, and Félix Guattari. 1988. *A Thousand Plateaus: Capitalism and Schizophrenia.* London: Athlone.

Demers, Joanna. 2010. *Listening through the Noise: The Aesthetics of Experimental Electronic Music*. London: Oxford University Press.

Derrida, Jacques. 1984. *Signéponge = Signsponge*. Translated by Richard Rand. New York: Columbia University Press.

Derrida, Jacques. 2005. *On Touching: Jean-Luc Nancy*. Translated by Christine Irizarry. Stanford, CA: Stanford University Press.

Derrida, Jacques. 2012. *Specters of Marx: The State of the Debt, the Work of Mourning and the New International*. Translated by Peggy Kamuf. New York: Routledge.

Descartes, René. (1637) 2006. *A Discourse on Method*. Translated and edited by Ian Maclean. Oxford, UK: Oxford University Press.

Dessal, Gustavo. 2017. "Psychoanalysis and Music: A Resonance." *OnScenes*, August 29. https://onscenes.weebly.com/music/psychoanalysis-and-music-a-resonance.

Duranti, Alessandro. 2015. *The Anthropology of Intentions: Language in a World of Others*. Cambridge, UK: Cambridge University Press.

Duranti, Alessandro, and Charles Goodwin. 1992. *Rethinking Context: Language as an Interactive Phenomenon*. New York: Cambridge University Press.

Dussel, Enrique. 1973. *Para una ética de la liberación latinoamericana*, vol. 2. Buenos Aires: Siglo 21.

Edelson, Marshall. 1975. *Language and Interpretation in Psychoanalysis*. New Haven, CT: Yale University Press.

Eisenlohr, Patrick. 2018. *Sounding Islam*. Berkeley: University of California Press.

Emmison, Michael. 2003. "Social Class and Cultural Mobility: Reconfiguring the Cultural Omnivore Thesis." *Journal of Sociology* 39, no. 3: 211–30.

Epele, María E. 2015. "Entre la escucha y el escuchar: Psicoanálisis, psicoterapia y pobreza urbana en Buenos Aires." *Physis: Revista de Saúde Coletiva* 25, no. 3: 797–818.

Erikson, Erik. 1993. *Childhood and Society*. New York: Norton.

Erikson, Erik. 1994. *Identity: Youth and Crisis*. New York: Norton.

Erlmann, Veit, ed. 2004. *Hearing Cultures: Essays on Sound, Listening, and Modernity*. New York: Berg.

Ervin-Tripp, Susan. 1972. "Sociolinguistic Rules: Alteration and Co-occurrence." In *Directions in Sociolinguistics*, edited by J. Gumperez and D. Hymes, 213–50. Cambridge, UK: Basil Blackwell.

Escalante, Candelaria, and Eduardo Leiderman. 2008. "Prevalencia de tratamiento psicoterapéutico en los habitantes de la Ciudad de Buenos Aires." *VERTEX: Revista Argentina de Psiquiatría* 19: 261–67.

Escuela de la Orientación Lacaniana. n.d. "El psicoanálisis y la orientación lacaniana." *EOL: Escuela de la Orientación Lacaniana*. Accessed December 17, 2021. http://www.eol.org.ar/template.asp?Sec=la_escuela&SubSec=el_psico&File=el_psico.html

Europa Press. 2020. "Las consultas psicológicas online crecen un 200% durante la cuarentena." *La Vanguardia*, March 3. https://www.lavanguardia.com/vida

/20200320/474274226329/consultas-psicologicas-online-crecen-cuarentena
-coronavirus.html.

Ey, Henri. 1935. "Hallucinations et délire: Les formes hallucinatoire de l'automatisme
verbale." *Journal of Nervous and Mental Disease* 81, no. 5: 604.

Facultad de Psicología. n.d. Universidad de Buenos Aires. Accessed February 2019.
http://www.psi.uba.ar.

Faurholt, Gry. 2009. "Self as Other: The Doppelgänger." *Double Dialogues* 10 (summer).

Feld, Steven. 1982. *Sound and Sentiment: Birds, Weeping, Poetics, and Song in Kaluli
Expression.* Philadelphia: University of Pennsylvania Press.

Feld, Steven. 2017. "On Post-ethnomusicology Alternatives: Acoustemology." In
*Perspectives on a 21st Century Comparative Musicology: Ethnomusicology or
Transcultural Musicology?*, edited by Francesco Giannattasio and Giovanni
Giuriati, 82–99. Udine, Italy: Nota.

Florence, Bruno de. 2011. "Lacan and Topology." *Lacanianworks* (blog). October 8.

Flores, Nelson, and Jonathan Rosa. 2015. "Undoing Appropriateness: Raciolinguistic
Ideologies and Language Diversity in Education." *Harvard Educational Review*
85, no. 2: 149–71.

Foucault, Michel. 1972. *The Archaeology of Knowledge.* Translated by Alan Sheridan.
New York: Pantheon.

Foucault, Michel. (1973) 2008. *Psychiatric Power. Lecturers at the Collegè de France,
1973–1974.* Baskingstoke, UK: Palgrave.

Foucault, Michel. 1977. *Discipline and Punish: The Birth of the Prison.* Translated by
Alan Sheridan. New York: Pantheon.

Foucault, Michel. 1986. *Foucault: A Critical Reader.* Edited by David Couzens Hoy.
New York: Blackwell.

Foucault, Michel. 1988. *Technologies of the Self: A Seminar with Michel Foucault.*
Edited by Luther H. Martin, Huck Gutman, and Patrick H. Hutton. Amherst:
University of Massachusetts Press.

Foucault, Michel. 2010. *The Birth of Biopolitics: Lectures at the Collège de France,
1978–1979.* Translated by Michel Senellart. New York: Picador.

Freud, Sigmund. (1900) 1953. *The Interpretation of Dreams (1900–1901).* Edited by
James Strachey. In *Standard Edition,* vol. 5, 35–616.

Freud, Sigmund. (1909) 1953. "Analysis of a Phobia in a Five-Year-Old Boy." Edited by
James Strachey. In *Standard Edition,* vol. 10, 3–149.

Freud, Sigmund. (1910) 1964. *Leonardo Da Vinci and a Memory of His Childhood.*
Edited by James Strachey. In *Standard Edition,* vol. 11, 59–137.

Freud, Sigmund. (1912) 1958. "Recommendation to Physicians Practicing Psychoanalysis." Edited by James Strachey. In *Standard Edition,* vol. 12, 109–20.

Freud, Sigmund. (1913) 1958. "On Beginning the Treatment." Edited and translated by
James Strachey. In *Standard Edition,* vol. 12, 123–44.

Freud, Sigmund. (1915) 1963. "The Unconscious." In *General Psychological Theory:
Papers on Metapsychology,* edited by Philip Rieff, 116–50. New York: Macmillan.

Freud, Sigmund. (1918) 2008. "Psychoanalytic Technique." In *Three Case Histories,*
edited by Philip Rieff, 1–280. New York: Touchstone.

Freud, Sigmund. (1923) 1995. *The Ego and the Id: And Other Works (1923–1925)*. London: Hogarth.

Freud, Sigmund (1926) 1959. "The Question of Lay Analysis." Edited and translated by James Strachey. In *Standard Edition*, vol. 20, 183–258.

Freud, Sigmund. (1930) 1962. *Civilization and Its Discontents*. New York: Norton.

Freud, Sigmund. 1953–74. *The Standard Edition of the Complete Psychological Works of Sigmund Freud*. Edited by James Strachey et al. London: Hogarth.

Freud, Sigmund. 1958. *The Case of Schreber, Papers on Technique, and Other Works (1911–1913)*. In *Standard Edition*, vol. 12, ii–vii.

Frittaoni, Verónica. 2020. "Aislamiento emocional: Coronavirus en Argentina; Con sesiones online y líneas gratuitas, aumenta la demanda de atención psicológica." *Buena Vida*, March 28. https://www.clarin.com/buena-vida/coronavirus -argentina-sesiones-online-lineas-gratuitas-aumenta-demanda-atencion -psicologica_0_fWvWGMcFF.html.

Frosh, Stephen. 1999. *The Politics of Psychoanalysis: An Introduction to Freudian and Post-Freudian Theory*. New York: New York University Press.

Frosh, Stephen. 2002. *Key Concepts in Psychoanalysis*. New York: New York University Press.

Frosh, Stephen. 2010. *Psychoanalysis outside the Clinic: Interventions in Psychosocial Studies*. New York: Palgrave Macmillan.

Gadamer, Hans-Georg. 1989. *Truth and Method*. Translated by Joel Weinsheimer and Donald G. Marshall. London: Continuum.

Gal, Susan. 1989. "Language and Political Economy." *Annual Review of Anthropology* 18: 345–67.

Gal, Susan. 1998. "Multiplicity and Contestation among Linguistic Ideologies." In *Language Ideologies: Practice and Theory*, edited by Bambi Schieffelin, Kathryn Woolard, and Paul Kroskrity, 317–31. New York: Oxford University Press.

García, Germán. 2005. *El psicoanálisis y los debates culturales: Ejemplos Argentinos*. Buenos Aires: Editorial Paidós.

García, Luciano Nicolás. 2016. *La psicología por asalto: Psiquiatría y cultura científica en el comunismo argentino (1935–1991)*. Buenos Aires: Edhasa.

García Badaracco, Jorge E. 1992. *Comunidad terapéutica psicoanalítica de estructura multifamiliar*. Madrid: Tecnipublicaciones.

García Badaracco, Jorge E. 2000. *Psicoanálisis multifamiliar: Los otros en nosotros y el descubrimiento del sí mismo*. Buenos Aires: Editorial Paidós.

Gauker, Christopher. 1992. "The Lockean Theory of Communication." *Noûs* 26, no. 3: 303–24.

Gay, Peter. 1988. *Freud: A Life for Our Time*. New York: Norton.

Germani, Gino, and Ruth Sautu. 1965. *Regularidad y origen social en los estudiantes universitarios*. Buenos Aires: Instituto de Sociología (Facultad de Filosofía y Letras, Universidad de Buenos Aires).

Gibb, R., and A. Good. 2014. "Interpretation, Translation and Intercultural Communication in Refugee Status Determination Procedures in the UK and France." *Language and Intercultural Communication* 14, no. 3: 385–99.

Goffman, Erving. 1964. "The Neglected Situation." *American Anthropologist* 66, no. 6, pt. 2: 133–36.

Goffman, Erving. 1974. *Frame Analysis: An Essay on the Organization of Experience.* New York: Harper and Row.

Goffman, Erving. 1981. *Forms of Talk.* Philadelphia: University of Pennsylvania Press.

Good, Byron. 1994. *Medicine, Rationality and Experience: An Anthropological Perspective.* Cambridge, UK: Cambridge University Press.

Gorney, J. E. 1978. "Resonance and Subjectivity: The Clinical Application of Lacan." *Contemporary Psychoanalysis* 14, no. 2: 246–73.

Gouk, Penelope. 1999. "Music, Melancholy, and Medical Spirits in Early Modern Thought." In *Music and Medicine,* edited by Patricia Horden, 147–53. Burlington, VT: Ashgate.

Gouk, Penelope. 2004. "Raising Spirits and Restoring Souls." In *Hearing Cultures: Essays on Sound, Listening, and Modernity,* edited by Veit Erlmann, 87–106. New York: Berg.

Guiraud, Paul. 1922. "Délire systématisé et inversion sexuelle." *Annales médico-psychologiques* 2, no. 12: 128–32.

Guiraud, Paul. 1925. "Les délires chroniques." *L'Encéphale,* no. 9: 669.

Guiraud, Paul, and Henri Ey. 1926. "Remarques critiques sur la schizophrénie de Bleuler." *Annales médico-psychologiques,* no. 1: 355–65. https://www.biusante .parisdescartes.fr/histoire/medica/resultats/?p=355&cote=90152x1926x01&do =page.

Gumperz, John J. 1982. *Discourse Strategies.* Cambridge, UK: Cambridge University Press.

Gumperz, John J., and Dell H. Hymes. 1972. *Directions in Sociolinguistics: The Ethnography of Communication.* New York: Holt, Rinehart and Winston.

Gupta, Dipankar. 2005. *Project Modernity: Intersubjectivity as Iso-Ontology.* London: Oxford University Press.

Hanks, William F. 1987. "Discourse Genres in a Theory of Practice." *American Ethnologist* 14, no. 4: 668–92.

Hanks, William F. 1990. *Referential Practice: Language and Lived Space among the Maya.* Chicago: University of Chicago Press.

Hanks, William F. 1993. "Notes on Semantics in Linguistic Practice." In *Towards a Reflexive Sociology: The Social Theory of Pierre Bourdieu,* edited by C. Calhoun and M. Pospone, 139–55. Oxford: Blackwell.

Hanks, William F. 1996. *Language and Communicative Practices.* Boulder, CO: Westview.

Heidegger, Martin. 1962. *Being and Time.* Translated by John MacQuarrie and Edward Robinson. Oxford, UK: Blackwell.

Hellman's Mayonnaise. 2004. YouTube. Accessed 23, 2021. https://www.youtube.com /watch?v=hkvjkycfJoY.

Hennion, Antoine. 2001. "Music Lovers: Taste as Performance." *Theory, Culture, Society* 18, no. 5: 1–22.

Hennion, Antoine. 2010. "Loving Music: From a Sociology of Mediation to a Pragmatics of Taste." *Comunicar* 17, no. 34: 25–33.

Hirschkind, Charles. 2004. "Hearing Modernity: Egypt, Islam, and the Pious Ear." In *Hearing Cultures: Essays on Sound, Listening and Modernity*, edited by Veit Erlmann. 131–51. New York: Berg.

Hirschkind, Charles. 2006. *The Ethical Soundscape: Cassette Sermons and Islamic Counterpublics*. New York: Columbia University Press.

Horowitz, Seth. 2012. *The Universal Sense: How Hearing Shapes the Mind*. New York: Bloomsbury.

Horrocks, Roger. 2001. *Freud Revisited: Psychoanalytic Themes in the Postmodern Age*. Edited by Jo Campling. New York: Palgrave.

Husserl, Edmund. 1982. *Ideas Pertaining to a Pure Phenomenology and to a Phenomenological Philosophy: First Book; General Introduction to a Pure Phenomenology*. Translated by F. Kersten. The Hague: Springer.

Hymes, Dell H. 1974. *Foundations in Sociolinguistics: An Ethnographic Approach*. Philadelphia: University of Pennsylvania Press.

Ihde, Don. 2007. *Listening and Voice: Phenomenologies of Sound*. Albany: State University of New York Press.

Inda, Jonathan Xavier, and Renato Rosaldo, eds. 2002. *The Anthropology of Globalization: A Reader*. Malden, MA: Blackwell.

Innis, Harold A. (1950) 2007. *Empire and Communications*. Toronto: Dundurn.

Inoue, Miyako. 2006. *Vicarious Language: Gender and Linguistic Modernity in Japan*. Berkeley: University of California Press.

Irvine, Judith T. 1989. "When Talk Isn't Cheap: Language and Political Economy." *American Ethnologist* 16, no. 2: 248–67.

Isakower, Otto. 1939. "On the Exceptional Position of the Auditory Sphere." *International Journal of Psychoanalysis*, no. 20: 340–48.

Izaguirre, Marcelo. 2009. *Jacques Lacan: El anclaje de su enseñanza en Argentina*. Buenos Aires: Catálogos.

Jackson, Donald. 1960. *The Etiology of Schizophrenia*. New York: Basic.

Jackson, Donald. 1964. *Myths of Madness: New Facts for Old Fallacies*. New York: Macmillan.

Jacquemet, Marco. 1996. *Credibility in Court: Communicative Practices in the Camorra Trials*. Cambridge, UK: Cambridge University Press.

Jakobson, Roman. 1960. "Linguistics and Poetics." In *Style in Language*, edited by Thomas A. Sebeok, 350–77. Cambridge, MA: MIT Press.

James, William. 1890. *Principles of Psychology*. New York: Holt.

Jauss, Hans Robert. 1974. "Levels of Identification of Hero and Audience." *New Literary History* 5, no. 2: 283–317.

Jauss, Hans Robert. 1982. "Theories of Genre and Medieval Literature." In *Toward an Aesthetic of Reception*, 76–109. Minneapolis: University of Minnesota Press.

Jay, Martin. 1993. *Downcast Eyes: The Denigration of Vision in Twentieth-Century French Thought*. Berkeley: University of California Press.

Jaynes, Julian. 1982. *The Origin of Consciousness in the Breakdown of the Bicameral Mind.* Boston: Houghton Mifflin Harcourt.

Johnson, James H. 1995. *Listening in Paris: A Cultural History.* Berkeley: University of California Press.

Johnson, Mark. 2007. *The Meaning of the Body: Aesthetics and Human Understanding.* Chicago: University of Chicago Press.

Jones, Maxwell. 1968. *Beyond the Therapeutic Community.* New Haven, CT: Yale University Press.

Jung, Carl Gustav. 1913. *The Theory of Psychoanalysis.* New York: Journal of Nervous and Mental Disease Publishing Company.

Juslin, Patrik N., and John A. Sloboda, eds. 2010. *Handbook of Music and Emotion: Theory, Research, Applications.* Oxford: Oxford University Press.

Kane, Brian. 2016. *Sound Unseen: Acousmatic Sound in Theory and Practice.* Oxford: Oxford University Press.

Karpf, Anne. 2006. *The Human Voice: How This Extraordinary Instrument Reveals Essential Clues about Who We Are.* New York: Bloomsbury.

Keane, Webb. 2001. "Voice." In *Key Terms in Language and Culture,* edited by Alessandro Duranti, 268–71. Malden, MA: Blackwell.

Kirmayer, Laurence J. 2002. "The Refugee's Predicament." *L'Évolution Psychiatrique* 67, no. 4: 724–42.

Kirmayer, Laurence J. 2003. "Failures of Imagination: The Refugee's Narrative in Psychiatry." *Anthropology and Medicine* 10, no. 2: 167–85.

Kittler, Friedrich A. 1999. *Gramophone, Film, Typewriter.* Stanford, CA: Stanford University Press.

Kivy, Peter. 2001. *New Essays on Musical Understanding.* Oxford, UK: Clarendon.

Kleinman, Arthur. 1980. *Patients and Healers in the Context of Culture: An Exploration of the Borderland between Anthropology, Medicine, and Psychiatry.* Berkeley: University of California Press.

Kohan, Martín. 2018. "Una Carta." *Perfil,* September 28. https://www.perfil.com/noticias/columnistas/una-carta.phtml.

Korman, Guido Pablo, Nicolás Viotti, and Cristian Javier Garay. 2015. "The Origins and Professionalization of Cognitive Psychotherapy in Argentina." *History of Psychology* 18, no. 2: 205–14.

Kristeva, Julia. 1984. *Revolution in Poetic Language.* New York: Columbia University Press.

Kristeva, Julia. 1987. *Tales of Love.* New York: Columbia University Press.

Kristeva, Julia, Josette Rey-Debove, and Donna Jean Umike-Sebeok. 1971. *Essays in Semiotics/Essais de Sémiotique.* The Hague: Mouton.

Lacan, Jacques. (1966) 2006. *Écrits: The First Complete Edition in English.* Translated by Bruce Fink. New York: Norton.

Lacan, Jacques. 1968. *The Language of the Self: The Function of Language in Psychoanalysis.* Translated by Anthony Wilden. Baltimore, MD: Johns Hopkins University Press.

Lacan, Jacques. 1977. *Écrits: A Selection.* Translated by Alan Sheridan. New York: W. W. Norton.

Lacan, Jacques. 1988. *The Seminar of Jacques Lacan*. Book 1, *Freud's Papers on Technique 1953–1954*. Edited by Jacques-Alain Miller. New York: Norton.

Lacan, Jacques. 1997. *The Seminar of Jacques Lacan*. Book 3, *The Psychoses, 1955–1956*. Edited by Jacques-Alain Miller. New York: Norton.

Lacan, Jacques. 1998. *The Seminar of Jacques Lacan*. Book 11, *The Four Fundamental Concepts of Psychoanalysis*. Edited by Jacques-Alain Miller. Translated by Alan Sheridan. London: Norton.

Lacan, Jacques. 2015. *The Seminar of Jacques Lacan*. Book 8, *Transference*. Translated by Bruce Fink. London: Polity.

Lacey, Kate. 2013. *Listening Publics: The Politics and Experience of Listening in the Media Age*. Cambridge, UK: Polity.

Lakoff, Andrew. 2006. *Pharmaceutical Reason: Knowledge and Value in Global Psychiatry*. Cambridge, UK: Cambridge University Press.

Latour, Bruno. 1993. *We Have Never Been Modern*. Cambridge, MA: Harvard University Press.

Latour, Bruno. 2001. *Science in Action: How to Follow Scientists and Engineers through Society*. Cambridge, MA: Harvard University Press.

Latour, Bruno. 2005. *Reassembling the Social: An Introduction to Actor-Network-Theory*. New York: Oxford University Press.

Launer, John. 2005. "Anna O and the 'Talking Cure.'" *QJM: An International Journal of Medicine* 98, no. 6: 465–66.

Lave, Jean, and Etienne Wenger. 1991. *Situated Learning: Legitimate Peripheral Participation*. Cambridge, UK: Cambridge University Press.

Lawler, Steph. 2000. *Mothering the Self: Mothers, Daughters, Subjects*. London: Routledge.

Leonard, Miriam. 2013. "Freud and Tragedy: Oedipus and the Gender of the Universal." *Classical Receptions Journal* 5, no. 1: 63–83.

Lézé, Samuel. 2006. "Convertirse en psicoanalista en Francia." *Política y sociedad* 43, no. 3: 73–87.

Lindner, Robert Mitchell. 1954. *The Fifty-Minute Hour: A Collection of True Psychoanalytic Tales*. New York: Rinehart.

Lipari, Lisbeth. 2014. *Listening, Thinking, Being: Toward an Ethic of Attunement*. University Park: Pennsylvania State University Press.

Locke, John. (1690) 1975. *Essay Concerning Human Understanding*. Edited by P. H. Nidditch. Oxford: Oxford University Press.

Longoni, Ana. 2017. *Oscar Masotta: La teoría como acción = theory as action*. Mexico City: Museo Universitario Arte Contemporáneo.

Marcuse, Herbert. 1955. *Eros and Civilization: A Philosophical Inquiry into Freud*. Boston: Beacon.

Markez, Iñaki. 2009. "Potencial del Psicoanálisis Multifamiliar. Entrevista a Jorge E. García-Badaracco." *Nortede de Salud Mental*, no. 34: 85–93.

Markez, Iñaki. 2010. "In Memoriam: A propósito de Jorge García Badaracco." *Norte de Salud Mental* 8, no. 38: 97–98.

Marshall, Collin. 2010. "Kant's Metaphysics of the Self." *Philosophers' Imprint* 10, no. 8: 1–21.

Marsilli-Vargas, Xochitl. 2014. "Listening Genres: The Emergence of Relevance Structures through the Reception of Sound." *Journal of Pragmatics* 69 (August): 42–51.

Marsilli-Vargas, Xochitl. 2015. "Anthropological Listening as a Genre." *Anthropology News*, September 29.

Marta, Jan. 1987. "Lacan and Post-structuralism." *American Journal of Psychoanalysis* 47, no. 1: 51–57.

Martínez Estrada, Ezequiel. (1933) 2007. *Radiografía de la Pampa*. Buenos Aires: Editorial Losada.

Mauss, Marcel. 1966. *The Gift: Forms and Functions of Exchange in Archaic Societies*. London: Cohen and West.

McLuhan, Marshall. 1962. *The Gutenberg Galaxy: The Making of Typographic Man*. Toronto: University of Toronto Press.

Melgar, Maria Cristina, and Raquel Rascovsky de Salvarezza. 2004. *Psicoanalisis y arte*. Buenos Aires: Lumen.

Menon, Vinod, and Daniel J. Levitin. 2005. "The Rewards of Music Listening: Response and Physiological Connectivity of the Mesolimbic System." *NeuroImage* 28, no. 1: 175–84.

Mikutta, Christian, Maissen Gieri, Altorfer Andreas, and Strik Werner. 2014. "Professional Musicians Listen Differently to Music." *Neuroscience* 268 (May 30): 102–11.

Mitchell, Juliet. 1974. *Psychoanalysis and Feminism*. New York: Pantheon.

Mitre, María Elisa. 2016. *Las voces del silencio*. Buenos Aires: Editorial Sudamericana.

Mon, Hugo Alconada. 2021. "Martin Seligman: 'La Argentina es uno de los países más atrasados en el campo de la psicología positiva.'" *La Nación*, January 23. https://www.lanacion.com.ar/el-mundo/martin-seligman-la-argentina-es-uno-paises-nid2580193/.

Morson, Gary S. 2006. "Addressivity." In *Encyclopedia of Language and Linguistics*, vol. 1, edited by Keith Brown, 55–58. Amsterdam: Elsevier.

Munro, G. C. 1850. "The Life Ransom." *North Star* (Rochester, NY), October 3.

Nancy, Jean-Luc. 2009. *Listening*. Translated by Charlotte Mandell. New York: Fordham University Press.

Novak, David, and Matt Sakakeeny, eds. 2015. *Keywords in Sound*. Durham, NC: Duke University Press.

"Nuevo Fernet 1882 RTD–Psicólogo." 2017. YouTube (Fratelli Branca advertisement). November 1. https://www.youtube.com/watch?v=yYx7nqRkpng.

Ochs, Elinor. 1979. *Developmental Pragmatics*. Cambridge, MA: Academic Press.

Ogden, Thomas H. 1999. *Reverie and Interpretation: Sensing Something Human*. London: Karnac.

Orozco, Ricardo. 2020. "El autoritarismo social en el combate del COVID-19." CLACSO (blog). March 30. https://www.clacso.org/el-autoritarismo-social-en-el-combate-al-covid-19/.

Oxford Dictionary of English, 3rd ed. 2010. New York: Oxford Univerity Press.

Park, Joseph Sung-Yul, and Mary Bucholtz. 2009. "Public Transcripts: Entextualization and Linguistic Representation in Institutional Contexts." *Text and Talk* 29, no. 5: 485–502.

Peirce, Charles S. 1998. *Collected Papers of Charles Sanders Peirce*. Edited by Charles Hartshorne and Paul Weiss. Bristol, UK: Thoemmes.

Peri, Mónica. 2009. "Aproximación psicoanalítica al Tango." *El Psitio*, March 19. http://www.elpsitio.com/Noticias/NoticiaMuestra.asp?Id=2033.

Peri, Mónica. 2010. *PsicoTango: Danza como terapia*. Buenos Aires: Corregidor.

Peri, Mónica. 2015. *Tango: Un abrazo sanador*. Buenos Aires: Corregidor.

Peterson, Richard A. 1992a. "How Musical Tastes Mark Occupation Status Groups." In *Cultivating Differences: Symbolic Boundaries and the Making of Inequality*, edited by Michèle Lamont and Marcel Fournier, 152–85. Chicago: University of Chicago Press.

Peterson, Richard A. 1992b. "Understanding Audience Segmentation: From Elite and Mass to Omnivore and Univore." *Poetics* 21, no. 4: 243–58.

Piangiani, Gaia. 2017. "Pope Francis Sought Psychoanalysis at 42, according to Book." *New York Times*, September 1. https://www.nytimes.com/2017/09/01/world/europe/pope-francis-psychoanalysis.html.

Pierce, Jennifer L. 1989. "The Relation between Emotion Work and Hysteria: A Feminist Reinterpretation of Freud's Studies on Hysteria." *Women's Studies: An Interdisciplinary Journal* 16, nos. 3–4: 255–70.

Plotkin, Mariano Ben. 2001. *Freud in the Pampas: The Emergence and Development of a Psychoanalytic Culture in Argentina*. Stanford, CA: Stanford University Press.

Plotkin, Mariano Ben. 2002. *Mañana Es San Perón: A Cultural History of Peron's Argentina*. Wilmington, DE: Scholarly Resources.

Plotkin, Mariano B., and Mariano Ruperthuz Honorato. 2017. *Estimado Doctor Freud: Una historia cultural del psicoanálisis en América Latina*. Buenos Aires: Edhasa.

Plotkin, Mariano B., and Nicolás Viotti. 2020. "Between Freud and Umbanda: Therapeutic Constellations in Buenos Aires Argentina." In *The Routledge International Handbook of Global Therapeutic Cultures*, edited by Daniel Nehring, Ole Jacob Madsen, Edgard Cabanas, China Mill, and Dylan Kerrigan, 257–67. London: Routledge.

Plotkin, Mariano B., and Sergio Visacovsky. 2007. "Saber y autoridad: Intervenciones de psicoanalistas en torno a la crisis en la Argentina." *Eial estudios interdisciplinarios de America Latina y el Caribe* 18, no. 1: 13–40.

Plotkin, Mariano B., and Sergio Visacovsky. 2008. "Los psicoanalistas y la crisis, la crisis del psicoanálisis." *Cuadernos LIRICO*, no. 4: 149–63.

Poe, Edgar Allan. 1887. *The Murders in the Rue Morgue: And Other Tales*. New York: Worthington.

Polack, María Elena. 2020. "COVID-19: Los psicólogos piden ser declarados personal esencial de salud." *La Nación*, June 25. https://www.lanacion.com.ar/sociedad/covid-19-los-psicologos-piden-ser-declarados-personal-nid2386155.

Portal de Noticias. 2018. "Palazzo: 'Hasta aquí llegó el ajuste de Mauricio Macri.'" *Portal de Noticias—Argentina* (blog). September 25.

Porter, Ted. 1996. *The Rise of Statistical Thinking, 1820–1900.* Princeton, NJ: Princeton University Press.

Ranzani, Oscar. 2020. "Gabriel Rolón: 'El aislamiento no es excusa para renunciar a vivir.'" *Página 12*, July 15. https://www.pagina12.com.ar/278456-gabriel-rolon-el-aislamiento-no-es-excusa-para-renunciar-a-v.

Reik, Theodor. 1948. *Listening with the Third Ear: The Inner Experience of a Psychoanalyst.* New York: Farrar, Straus.

Reik, Theodor. 1949. *Fragment of a Great Confession: A Psychoanalytic Autobiography.* New York: Farrar, Straus.

Reik, Theodor. 1964. *Voices from the Inaudible: The Patients Speak.* New York: Farrar, Straus.

Rentfrow, Peter, and Jennifer A. McDonald. 2010. "Preference, Personality, and Emotion." In *Handbook of Music and Emotion: Theory, Research, Applications*, edited by Patrick Juslin and John Sloboda, 669–95. Oxford, UK: Oxford University Press.

Rice, Tom. 2013. *Hearing and the Hospital: Sound, Listening, Knowledge and Experience.* Canon Pyon, UK: Kingston.

Ricoeur, Paul. 1975. "Phenomenology and Hermeneutics." *Noûs* 9, no. 1: 85–102.

Rodríguez, Cristian. 2019. "El Ejército de Ocupación." *Página 12*, August 15. https://www.pagina12.com.ar/212309-el-ejercito-de-ocupacion.

Rodríguez, Sergio. 1998. "Efectos de Lacan en la Argentina." *Topía*, March 29. https://www.topia.com.ar/articulos/efectos-de-lacan-en-la-argentina.

Rolón, Gabriel. 2020. "La importancia de sentirse escuchado." YouTube, July 17. https://www.youtube.com/watch?v=5sR8kgkmprE.

Romero, Simon. 2012. "Do Argentines Need Therapy? Pull Up a Couch." *New York Times*, August 18.

Rosa, Jonathan. 2019. *Looking Like a Language, Sounding Like a Race: Raciolinguistic Ideologies and the Learning of Latinidad.* New York: Oxford University Press.

Rose, Mary Beth. 1991. "Where Are Mothers in Shakespeare? Option for Gender Representation in the English Renaissance." *Shakespeare Quarterly* 42, no. 3: 291–314.

Roudinesco, Elisabeth. 1990. *Jacques Lacan and Co.: A History of Psychoanalysis in France, 1925–1985.* Translated by Jeffrey Mehlman. Chicago: University of Chicago Press.

Roudinesco, Elisabeth. 2003. *Why Psychoanalysis?* New York: Columbia University Press.

Rudaeff, Marcelo. 2018. "Love $tory: Amar es nunca tener que pedir un crédito." *Pagina 12*, September 29. https://www.pagina12.com.ar/145412-love-tory.

Salvatto, Augusto. 2020. "El coronavirus y la tentación autoritaria." *El Economista* (blog). March 30. https://eleconomista.com.ar/2020-03-el-coronavirus-y-la-tentacion-autoritaria/.

Sarmiento, Domingo Faustino. (1845) 2005. *Facundo*. Edited by Roberto Yahni. Buenos Aires: Ediciones Cátedra.

Savage, Mike, and Modesto Gayo. 2011. "Unravelling the Omnivore: A Field Analysis of Contemporary Musical Taste in the United Kingdom." *Poetics* 39, no. 5: 337–57.

Schaeffer, Pierre. 1952. *A la recherche d'une musique concrète*. Paris: Éditions du Seuil.

Schaeffer, Pierre. 1966. *Traité des objets musicaux: Essai interdisciplines*. Paris: Éditions du Seuil.

Schafer, Murray. 2003. "Open Ears." In *The Auditory Culture Reader*, edited by Michael Bull and Les Back, 25–40. Oxford, UK: Berg.

Schegloff, Emanuel A. 1987. "Some Sources of Misunderstanding in Talk-in-Interaction." *Linguistics* 25, no. 1: 201–18.

Schmidt, Leigh Eric. 2000. *Hearing Things: Religion, Illusion, and the American Enlightenment*. Cambridge, MA: Harvard University Press.

Schujman, Alejandro. 2019. "Aplicá el método Marie Kondo para ordenar tu vida y tus vínculos." *Clarín*, May 28. https://www.clarin.com/buena-vida/aplica-metodo -marie-kondo-ordenar-vida-vinculos_0_POkKphPE6.html.

Schwarz, David. 1997. *Listening Subjects: Music, Psychoanalysis, Culture*. Durham, NC: Duke University Press.

Schwarz, Katharina A., and Roland Pfister. 2016. "Scientific Psychology in the 18th Century: A Historical Rediscovery." *Perspectives on Psychological Science* 11, no. 3: 399–407.

Sehinkman, Diego. 2014. *Políticos al diván: Cómo piensan los inconscientes que nos gobiernan*. Buenos Aires: Sudamericana.

Shullenberger, Geoff. 2016. "Oscar Masotta and the Decentering of Lacanian Psychoanalysis." *Revista Landa* 5, no. 1: 416–26.

Silverstein, Michael. 1979. "Language Structure and Linguistic Ideology." In *The Elements: A Parasession on Linguistic Units and Levels*, edited by Paul R. Clyne, William F. Hanks, and Carol L. Hofbauer, 193–247. Chicago: Chicago Linguistic Society.

Silverstein, Michael. 2003. "Indexical Order and the Dialectics of Sociolinguistic Life." *Language and Communication* 23, nos. 3–4: 193–229.

Silverstein, Michael, and Greg Urban. 1996. *Natural Histories of Discourse*. Chicago: University of Chicago Press.

Siminovich, Maya. 2020. "Cómo apaciguar la incertidumbre en tiempos del coronavirus." *Infobae*, March 20. https://www.infobae.com/america/america-latina/2020 /03/20/como-apaciguar-la-incertidumbre-en-tiempos-del-coronavirus/.

Sinatra, Ernesto S. 2004. *Las entrevistas preliminares y la entrada en análisis*. Buenos Aires: Cuadernos del Instituto Clínico de Buenos Aires.

Smith, Bruce. 1999. *The Acoustic World of Early Modern England: Attending to the O-Factor*. Chicago: University of Chicago Press.

Smith, Mark M. 2001. *Listening to Nineteenth-Century America*. Chapel Hill: University of North Carolina Press.

Smith, Mark M. 2003. "Listening to the Heard Worlds of Antebellum America." In *The Auditory Culture Reader*, edited by Michael Bull and Les Back, 137–63. New York: Berg.

Sokolowski, Robert. 1964. *The Formation of Husserl's Concept of Constitution*. The Hague: Nijhoff.

Sorokowska, Agnieszka, Piotr Sorokowski, Peter Hilpert, Katarzyna Cantarero, Tomasz Frackowaik, Khodabakhsh Ahmadi, Ahmad M. Alghraibeh, et al. 2017. "Preferred Interpersonal Distances: A Global Comparison." *Journal of Cross-Cultural Psychology* 48, no. 4: 577–92.

Spivak, Eduardo D., Nahuel Emiliano Farias, Emiliano Hernán Ocampo, Gustavo A. Lovrich, and Tomás A Luppi. 2019. "Annotated Catalogue and Bibliography of Marine and Estuarine Shrimps, Lobsters, Crabs and Their Allies (Crustacea: Decapoda) of Argentina and Uruguay (Southwestern Atlantic Ocean)." *Frente Marítimo* 26 (April): 1–164.

Spivak, Gayatri Chakravorty. 1987. *In Other Worlds: Essays in Cultural Politics*. New York: Methuen.

Stauffer, Jill. 2015. *Ethical Loneliness: The Injustice of Not Being Heard*. New York: Columbia University Press.

Sterne, Jonathan. 2001. "Mediate Auscultation, the Stethoscope, and the 'Autopsy of the Living': Medicine's Acoustic Culture." *Journal of Medical Humanities* 22, no. 2: 115–36.

Sterne, Jonathan, ed. 2012. *The Sound Studies Reader*. New York: Routledge.

Stoever, Jennifer Lynn. 2016. *The Sonic Color Line: Race and the Cultural Politics of Listening*. New York: New York University Press.

Stolorow, Robert D. 2006. "Autobiographical and Theoretical Reflections on the Ontological Unconscious." *Contemporary Psychoanalysis* 42, no. 2: 233–41.

Tichenor, Marlee. 2020. "Metrics." In *The Cambridge Encyclopedia of Anthropology*, edited by F. Stein. (Article first published October 14, 2020.) https://www.anthroencyclopedia.com/entry/metrics.

Todorov, Tzvetan. 1980. *The Fantastic: A Structural Approach to a Literary Genre*. Ithaca, NY: Cornell University Press.

Toop, David. 2010. *Sinister Resonance: The Mediumship of the Listener*. New York: Continuum.

Townsend, Dann O. 1992. "The Isakower Phenomenon Revisited: A Case Study." *Journal of Psychoanalysis* 73, no. 3, pt. 3:481–91.

Tschemplik, Andrea. 2008. *Knowledge and Self-Knowledge in Plato's Theaetetus*. Lanham, MD: Lexington Books.

Turkle, Sherry. 1992. *Psychoanalytic Politics: Jacques Lacan and Freud's French Revolution*. London: Free Association Books.

Tute. 2013. *Tuterapia*. Buenos Aires: Sudamericana.

Tute. 2017. *Humor al Diván*. Buenos Aires: Sudamericana.

Tute. 2018. Presentation on *Humor al diván* at the Asociación Psicoanalítica Argentina (APA) conference, Buenos Aires, July 12, 2018. YouTube, September 14, 2018. https://wwwyoutube.com/watch?v=77-Qgh9914I.

Universidad de Buenos Aires, Secretaría de Asuntos Académicos. 2004. *Censo estudiantes.* https://www.uba.ar/institucional/censos/Estudiantes2004/censo-estudiantes.pdf.

Urban, Greg. 1996. *Metaphysical Community: The Interplay of the Senses and the Intellect.* Austin: University of Texas Press.

Vainer, Alejandro. 2014. "Psicoanálisis y salud mental: Definiciones, experiencias y perspectivas." *Topía,* November. https://www.topia.com.ar/articulos /psicoan%C3%A1lisis-y-salud-mental.

Verdon, Michel. 2007. "Franz Boas: Cultural History for the Present, or Obsolete Natural History?" *Journal of the Royal Anthropological Institute* 13, no. 2: 433–51.

Verztman, J., and Daniela Romão-Dias. 2020. "Catástrofe, luto e esperança: O trabalho psicanalítico na pandemia de COVID-19." *Revista Latinoamericana de Psicopatologia Fundamental* 23, no. 2: 269–90.

Vezzetti, Hugo. 1983. *La locura en la Argentina.* Buenos Aires: Folios Ediciones.

Vezzetti, Hugo. 1996. *Aventuras de Freud en el país de los argentinos: De José Ingenieros a Enrique Pichon-Rivière.* Buenos Aires: Editorial Paidós.

Vezzetti, Hugo. 1998. *Las promesas del psicoanálisis en la cultura de masas.* Buenos Aires: Aguilar.

Vezzetti, Hugo. 2009. *Sobre la violencia revolucionaria: Memorias y olvidos.* Buenos Aires: Siglo Veintiuno.

Visacovsky, Sergio E. 2001. "Memorias fracturadas: Usos del pasado, política y filiación en el psicoanálisis argentino." *Quaderns de l'Institut Català d'Antropologia,* nos. 15–16: 113–33.

Visacovsky, Sergio E. 2002. *El Lanús: Memoria, política y psicoanálisis en la Argentina (1956–1992).* Buenos Aires: Alianza Editorial.

Visacovsky, Sergio E. 2008. "Usos del espacio y creencias encarnadas: Psiquiatría y psicoanálisis en un servicio psiquiátrico Argentino." *Antípoda: Revista de antropología y arqueología,* no. 6: 91–111.

Voloshinov, Valentine. 1973. *Marxism and the Philosophy of Language.* Translated by Ladislav Matejka and I. R. Titunik. New York: Seminar.

Walkerdine, Valerie, and Helen Lucey. 1989. *Democracy in the Kitchen.* London: Virago.

Warde, Alan, David Wright, and Modesto Gayo. 2008. "The Omnivorous Orientation in the UK." *Poetics* 36, nos. 2–3: 148–65.

Werker, Janet F., and Christopher T. Fennell. 2004. "Listening to Sounds versus Listening to Words: Early Steps in Word Learning." In *Weaving a Lexicon,* edited by Sandra Waxman and Geoffrey Hall, 79–109. Cambridge, MA: MIT Press.

Wilberg, Peter. 2004. *The Therapist as Listener: Martin Heidegger and the Missing Dimension of Counselling and Psychotherapy Training.* London: New Gnosis.

Wiley, Clare. 2020. "Why Argentinians May Be Finding Social Distancing Harder Than the Rest of Us." *Daily Telegraph,* April 23. https://www.telegraph.co.uk/travel /destinations/south-america/argentina/articles/argentina-personal-space/.

Woolard, Kathryn Ann. 1985a. "Language Ideology: Issues and Approaches." *Pragmatics* 2, no. 3: 235–49.

Woolard, Kathryn Ann. 1985b. "Language Variation and Cultural Hegemony: Toward an Integration of Sociolinguistic and Social Theory." *American Ethnologist* 12, no. 4: 738–48.

World Health Organization. 2015–17. "Mental Health Atlas 2017 Country Profile: Argentina." https://www.who.int/publications/m/item/mental-health-atlas-2017-country-profile-argentina.

World Health Organization. 2021. "Psychologists Working in Mental Health Sector (per 100,000)." https://www.who.int/data/gho/data/indicators/indicator-details/GHO/psychologists-working-in-mental-health-sector-(per-100-000).

Wright, Silvia. 1954. "The Death of Lady Mondegreen." *Harper's Magazine*, November, 48–51.

Ysseling, Samuel. 1970. "Structuralism and Psychoanalysis in the Work of Jacques Lacan." *International Philosophical Quarterly* 10, no. 1: 102–17.

Zelizer, Barbie. 1992. *Covering the Body: The Kennedy Assassination, the Media, and the Shaping of Collective Memory*. Chicago: University of Chicago Press.

INDEX

Note: Page numbers in italics indicate figures.

acoustemology, 189n24, 190n26
action contexts, 65–66
Adela, 62–63, 68
Adler, Alfred, 114
Adriana, 101–4
advertisements, 138–39, 142, 166–72
Agha, Asif, 87, 188n15, 199n4
Aislamiento Social Preventivo y
    Obligatorio (Preventive and Com-
    pulsory Social Isolation; ASPO),
    176, 181
Akhtar, Salman, 28, 40, 61–62
Alfandary, Isabelle, 78
Alicia, 126
Alonso, Modesto, 11, 14–15, 16, 109
alterity, 21, 70–71, 122, 198n24; created
    through reported speech, 96–100;
    inside one's self, 100–105; 198n24.
    See also the Other; otherness
Althusser, Louis, 18
Althusserian structuralism, 116
Alvear, T. de, 124
analysand-analyst relationship, 7, 19–20,
    25, 28, 39–40, 42–44, 48–53, 130, 139;
    during COVID-19 pandemic, 175–77;
    inference and, 189n18; intersubjec-
    tive dialogue of, 47; mediatization of,
    117–18, 149–55, 166–67; MFSPT and,
    20–21, 54–55, 58–61, 67–71, 74–78,
    82; professionalization of, 143–44;

relations outside the clinic, 99, 117–18;
    replication of, 172; resonance and,
    45–47, 129, 133; subjectivity of, 46;
    technology and, 175–77, 200–201n3.
    See also analyst
analyst(s), 7, 19, 25; in Buenos Aires, 49,
    109–10; figure of, 138–39; "intellectual
    psychoanalysts," 115; psychoanalytic
    listening genre constituted by, 44; task
    of achieving state of resonance, 45;
    training of, 22; See also psychoana-
    lytic training
Andrés, 52–53, 62, 64
El ángel de la medianoche, 138
Ángel Garma Institute, 58, 191–92n15
Animales sueltos, 137, 138, 163
antebellum America, constitution of
    meanings and sounds in, 90
anthropology, 18; anthropological genre
    of listening, 6; anthropological theory,
    23
Argentina: modernization and social
    restructuring in, 112
Argentine cultural history, 23
Argentine cultural production: psycho-
    analysis and, 137–43
Argentine exceptionality, 111
Argentine Federation of Psychiatrists,
    197n16
Asociación Bancaria, 81

Asociación Psicoanalítica Argentina (rgentine Psychoanalytic Association; APA), 3, 22, 49, 54, 57–59, 197n16, 197n17; mass mediation of psychoanalytic listening and, 149–51; psychoanalytic field and, 112–13, 115–17, 127, 133–35
assimilation, 71–72
associations, 88
attention, 28–29, 31–32, 189n23
auditory ideology, 91–92
auditory perception, 187n9
auditory sphere, theory of, 41–42
aural ideologies, 88–91. See also listening ideologies
Austin, J. L., 34
authenticity, 152

Bachrach, Estanislao, 16
Bakhtin, Mikhail, 71–72, 80, 83, 94, 97, 100, 172, 185n6, 195n9
Bäl, Federico Fernando, 161
Balán, Jorge, 111–12
Basso, Keith, 166–67
Bauman, Richard, 37
Becker, Judith, 65, 73
Benveniste, Émile, 104
Biglieri, Jorge A., 177
Bijsterveld, Kerin, 90, 91
Bleger, José, 114, 197n17
Bleichmar, Silvia, 121, 197n13
Boas, Franz, 18
bonds (vínculos), 139
Borch-Jacobsen, Mikkel, 80
Borges, Jorge Luis, 108
Borussia Dortmund, 174
boundaries, 35
Bourdieu, Pierre, 18, 108
Briggs, Charles, 148
Buenos Aires, Argentina: as city of listeners, 1; COVID-19 lockdown in, 175–76; embrace of Lacanian psychoanalysis in, 108–9, 110 (see also Lacanian psychoanalysis); as epicenter of diffusion of Lacanian psychoanalysis, 186n9;

protests in, 80–82; psychoanalysis in, 106–36; ubiquity of psychoanalysis in, 11–14, 49, 109
Buenos Aires National University (UBA), 109. See also University of Buenos Aires (UBA)
Butelman, Enrique, 114, 117

Cage, John, 185n2
Caloi (Carlos Loiseau), 150
Carlos, 26–27, 75
Carr, E. Summerson, 74, 77
cathetic energy, 189n19
Celia, 125–26
Central de Trabajadores de la Argentina (Argentine Workers' Central Union), 80–81
Centro DITEM (Diagnóstico, Investigación, y Tratamiento de Enfermedades Mentales; Center for Diagnosis, Research, and Treatment of Mental Diseases), 49, 50, 51–52, 54, 57–59, 73–74, 75, 177
Chakrabarty, Dipesh, 94
Chion, Michel, 32, 186n3
Cibecue, 166–67, 169
Clarín (newspaper), 139, 153
class, listening ideologies and, 90–91, 92–93
Clifford, James, 187n9
clinic, the, 144
commercials. See advertisements
commoditization, 145, 152, 155, 166, 171, 199n4
communicability, 22–23, 166, 169, 172
communication, 145, 152; ethnography of, 87; metacommunication, 142–43, 166–67; sounds and, 29
communion, 57
Communist Party, 113, 114
communities of practice, 66
"concealment of truth," 18
conceptualization, 162
concurrencias, 120, 122–24, 126, 198n25

Connor, Steven, 31, 200n9
conscious, the, 50
consciousness, suspension of, 187n7
consumers, 157, 166, 171
contextualization, 145
Contorno (journal), 116
co-occurrence, 188n14, 188n15
Cook, Nicholas, 6–7
coparticipation, 66
Cortá por Lozano (television show), 138, 157–58, 199n8
Cosse, Isabella, 199n7
countertransference, 51
COVID-19, 174, 175–78, 179, 181, 200n1, 200n2
cultivation, 64–68, 78
"cultural authority," 145
cultura psi, 25, 26–27, 37, 47
culture of listeners, 65, 177–78

Dagfal, Alejandro, 110–11
Dalí, Salvador, 111–12
Damousi, Joy, 186n9
dance, 142
Daniel, 179
Dasein, 46
day-to-day interaction, psychoanalytic listening in, 80–105
denotation, 173, 185n5
Derrida, Jacques, 48, 72–73
De Saussure, Ferdinand, 44, 45–46
Descartes, René, 50, 157
Descartes Center, 110
Descola, Philippe, 10
desire, 122
dialectics, 114
dialogism, 100, 143, 177, 182, 185n6
dialogue, 100–101, 132
Diana, 57, 75–76
directionality, 28–29, 31–32, 39, 72, 76–77, 182
disseminators, 157, 166, 171
Di Tella University, 115
Documento, 115, 197n16
doppelgängers, 52, 70, 77, 83, 190n6

dreamwork, 50
Dussel, Enrique, 182, 195n8

ear, anatomy of, 189n21
"earslips," 182
École Freudienne de Paris, 115
ego, 50
Eisenlohr, Patrick, 185n3
Electra Complex, 171
emphatic listening, 61
encuadre espontáneo (spontaneous framework), 55
En el margen (magazine), 152
entextualization, 72, 145
enunciation, prosodic, 53, 73–78
Epele, María E., 11
Erlmann, Veit, 187n9
Ernesto, 27
Ervin-Tripp, Susan, 188n13
Escalante, Candelaria, 186n7
Escobar, Laura, 139
Escuela de la Orientación Lacaniana (School of the Lacanian Orientation; EOL), 127–33
Escuela Freudiana de Buenos Aires (Freudian School of Buenos Aires), 115, 134
ethical listening, 4, 9, 27, 34–35
experience, embodied, 23
the experiential, 52–53, 61, 69–73
experiential scene, 52
expertise, tropes of, 157
experts, 157
Ey, Henri, 54, 121, 191n12

Facebook, 177, 179
"false consciousness," 18
Fantino, Alejandro, 163–64, 165
FC Schalke 04, 174
Fédération Internationale de Football Association (FIFA), 174
Feld, Steven, 46, 189n24, 190n26
female sexuality, 171, 200n10
female subjectivity, in Japan, 91–92
Fernández, Alberto, 200n1

Fernet, 167–69, 171–72
fetishism, 18
figurative meaning, 107
Firstness, 67–68, 78
Florentino Ameghino hospital, 126
Foucauldian analysis, 9
Foucault, Michel, 9, 186n4
France, 108, 111, 145–46
Francis, Pope, 84
Frankfurt School, 18
"free associations," 37
Freud, Sigmund, 4, 18, 20, 22, 28, 138, 145, 166, 173; APA and, 133, 134–35; classes at UBA devoted to, 119; conscious-ness and, 44; determinism and, 108; divided subjectivity and, 50, 94; on dreamwork, 50; female sexuality and, 200n10; gleichschwebend and, 189n23; idea of "floating attention," 68; meth-odology of, 50–51; on necessity of payment, 198n20; Oedipus complex and, 170–71, 200n11; "preliminary treatment" and, 130; psychoanalytic pedagogy and, 66, 113–16, 121, 127; resonance and, 46, 94; return to, 145; on role of auditory traces, 40–41; Rolón and, 156–57, 159; on transfer-ence, 51; the unconscious and, 44–45; Zunino and, 177–78
Freudiana radio; La voz psicoanalítica del mundo (radio program), 138
Freudianism: and the Left, 113
Freudian slips, 160–61, 200n9
Frog, 188n15
Frosh, Stephen, 145–46
functional psychical repression, 139
fútbol, 73–74, 174, 182

Gadamer, Hans-Georg, 1
Gago, Paula, 14–15, 109
Gal, Susan, 87
García, Germán, 109–10
García, Luciano, 113
García Badaracco, Jorge, 49, 51–52, 54–68, 192n18, 192n19

Gardel, Carlos, 199n7
Garma, Ángel, 44, 133–34
Garma Zubizarreta, Ángel, 191–92n15
gaze, the 183
Gée, Alejandro, 181
gender, listening ideologies and, 91–92
genre(s), 188–89n16; as kinds of discourse, 37–38; theory of, 20. See also genres of listening
genres of listening: action oriented by, 65–66; context created by, 38–39; cultivation of, 64–68, 78; as frame-works of relevance, 38–39; historically constituted, 36–37; performative aspect of, 105; shaped by "normative basic patterns," 36–37; temporality of, 62–64; theoretic underpinnings of, 19; theory of, 25–47; why genres, 35–39
German Bundesliga, 174
Germani, Gino, 117
gleichschwebend, 189n23
Goffman, Erving, 68, 195n9
Gonzalo, 75–76, 77
Google Meet, 177
Grabois, Juan, 80
Gramsci, Antonio, 115
graphic humor, 137, 139, 140–41, 142, 149–55
Guevara, Ernesto "Che," 199n7
Guiraud, Paul, 54, 191n12
Gupta, Dipankar, 19

"habitus of listening," 65, 66
Hanslick, Eduard, 6
health, biomedical discourse of, 148
hearing, vs. listening, 189–90n25
Hegel, G. W. F., 114
Heidegger, Martin, 185n1, 185n6
Hellman's mayonnaise, 170–72
Hennion, Antoine, 194–95n7
heteroglossia, 83, 185n6
Hirschkind, Charles, 33
Hitchcock, Alfred, 111–12
homeostasis, 55
horizontal co-occurrence, 188n13

Hospital Borda, 17, 55, 56
Hospital San Isidro, 57
Hugo, 48–49, 63, 64
Husserl, Edmund, 187n6
hysteria, 200n10

ICdeBA (Clinical Institute of Buenos
 Aires), 128, 130–31
id, 50
ideology, 18, 22–23, 86; auditory ideology,
 91–92; "ideology of inner reference"
 (IIR), 77; of knowledge, 86, 92–93;
 linguistic ideology, 87–88; listening
 ideologies, 86, 87–94
illness, biomedical discourse of, 148
illocutionary speech acts, 34
imprints, 46
indexical transposition, of present dyad
 into psychoanalytic dyad, 93–94
inference, 8, 99, 189n18
"inner voice," 63
Inoue, Miyako, 91–92, 104
Instituto del Campo Freudiano en París
 (Institute of the Freudian Field in
 Paris; ICFP), 127
Instituto de Psicoanálisis Ángel Garma,
 134–35
Intention: interpretations of, 8–9
"intentional acts," 187n6
International Monetary Fund, 82
International Psychoanalytic Association (IPA), 111–12, 113, 114, 127, 133, 150,
 197n15
interpellation, 9, 26, 37, 93, 167
interpretation: overinterpreting, 131–32;
 resistance to, 132; surplus of, 162;
 suspension of, 78
interpretive framework, psychoanalysis
 as, 143–47
intersubjectivity, 19, 21, 47, 61, 95, 182
Isakower, Otto, 40, 41–42, 44, 127, 189n20
iso-ontology, 19
Itzigsohn, José, 113, 197n17
Izaguirre, 196n6
izquierdismo plebeyo de masas, 113

Jackson, Donald, 55
Japan, female subjectivity in, 91–92
Jauss, Hans, 188–89n16
Johnson, James, 88–89
Johnson, Mark L., 23
Jones, Maxwell, 55
Journal of Psychoanalysis Today,
 150
journals, 116–18. See also specific
 journals
Juan, 62–63, 68
Jung, Carl, 114, 145, 170–71

Kant, Immanuel, 50
Karpf, Anne, 189n22
Klein, Melanie, 22, 114, 121
Kleinian theories, 115, 116
Klinar, Doménica, 14–15, 109
knowledge: ideology of, 86, 92–93; as
 structural dynamic, 132
Kohan, Martín, 81, 82
Kondo, Marie, 139, 141
Kristeva, Julia, 185n5

Lacan, Jacques, 4, 20, 22, 28, 40, 48,
 52, 66, 192n19; daughter of, 128; on
 "discourse of the other," 69; early
 theory of language, 44–45; in France,
 145–46; on language, 161; on "learned
 ignorance," 132; mass mediation of
 psychoanalysis and, 138, 156–57,
 177–78; personality cult around,
 128–29; on psychoanalysis beyond
 clinic setting, 198n21; psychoanalytic
 pedagogy and, 119, 121, 125–28; quoted
 by Palazzo, 81–82; on radical alterity,
 198n24; the Real and, 77; resonance
 and, 8, 45–46, 68, 74–75, 133, 185n5;
 Rolón and, 156–57; on scansion, 78;
 theory of "radical otherness," 70;
 theory of the Real, the Symbolic, and
 the Imaginary, 194n36; transference
 and, 51, 190n7; the unconscious and,
 44–45, 133, 161; Zunino and, 177–78.
 See also Lacanian psychoanalysis

Lacanian psychoanalysis, 116, 122, 127, 128–30; Buenos Aires as epicenter of diffusion of, 186n9; criticism of, 116; embraced in Buenos Aires, 108–9, 110; emphasis on reading texts, 116; entry into Argentina in 1960s, 113, 114–15; individualism of, 116; "preliminary interview" and, 129–31; in Spain, 196n3

Lagache, Daniel, 114

Lagarde, Christine, 82

Lagarrigue, Alicia, 149

Langer, Marie, 113, 197n17

language, 153, 161; capacity to create subjectivities, 72–73; dialogic nature of, 83; language structural co-occurrence, 188n13; polysemic reception of, 162; prosodic enunciation, 73–78; psychoanalysis and, 125; as transindividual, 44–47; understandings of, 8–9

la langue, 4

Laurent, Eric, 121

Lave, Jean, 67, 192n24

"learn by unlearning," 133

the Left: Freudianism and, 113; psychoanalysis and, 113

"legitimate peripheral participation," 67

Leiderman, Eduardo, 186n7

Lerner, Max, 145

Lévi-Strauss, Claude, 10

Lewin, Kurt, 114

liberal theory, 8

licenciaturas, 118–19, 120, 128

Lindner, Robert, 145

linguistic anthropology, 23

linguistic ideology, 87–88

linguistics, 115

listeners: embodied, 33, 39; as individual agents, 33; personal history of, 37; role as active agent of value, 6; social identity and, 32–34; as translators, 33

listening, 23; active, 66; active character of, 20; as active mode of reception, 32–33; act of, 23, 88; as act of inter-

pretation vs. mode of being in the world, 33; circulation of psychoanalytic discourses and, 172–73; conceptualizations of, 20; contextual nature of, 187n8; cultivation of, 64–68; culturally situated, 32; as dialogue within the psyche, 42–44; directionality provided by, 182; as embodied experience, 39; as embodied practice, 185n3; ethics of, 21; as a genre, 20; genres of, 19, 25–47, 35–39, 62–68, 78, 105 (*see also* genres of listening); "habitus of listening," 65, 66; vs. hearing, 189–90n25; ideological component of, 21; intersubjective listening, 61; listening discourses, 37; listening ideologies, 86, 87–94; listening practices, 33, 78, 80–105, 126–27, 187–88n11; "listening slips," 161; mastery of, 32, 34, 182; medical science and, 186n4; metalistening, 78, 88; modernity and, 95; modes of, 35, 182; as most important sense in infants, 189n22; multimodal, 182; musical listening, 6–7; musicological listening, 6; Nancy's conceptualization of, 46; objective listening, 61; to oneself, 9; other sensory experiences and, 30; performativity of, 20, 32–35, 39, 182; perlocutionary force of, 182; phenomenological approaches to, 185n2, 186n2; pragmatics of, 32; as process of ordering, 20; properties of, 181–82; psychoanalysis and, 39–40; psychoanalytic listening; "residual listening," 71; semantic listening, 32; semiotics of, 20, 28–32; situated listening, 35; "social listening," 65; specialized types of, 5; structuring of, 181–82; subjective listening, 61; suspicious listening, 5–6; temporality of, 62–64; to "that which is not said, 80–105; theory of, 20; transference and, 51; transformative force of, 187n9

listening discourses, 37

listening genres. *See* genres of listening

listening ideologies, 86, 87–94; class and, 90–93; gender and, 91–93; music and, 87–88; race and, 92–93; social relations and, 90–94

listening practices, 33, 89, 126–27; in day-to-day interaction, 80–105; discussions of, 78; race and, 92; "setting boundaries" to, 187–88n11; sociability enacted through, 86; social relations and, 86; sociopolitical forces and, 94–105

"listening slips," 161

Locke, John, 8

locutionary speech acts, 34

Loiseau, Juan Matías, 149

Lozano, Verónica, 158, 160, 161–63, 173, 199n8

Lucey, Helen, 168

Lucía, 69–70, 71, 72–73, 77, 83

Macri, Mauricio, 80–82, 83, 200n1

Mafalda, 153

magazines, 116–18

male subjectivity, 171–72

Mandelbaum, Eduardo, 40

Marcelo, 75–76, 177

Marcus, George, 187n9

Marx, Karl, 18

Marxism, 114

Masotta, Oscar, 115, 116

materialism, 114

Mauss, Marcel, 9, 84, 163

meaning, 89; beyond denotation, 165; creation of, 23; figurative, 107

mediation, 67

mediatization, 22–23, 137–73, 178

medical-psychological anthropology, 23

mental health institutions, 124. See also public hospitals

Messi, Lionel, 73, 75

metacommunication, 142–43, 166–67

metalistening, 78, 88

metonymy, 99

Miller, Jacques-Alain, 128, 130

"misrecognition," 18

Mitre, María Elisa, 51–53, 56, 62, 63, 64

modernity: listening and, 95; psychoanalytic listening and, 94–105; subjectivity and, 94–105

modes of listening, boundaries and, 35

mondegreens, 31, 182, 200n9

"mother," figure of, 23

motherhood, 168–72

Movimiento de Trabajadores Excluídos (Movement of Excluded Workers), 80

Multi-Family Structured Psychoanalytical Therapeutic communities (MFSPT), 3–4, 8, 20–21, 40, 118, 134, 177–78; analysand-analyst relationship and, 54–55, 58–61, 67–71, 74–78, 82; coparticipation and, 66; democratic format of, 57, 62, 66–67; description of, 49–50; history of, 54–58; humanistic dimension of, 56–57; listening inside, 60–78; psychoanalytic listening among, 53–60; setting of the, 58–60; temporality and, 62–64; themes of sessions, 60

mundo psi, 2–3, 21–22, 110, 118

music, 142, 149, 153; definition of, 76; listening ideologies and, 87–88; of words, 74–78

musical listening, 6–7

musicological listening, 6

La Nación (newspaper), 139, 141, 177, 183, 196n6

names, cultural knowledge and, 166–67

Nancy, Jean-Luc, 46

Natalia, 26

neuroscience, 16, 17

newspapers, 139

Nietzsche, Friedrich, 157

la noche de los bastones largos, 114

Noches de diván (radio program), 156

"noise etiquette," 90

Nosotros (literary magazine), 113

objective listening, 61

Oedipus complex, 23, 168–71, 200n11

online psychotherapy, 176–77, 200–201n3
"ontological generosity," 182
ordering, 28–29, 31–32, 38
"orders of knowledge," 37
Other, the, 71, 122, 132, 195n8, 198n24; listening to, 94; polyphony of discourse of, 46
otherness, 70–71, 198n24. *See also* alterity
others, 83
overinterpreting, 131–32
overtly occurring discourse, 39

Los padecientes (*The Sufferers*; Rolón), 157–58
Página 12 (newspaper), 139
Paidós (book publisher), 117
Palaemon, 41–42, *42*, 43
Palazzo, Sergio, 80–82, 83, 85, 86, 99
Paris Opera, 88–89
Paris Psychoanalytic Association, 54
Pavlov, Ivan Petrovich, 113, 114
Pavlovian school, 113–14
Pedrón, Liliana, 150, 151
Peirce, Charles S., 67, 68
"Pentecostal arousal," 65, 66, 73
performative experience, 72–73
performative listening, 32–35, 39
performative utterances, 34, 39
Peri, Mónica, 142
periodicals, 116–18
perlocutionary speech acts, 34–35, 167, 171–72, 182
Perón, Evita, 199n7
Perón, Juan, 112, 114
Piazzolla, Ástor, 142
Plataforma, 115, 197n16
Plato, 50, 157
Plotkin, Mariano Ben, 10, 15, 22, 106, 107–8, 112, 142, 186n9
Podetti, Esteban, *180*
Poe, Edgar Allan, 29–31, 32, 35
Políticos al diván, 138, 141
Politzer, Georges, 114

popular press, psychoanalysis in, 116–17
porteños, 1, 25–26
postgraduate psychoanalytic training institutions, 127–35
postmodern theory, 145
potentiality, 67–68
pragmatics, 187n5
the preconscious, 50
"preliminary interview," 129–31
primary processes, 44–45
producers, 171
Programa radial psi (radio program), 138
prosodic enunciation, 53, 73–78
psychiatry, 21–22, 110
psychoanalysis, 21–22, 145; in Argentine context, 108–36; beyond the clinical setting, 80–105, 145–46, 198n21; in Buenos Aires, 106–36; circulation of, 22, 116–18; as clinical theory of universal properties, 107; consumption of, 199n4; as creative technique, 152; critical to Argentinian cultural field, 9–10; as cultural practice, 135, 1, 147–72; cultural representations of, 22–23, 137–43 (see also mediatization); decline/rejection of, 18; degrees in, 149; earlier theorists of, 42–43; as a field, 107–8; focus on individual subjects as such, 19; hegemonic position of, 15–17, 22, 145; history in Buenos Aires, 21–22, 109–17; as interpretive framework, 143–47; language and, 3, 125; the Left and, 113; listening and, 39–40; as "listening cure," 7; as live encounter, 144; in the media, 22–23; as medical science, 144, 148–49; misuse of, 145; in national health system, 17; as negative methodology, 183; noninstitutionalized, 115; permeation of different fields, 17; in the press, 116–18; privacy and, 49–50; professionalization of, 143; public group sessions of, 49; social analysis and, 144–45; speaking and, 7, 11, 39–40, 95, 105, 125; as "talking cure," 7, 11, 95, 105, 125;

terminology borrowed from medicine, 143; as therapeutic encounter, 145; as way of relating to the world, 106–7, 135–36; "wild" form of, 19

psychoanalysts. *See* analysts

psychoanalytic discourses, 147–49; "authoritative," 148–49; circulation of, 137–72; communicability of, 147–49, 166–72; lay representations of, 148; mediatization of, 137–72; metacommunication and, 142–43

psychoanalytic ear, training of, 120–35

psychoanalytic gaze, 183

psychoanalytic genre, signature formula of, 20

psychoanalytic jargon, 84

psychoanalytic listening, 73, 92–93, 125–27, 142–43; among MFSPT communities, 53–60; cultivation of, 64–68; culture of, 17–18; as cumulative, 101; in day-to-day interaction, 80–105; defined through analysis of overtly occurring discourse, 39; embodied nature of, 6–7; genealogies of, 39–47; genre of, 4; as heteroglossic, 83; mass mediation of, 137–73; modernity and, 94–105; pedagogy of, 117; performative aspect of, 24; temporality of, 68, 69

psychoanalytic therapy, 49. *See also* Multi-Family Structured Psychoanalytical Therapeutic communities (MFSPT)

psychoanalytic training, 110–11, 117–35

psychology, 21–22, 109–10, 112; defining boundaries of the field, 124–25; popularity of degree in, 120

psychology students, 17, 120, 197n10

psychopathology, 119

psychotango, 149

psychotherapy, online, 176–77, 200–201n3

psytrance music, 149

public clinics, 118

public hospitals, 118, 120–27. *See also* *specific hospitals*

public universities, 119–20; "hegemonic presence" of psychoanalysis in, 145; role of, 21–22. *See also specific universities*

Pura química (television show), 138

Quino (Joaquín Lavado), 153

Rabinovich, Diana, 121

race, listening ideologies and, 92–93

raciolinguistics, 92

radical alterity, 198n24

radio, 137–38

Radio Lacan (radio program), 138

Rafael, 177–78

Ramiro, 25–28, 32, 34–37, 38, 39, 46–47

Rascovsky, Andrés, 150–51

rationalizations, 18

reading, 36

reception, 36, 38–39; context and, 39, 89; local conditions of, 108; modes of, 88–89; structural and personal aspects of, 88–89

"reflective appraisals," 61

reflexivity, 67

reflexology, 113, 114

regional soundscapes, social relations and, 90–91

Reik, Theodor, 25, 39, 40, 43–44, 69, 105, 127, 133–35

Rep (Miguel Repiso), 153, *154*

reported speech, 96–100

residencias, 120–23, 124, 126

"residual listening," 71

Resolution 2282, 112

resonance, 24, 28, 33–34, 44–47, 58, 63, 94, 177; analysand-analyst relationship and, 45–47, 129, 133; Freud and, 46, 94; Lacan and, 8, 45–46, 68, 74–75, 133, 185n5; as a sort of Dasein, 46; "states of resonance," 1–2, 45

Revista de Filosofía (journal), 113, 197n14

Revista de Psicoanálisis (Psychoanalysis magazine), 135

Roberto, 64–65, 66, 67, 68

Rodríguez, Cristian, 139
Rodríguez, Sergio, 115
Rolón, Gabriel, 16, 137, 153, 156–58,
  160–65, 172–73, 178–79, 199n5, 200n9
Rozitchner, León, 116
Rudaeff, Marcelo ("Rudy"),
  Rudy (Marcelo Rudaeff), 81–82, 153, 155
Ruperthuz Honorato, Mariano, 107–8

Sartre, Jean-Paul, 115
Sartrean humanism, 116
scansion, 78
Schaeffer, Pierre, 30, 185n2, 189–90n25
Schafer, R. Murray, 89
Schenker, Heinrich, 6
School of Lacanian Orientation (EOL), 22
Schopenhauer, Arthur, 90
Schujman, Alejandro, 139
secondary processes, 44
secondary rationalizations, 18, 19
Secondness, 67–68, 78
Sehinkman, Diego, 141–42, 173, 196n6
self, 22, 83; conceptualizations of, 8–9;
  constructs of, 86; emergence of new,
  103–4; neoliberal conceptualizations
  of, 16; true, 52–53, 86, 95
self-alienation, 70
self-sufficiency, paradigm of, 183
Seligman, Martin, 182–83
semantic listening, 32
semiosis, 67
semiotic chains, 23, 167, 169, 171, 171–73,
  199n4
Sendra, Fernando, 141, 153, 168
sermons, listening to, 33, 34, 35, 47, 185n3,
  187n10
Shpirer, Iafi, 179
Siempre listos (television show), 156
signifying chain, 4, 7, 9, 19, 45–46, 68, 94,
  129, 131, 192n19
Silverstein, Michael, 91
Siminovich, Maya, 179
Sinatra, Ernesto, 130–33
situated listening, 35
Smith, Mark, 90

Smith, Yvonne, 74
social analysis, psychoanalysis and,
  144–45
social facts, 84, 173
social identity, 70; listeners and, 32–34
"social listening," 65
social media, 179–80
social positionality, 182
social relations, 182; created and sus-
  tained by listening, 23–24; listening
  ideologies and, 90–94; listening practices and, 86; regional soundscapes
  and, 90–91; structured by genres, 38
society, 22
sociopolitical forces, listening practices
  and, 94–105
Sofia, 17
sound images, 64
sounding, 4
"sounding atmosphere," 185n3
sounds: apprehension of, 38; communication and, 29; perception of, 29–30
soundscapes, 174–75
sound studies, 23
speaking, psychoanalysis and, 39–40
speech acts, 34, 167, 171–72
speech genres, 38
Stoever, Jennifer Lynn, 92
Stravinsky, Igor, 25, 32
structuralism, 115, 116
structures of relevance, 39
subject, modernity and, 94–105
subject, decentered, 50–51, 70–73, 77,
  94, 95
subjective listening, 61
subjectivity: created by language, 72–73;
  modernity and, 94–105
super ego, 50
suspicious listening, 5–6
symbolic, the, 51, 77
symbolic capital, 81
"symbolic exchange," 9

tango, 142, 180, 181
Tango-Psi, 142

television, 137–38, 142, 155–66, 196n6,
199n8. *See also* advertisements
temporality, 62–64; of psychoanalytic
listening, 68, 69
Terapia de Noticias (online newspaper
program), 141, 196n6
"textual paradigm," 187n9
theater, 142, 178
"therapeutic community," 55
therapeutic constellations, heterogeneity of, 10
therapist, as translator, 45
the "third ear," 40–44, 63
Thirdness, 67–68
Tiene la palabra (television show), 138
Tobar García hospital, 125–26
Todorov, Tzvetan, 188n14
Todos al diván, ¿A vos quién te ama?
(television show), 156
Toop, David, 30–31
transference, 51–52, 57, 190n7
transformation, 33
translation, 45, 165
transposition, 93, 98
transubjectivity, 139
Turkle, Sherry, 108
Tute (Juan Matías Loiseau), 26–27, 137,
149–53, *151*, 173

uncanny, the (*unheimlich*), 4
unconscious, the, 18, 44–45, 50–51,
70–71, 76, 100–105, 122, 135; Freudian
theory of, 18; knowledge and, 132–33;
structured like a language, 45, 133;
structure of, 18
United States, 108, 109
United States Citizenship and Immigration Services (USCIS), 5
universities, 21–22, 119–20, 145. *See also*
specific universities
University of Buenos Aires (UBA),
17, 22, 113–14, 118–20, 128, 134, 144,

194n3, 197n17. *See also* Buenos Aires
National University (UBA)
Urlinie, 6

Vainer, Alejandro, 112
Valeria, 48–49
Va X Vos (television show), 156
verbal performance, mastery of genres
of, 157
Vezzetti, Hugo, 113
Vicentico, 170
Viotti, Nicolás, 10, 15, 142
lo vivencial. See experiential voices,
100
Volnovich, Juan Carlos, 113, 195n11
Voloshinov, Valentine, 97

Wagner, Richard, 38
Walkerdine, Valerie, 168
Wenger, Etienne, 67, 192n24
Western Apache of Cibecue, 166–67,
169
WhatsApp, 179
Wila, Cynthia, 178
Wiley, Clare, 180, 181
Winnicott, Donald, 22, 121
women's magazines, 116–17
words: meaning of, 73–78; music of,
48–78; sound of, 3–4, 9, 23, 48–78,
73–74. *See also* language
World Health Organization, 13, 109
World War I, 145
Wright, Sylvia, 31

X-rays, metaphor of, 141

Yamil, 17, 145
Yseling, Samuel, 45

Žižek, Slavoj, 81
Zuckerberg, Mark, 179
Zunino, Pablo, 177